Wrecks of Human Ambition

Wrecks of Human Ambition

A History of Utah's Canyon Country to 1936

Paul T. Nelson

The University of Utah Press

Salt Lake City

The Defiance House Man colophon is a registered trademark
of the University of Utah Press. It is based on a four-foot-tall
Ancient Puebloan pictograph (late PIII) near Glen Canyon, Utah.

18 17 16 15 14   1 2 3 4 5

LIBRARY OF CONGRESS CATALOGING-IN-PUBLICATION DATA
Nelson, Paul T.
  Wrecks of human ambition : a history of Utah's Canyon Country to 1936 / Paul T.
Nelson.
      pages cm
  Includes bibliographical references and index.
  ISBN 978-1-60781-333-0 (pbk. : alk. paper) — ISBN 978-1-60781-334-7 (ebook)
1. Utah—Discovery and exploration. 2. Canyons—Utah. 3. Mormons—Utah—
History—19th century. 4. Utah—History. 5. Utah—Description and travel. I. Title. II.
Title: History of Utah's Canyon Country to 1936.
  F826.N46 2014
  979.2—dc23
                              2013042707

COVER PAINTING: *View of Lake Powell* © Harrison Thomas Groutage, circa 1970. Used
by permission.

Printed and bound by Sheridan Books, Inc., Ann Arbor, Michigan.

The river is of no help for farming near it.

—Silvestre Vélez de Escalante, 1776

No good country over there.

—Wakara, 1849

Wrecks of human ambition lie scattered all about.

—John Widtsoe, 1922

Contents

Illustrations

Acknowledgments

The ideas for this book began in Dallas, Texas, fermented in the desert of Castle Valley, Utah, and were finally completed in the greenery of central Ohio. During the course of researching and writing about this landscape, countless individuals—within and beyond academic circles—have spurred me to think about the Canyon Country's history from different perspectives. Most importantly, my academic mentor at Southern Methodist University, David J. Weber, was a constant inspiration and motivator as I began to put this project's ideas into my doctoral dissertation. From its very inception he urged me to think of it as a book, not a dissertation. As my graduate studies progressed, my originally intended research topics of Spanish colonization and exploration gradually blended with my older sentimental attachment to the Canyon Country. Through every step of this evolution, David Weber was there with a perfect blend of criticism and encouragement and above all a deep sense of what happens at the intersection of history and landscape. Sadly, David passed away as I was revising my dissertation into this book. I sincerely hope that this work will at least in small part carry on this brilliant scholar's legacy.

I also thank other readers of this manuscript when it was in dissertation form at Southern Methodist University. Benjamin Johnson and Sherry Smith, both excellent researchers and writers of the American West, pushed and questioned my ideas. Jared Farmer, whose own book *Glen Canyon Dammed* first showed me how to approach this beautiful landscape from a historical and analytical perspective, also sat in on my dissertation committee. I value his insight and critiques. Although they did not read this work in its entirety, John Mears and Edward Countryman also provided encouragement through my years of graduate school. In particular Professor Countryman allowed me to veer off on material from chapter 1 during one of my first lectures as a student teacher for his Early American History survey. Finally, and most basically, the dissertation from which this book originated would have been impossible without a generous endowment by the late Texas governor William Clements, which paid nearly all of my expenses through five years of graduate school.

Many other scholars beyond the borders of my graduate institution provided encouragement and criticism over the years, although some may not even remember it. When I was an undergraduate at Utah State University, Mark Damon's classics courses first convinced me to make history a profession, for better or for worse. Clyde A. Milner II steered me toward graduate studies in southwestern history when I took his U.S. West class. Brief but enlightening conversations with James P. Ronda and Richard Francaviglia spurred me to consider the more mythical aspects of exploration and geography as I began researching this project. During my time as a visiting lecturer at Austin College, Professor Light Cummins showed more interest in and insight into this project (specifically the legend of Everett Ruess) than I ever would have expected from a Texas historian. David Rich Lewis of Utah State University was an excellent academic "life raft" for two years in Utah as I attempted to research and write, far from the watchful eyes of my dissertation advisors.

Several historians whom I have never met helped this project immensely: Charles S. Peterson's books were constantly at my side, and Gary Topping's papers at the Utah State Historical Society were a veritable gold mine. Allan Kent Powell read my first manuscript submitted to the University of Utah Press, with valuable insight and comments. Two students of the Canyon Country even serendipitously made my new home in central Ohio a trove of Canyon Country information: the late Dwight Smith, who compiled the Robert Stanton collection at Miami University, and the gentleman-explorer of chapter 9, Julius F. Stone, whose papers at the Ohio State University archives transported me back to the desert as I struggled to acclimate to the sprawling, humid flatlands of the Midwest. Other scholars that I am fortunate enough to have met—some in depth, others in passing—have helped me through the years in Utah, Texas, and Ohio, as this project moved from research project to dissertation to book manuscript. These include, in no particular order: Anna Banhegyi, George Díaz, David Rex-Galindo, Alicia Dewey, Helen McClure, J. Gabriel Martínez-Serna, Dale Topham, Matt Babcock, Michael Scott Wagenen, Benedict J. Colombi, Brian Frehner, Joaquín Rivaya-Martínez, David Bernstein, Richard Yntema, Sarah Fatherly, Kerwin L. Klein, Jeff Nichols, and Jedediah Rogers.

The staffs and archivists of the Utah State Historical Society, Utah State University's Special Collections, Brigham Young University's Special Collections, Southern Methodist's DeGolyer Library, Miami University's Special Collections, and the Ohio State University's Archives were all very helpful as I poured through their collections. Russell Martin at the DeGolyer Library was particularly helpful in suggesting diverse sources in his collection. I especially thank David Rumsey both for putting together his incomparable website of period maps and for giving me permission to use his scan of the Humboldt map. On one occasion at the Utah Historical Society's archives, I ran into Canyon Country hiking guidebook author Steve Allen, whose books spurred my youthful interest in the region years ago. We discussed the region's history and our respective projects enthusiastically; I hope that someday he will read this. Professor Jonathan Johnson and his work study assistant Rebecca Copper of Otterbein University did a splendid job of photographing the painting on this book's cover, capturing the beauty of the original. John Alley and Peter DeLafosse of University of Utah Press were both extremely helpful and interested as I worked toward turning a dissertation into this book. Finally, very special thanks and an apology to the kindly, well-intentioned missionary volunteer at the LDS Church Archives, who accidentally allowed my laptop computer case into the archival reading room and was harshly berated by his younger supervisor. I still feel guilty.

Well before I began this dissertation, my employers and friends Pat and Gary George of the outfitter Hondoo Rivers and Trails in Torrey, Utah, instilled in me a deep love for the Canyon Country that can only come from years of toiling through the region's Bad Lands and Good Lands. The hundreds of clients that we guided through the canyons and rivers likewise refined the way that I viewed the region with their ever-fresh questions and curiosity. Local ranchers and farmers whom I met while working as a guide—most notably Richard "Dickie" Pace—gave me firsthand insight into their heritage. Other guides with whom I worked also tolerated my constant historical bantering and provided insight into their decades of experience in the region, including Roger Murphy, Myron Cook, and Bob Poulton. Fred Blackburn, a southwestern Colorado archaeologist and historian, spurred my early interest in regional history years ago as we hunted 100-year-old carvings on the aspen trees of Thousand Lake Mountain.

I also thank my close friends and family, all "desert rats," who have accompanied me on forays into the region's backcountry, down its rivers, and up its cliffs: Dylan Brown, Casey Anderson, Greta Schen, Mike Langenheim, Andrew Gram, Annelise Nelson, Jackson and Maggie Evans, Kevin Conti, John Langston, Amanda Smith, Stephanie Hong, and Mike Nelson. Extra thanks to Amber Shafer, for taking pity on my technological ineptitude with much-needed Photoshop expertise, and Dan Brayack, for generously allowing me to use one of his beautiful landscape photos of the Sixshooter Peaks. Dean Kerkling rented me a lovely house in Castleton, Utah, as I began writing this manuscript and provided excellent food, drink, and conversation as we watched countless sunsets over the Wingate cliffs of Parriot Mesa. My uncle Michael Nelson, professor and mining engineer, specifically helped me as I attempted to navigate the complex waters of Mormon doctrine, culture, and history. Many thanks to my parents, Eric and Farol Nelson, who both supported and accompanied me on many trips through the canyons, and to my grandmother, Iva Lou Groutage, who at eighty-eight is still one of the most inquisitive critics of all my historical work. My other grandparents, Tom and Shirley Nelson, were also essential in instilling a deep sense of regional and cultural history in me through childhood, and their influence flows through this book. Special thanks to Christina Austin, whom I introduced to the Canyon Country years ago by way of an unfortunate raft flip in Cataract Canyon. Through the final stages of the writing and revision process, she tolerated my complaints and revelations, reading and scrutinizing chapter drafts and ideas with the eye of a research scientist. Though we have since parted ways, her love and support through this entire project was indispensable.

Finally, I am dedicating this book to my grandfather, Harrison Thomas Groutage, who unfortunately passed away in February 2013. For over sixty years "Grout" depicted western American and Mexican landscapes in water-color and oil as no other artist has or will, perfectly capturing their fore-boding beauty (see the cover). My best memories from childhood are of his vacation home just south of Zion National Park. I fondly recall wandering the desert back roads of the Canyon Country, Mojave Desert, Arizona Strip, and Grand Canyon region through the years with him, with sketchbook and camera in hand, as he explored and searched for another sublime panorama of rock, sand, water, and sky.

Introduction

LINEAR AND CROOKED LANDSCAPES

*I cannot conceive of a more worthless and impractible region
than the one we now find ourselves in.*
—Capt. John N. Macomb, on the future Canyonlands National Park, 1859

*The worst places in the land we can probably get, and we must
develop them. If we were to find a good country how long
would it be before the wicked would want it and seek to strip us
of our possessions?*
—Apostle George Q. Cannon, addressing his Mormon congregation, 1873

Deserts have made fools of the wisest people.
—Patricia Nelson Limerick, *Desert Passages* (1985)

Just south of the San Juan River and northwest of Shiprock, New Mexico, is a
monument. Tourists visiting this attraction walk past booths selling trinkets of
the Navajo Reservation, perhaps buying a few souvenirs before reaching their
destination, a granite platform. Engraved upon the platform is a circle, neatly
quartered by two straight lines. Each quadrant contains two words, forming
the statement "Four States Here Meet in Freedom under God." This granite

base is the only place in the United States where four states meet at a common point. The tourists can walk onto the platform to spread themselves over the quartered circle, experiencing the novelty of being in Utah, Colorado, Arizona, and New Mexico at the same time. This is Four Corners Monument. The desert stretches away in all directions, oblivious to the boundaries.

A map of the region surrounding Four Corners shows dozens of other state and national parks, monuments, recreation areas, primitive areas, wilderness areas, and scenic overlooks. Indeed, this area has the greatest concentration of such parks and monuments in the United States. Tourism promoters and local chambers of commerce realize this and aggressively promote an automobile tour of the "Grand Circle" as the Great American Vacation: fly cheaply into Las Vegas, rent a car, drive to the Grand Canyon, then go east through the Navajo reservation, stopping at Canyon de Chelly, Mesa Verde, and the Four Corners before cutting back to the northwest through Monument Valley to Arches, Canyonlands, back south to Powell Reservoir, Capitol Reef, Grand Staircase–Escalante, Bryce, and Zion, returning to Las Vegas.

Four Corners stands out among these monuments, parks, and recreation areas. It does not have the deepest canyon gorge, the widest scenic vista, or the highest rock pinnacles—quite the opposite. Four Corners has nothing naturally spectacular or unique. Here lies the irony. In a region so distinguished for its natural landscapes, where the mark of humankind appears to be completely absent, this monument is dedicated to contrived political boundaries, having absolutely nothing to do with the natural topographic shapes of the land. In a place of sinuous canyons and rivers that may flow through miles of goosenecks and oxbows just to travel one linear mile, where cliffs and gorges force travelers to make crooked and convoluted detours, we have a monument dedicated to straight lines: meridians and parallels, invisible and invented.

In a way, this is the story I have attempted to tell here—the mixed successes and failures involved in imposing straight lines upon a crooked landscape. Even beyond the literal imposition of linear divisions and thoroughfares upon this landscape in the form of railroads, highways, or political boundaries are the many ways in which we have approached the region with rigid, straight ideas of what it should be and how it should fit into the greater scope of a continent-spanning nation. This approach has not been unique to American culture, however. The long process of all Euro-American Christians envisioning, exploring, settling, and ultimately exploiting the area around the Four Corners has been driven by a desire to shape the landscape to preexisting expectations.

This desire is in no way limited to a specific region or landscape. The yearning for an ordered, efficient, and utilitarian landscape is one of the most basic themes of European Christianity's spread across the globe in the last five hundred years, if not the past fifteen hundred. In countless reports promoting exploration and colonization in the New World, from Christopher Columbus's vision of a direct water route to the Orient to Thomas Jefferson's idealized uniform Yeoman Democracy, we see a repetition of the same expectations. New land would have fertile, well-watered soil; its rivers and ocean inlets would be direct natural highways for commerce on a transcontinental scale; topographical features would be little more than low hills directing the courses of these rivers, in no circumstances presenting barriers to passage. Ultimately, all of this geography would aid the Americas to become the new center for commerce between Europe and Asia. To colonize and incorporate was to map straight lines and ideas across the continent, literally and metaphorically.[1]

The story of Euro-American Christianity's encounters and compromises with this specific region shows the profundity of ideas concerning the transformation of useless desert—Bad Land—into a fertile, ordered, Christian garden—Good Land. Good Land, in an intellectual tradition stretching from the Old Testament to agrarian Mormon settlers and beyond, is straight and well watered, with uniform, nonabrupt topography.[2] The Canyon Country's topography is crooked, its environs arid. As Captain Macomb complains in disgust in the epigraph above, it has been completely contrary to the idea of practicable land that presumably fostered decent Americanness elsewhere. As a landscape of the "other," the Canyon Country has long encouraged visitors to view it in very dualistic, polarized perspectives: Good Land versus Bad Land, desert versus garden. The story of the Canyon Country's environmental, intellectual, and geographical histories and of the unfolding processes of hope, experience, compromise, and failure in the region exemplifies a sort of worst case scenario as Euro-Christianity encountered the worst of the Bad Land.

This book traces the broad patterns of experience as visitors encountered this perplexing landscape and struggled to fit it into their own notions of what Good Land was supposed to be or what Bad Land could be. It is almost exclusively a story of those coming from a background of white European Christianity. The religious compulsion of Spanish Catholics and Mormons to convert the landscape as thoroughly as they wished to convert its Indian inhabitants is a prominent theme. Equally important is the trend of broad sentiments toward the Canyon Country moving from disgust to curiosity, intrigue, and even love as this narrative concludes and as the United States beyond the region became more industrialized and developed. While in some ways this theme mirrors the development of the preservation movements on a national level, the Canyon Country offered unique challenges to the idea of what was "wilderness" or "beautiful." It is comparatively easy to make a case for preserving or conserving soaring mountain peaks or verdant forests, but the depths of the Canyon Country had neither of these more aesthetically pleasing landscapes.

More specifically, this story begins with the grafting of incomplete conceptions onto the terrain of the New World and the creation of an alternate geography of optimism far from the rivers and canyons of what was to become southeastern Utah. After 1492 optimistic "Geographies of Hope" were strongest when flowing from the pens of intellectuals, geographers, and theologians with little or no experience in actually exploring the farthest reaches of the claims of their respective nations or monarchs.[3] The exploration of the New World has always involved a conflict between expectation and reality, hope and experience. As Stephen Pyne writes, "Scholars who constructed gorgeous *mappae mundi* with Jerusalem squarely in the center of the world had little in common with pilots who kept rutters and consulted empirically drawn portolan charts."[4] The first chapter examines this displaced geographical optimism (which almost always had religious, millenarian, and even Edenic undercurrents) that accompanied early theories of exactly what the interior of North America held. Growing out of broad, continental expectations first envisioned and applied by Christopher Columbus, these hopes gradually focused upon a place and a name by the late 1600s. "Teguayo," the promising region north of Spanish New Mexico between the Great Plains and Pacific Coast of North America, was a mythical realm that the Spanish imagination superimposed over the realities of the Canyon Country's Bad Land.

As the second chapter on the eighteenth century indicates, the earliest Spanish explorers found that much of the Teguayo region was in fact the complete opposite of their expectations. Teguayo was supposed to be Good Land, with a uniform, unabrupt topography, rivers that both watered the land and provided easy passage across it, and perhaps meek, sinless Indians awaiting conversion to Christianity. The actual Canyon Country that lay beneath the idea of Teguayo was Bad Land, with cliffs and canyons preventing easy travel or extensive agriculture, rivers that flowed violently through inaccessible canyons, and Indians whose very ways of subsistence in the desert disgusted their would-be converters. Many of the region's earliest visitors were so horrified that they saw the landscape not only as Bad Land but as fallen land: once lush, productive, and civilized but now decaying, eroding, and savage. It was becoming clear that the continental interior was not at all the divinely created Eden of arable land and straight lines that the earliest geographical theorists had anticipated.

As the invisible political orientation of the Canyon Country shifted from its position as the Far North of Spain and Mexico to the Far West of the United States, supposedly more rational and learned scientist-explorers began trying to understand it more fully. At least this was the perspective of American explorers and geographers. Compared to neighboring regions such as the Rocky Mountains or the Great Basin that had been explored earlier, however, the nature of the Canyon Country was quite difficult to grasp even for those who intentionally sought it out. For the most part U.S. government explorers such as John Gunnison and John Frémont intentionally avoided the most complex areas of the region, only brushing across its northern fringes. Expeditions such as the one led by John Macomb that purposefully delved into the heart of the Canyon Country deplored and dismissed the region.

But the surveys of John Wesley Powell through the early and mid-1870s brought scientists to the area who explicitly attempted to understand its geography and geology. To a degree Powell and his surveyors succeeded in their objectives. They did not simply dismiss the region as "worthless and impractible," as Macomb had,[5] but for the most part they avoided the optimism of earlier Spanish theorists and contemporary promoters of desert development such as William Gilpin and William Ellsworth Smythe. Instead they valued the region as an outdoor laboratory for future research and as an aesthetically valuable landscape, setting the stage for its later designation into national parks and wilderness areas.

As the sixth, seventh, and eighth chapters show, however, the older notions of a religious obligation to convert the Canyon Country to a productive garden that had originated in the Spanish period actually experienced a rebirth with the Mormons, who had begun settling northwest of the Canyon Country in the late 1840s. Mormon notions of cooperative irrigation and moderated resource consumption actually fostered successful settlement around the edges of the Canyon Country. But by the 1870s new settlements were pressing even farther into the interior of the Bad Land, carrying the well-tested confidence of a divinely chosen people, but with none of earlier generations' careful moderation or selection of more forgiving landscapes. These settlements in the interior of the Canyon Country either failed or were forced to compromise elements of the traditional Mormon village model.

As these settlements withered away in the Canyon Country during the first decade of the twentieth century, two outside forces took interest with new strength and set the stage for today's continuing exploitation of the region's scenic and mineral resources. The first was mineral extraction: although Glen Canyon's gold rush was a bust for nearly all involved, it represented a distinct digression from previous attempts at exploiting the area agriculturally. Seeking mineral wealth, especially for personal profit, was long discouraged by Mormon leadership. Much more than the cultivation of farmland, minerals enticed outside ideas and capital to the Canyon Country. Wealthy investors poured hundreds of thousands of dollars into schemes concocted by bright engineers who believed that modern technology and ingenuity could finally force the Bad Land to produce where religious faith had failed. Few of these mineral speculators made any profit, and none would become truly wealthy until the 1940s uranium boom.

The second new outside force involved the successors to Powell's hinted aesthetic appreciation, who began seeing the region not only as something unique but as an area worth visiting simply for the experience. Most of the themes of early tourism, wilderness appreciation, and federal designation of national parks and monuments throughout the United States have already been well documented by historians such as Hal Rothman, Roderick Nash, and Richard Sellers.[6] But the Canyon Country of the early 1900s offered an experience very different from, say, viewing the Grand Canyon from a manicured trail with guardrails and interpretive signs or visiting Yosemite Valley while staying in a luxurious grand lodge. It was so remote that its most complicated and arguably beautiful interior regions such as the confluence of the Green and Colorado Rivers did not even gain official national park status until well into the 1960s. The remoteness and unfamiliarity of the Canyon Country encouraged early visitors to view themselves as expeditionary "explorers" rather than as mere "tourists."

Throughout this broad chronological scope are many stories that I do not cover here; this is not a comprehensive human history of even the pre–twentieth century Canyon Country. Rather than document every human to have entered and/or written about the region, I have concentrated more on farming expectations than on ranching or mining, and primarily on the experiences of Mormons who approached the canyons from the Northwest. Cultivation was the primary concern of those who wrote the most on the region before it was well known and of those who explored it into the 1870s. For Mormons, the literal transformation of a useless brown landscape into a productive green one was heavy with biblical symbolism in a way that mining and even ranching never were. Farming was an explicit charge from their creator. Ultimately, it was these agricultural expectations that failed most dramatically when they met the Canyon Country. As the case of the San Juan settlers of the 1880s shows, livestock ranching was slightly more sustainable than farming in this Bad Land, and mineral exploitation, despite its rough "boom and bust" cycles, continues to receive serious attention in today's modern Canyon Country.[7]

Similarly, I do not give the Indian groups in and around the Canyon Country ample attention. My neglect of Indian history would be inexcusable if this book was simply a human history of the region. The Canyon Country shares most of its southern border with the largest Indian reservation in the United States. Navajos and Utes no doubt knew its trails and river fords better than any American or European "explorer" of the eighteenth or nineteenth centuries. Nonequestrian Paiutes, long denigrated and abused by both white society and other Indians as lowly "diggers" and slaves actually managed to live sustainably in this desert longer than any more sedentary society, white or Indian. But I have chosen to focus upon what happened when Euro-Christian ideas of deserts, wildernesses, and productivity encountered the Canyon Country, since they seem to be in many ways so completely incompatible with the region. This is not to say that all Indian groups had some sort of innate knowledge of how to live successfully in the region—the romanticized idea of ecologically neutral Indians has been soundly refuted by historians and anthropologists.[8] Specifically, much evidence indicates that the Ancestral Puebloans of Mesa Verde and Chaco Canyon, who spread into the Canyon Country several centuries before Columbus, failed because of unwise resource consumption and unsustainable relationships with the desert.[9] But in the end this is almost exclusively a story of European, Christian, and ultimately mainstream American colonization.

My narrative examines the Canyon Country when it was even more isolated from the rest of the United States than it is today. It is impossible to pinpoint a specific date when American "modernity" fully incorporated the region and its surrounding "island communities" (arguably this still has not happened).[10] By 1936, however, the rest of the nation was taking an interest in the Canyon Country as never before. New Deal legislation like the Taylor Grazing Act of 1934 imposed new federal regulations on livestock use in the West. The U.S. Department of the Interior proposed a huge new national monument that would have included the bulk of the Canyon Country. Though this monument never came to be, it set the stage for a more approachable, American Canyon Country.

Beyond federal legislation, the Canyon Country was still remote by the 1930s but well on its way to incorporation into the rest of the United States. Transportation through the Canyon Country continued to be difficult throughout the 1930s: the small town of Boulder actually still received its mail via mule train. But at least the rudimentary trails and paths that would later become highways were well established by this point. Boundaries of national parks and monuments were not as extensive as they are today, but most of the major points of interest—Arches, Capitol Reef, Rainbow Bridge, Natural Bridges—were designated and protected in some way. The uranium boom of the 1940s and 1950s had not yet happened, but geologists had at least identified the presence of radioactive minerals in the Chinle Formation of the region. The most drastic human-caused environmental change, Glen Canyon Dam, was still decades away, but U.S. Geological Survey workers under Claude Birdseye had thoroughly examined the Colorado River system and identified nearly all of its potential dam sites. Thus by the 1930s the Canyon Country was no longer the blank place on a map that it had been for so many centuries. At least conceptually, modernity had reached the Bad Land.

DEFINING CHARACTERISTICS: DESERTS, RIVERS, AND CANYONS
Above all other characteristics, the Canyon Country is a desert. Sun, wind, sand, and rock abound. Aridity lays the rocks bare of most vegetations and loamy soils, exposing the colorful cliffs that draw so many tourists to the region. But aridity alone does not distinguish the Canyon Country. Other deserts certainly have repelled or disgusted explorers and settlers in the Americas: California's Death Valley and Mojave Desert, the Chihuahuan region of Texas and Mexico, and the most arid of them all, Chile's Atacama Desert. All of these deserts are actually much hotter, drier, and "worse" than the Canyon Country. But they lack some of its other characteristics.

The second major feature of the Canyon Country is its rivers. Two great streams, the Green and the Colorado, meet in the heart of Canyon Country to form one of America's longer waterways, which drains about one-twelfth of the contiguous United States.[11] Although the Colorado's flow can be substantial—especially during the spring runoff in May and June when mountain snowmelt funnels into the channels—the river's overall volume is quite small given its length and drainage basin.[12] Adding tributaries such as the sizable San Juan and the smaller Dolores, San Rafael, Dirty Devil, Paria, and Escalante Rivers shows that even this desert has a significant web of waterways. These rivers set the Canyon Country apart from deserts such as the

Mojave or the Great Basin, which lack the orderly outlet of a master stream that drains into the ocean.

Although only the Green, Colorado, and perhaps San Juan Rivers are large enough for even small year-round boat traffic, we might assume that all these rivers are a benefit to the surrounding badlands. River bottoms attract settlement, offering the promise of an oasis in the desert. Unfortunately, however, rivers are also floodways. Many settlements built with hope along Canyon Country rivers failed not because of drought but because of floods. Again, the Canyon Country is not unique in being an arid region transected by a great river. The lower Colorado River valley, the valleys of the Rio Grande through New Mexico and Texas, and even the Cradles of Civilization along the Tigris, Euphrates, and Nile corridors of the Middle East also share this same characteristic.

Its namesakes ultimately set the region apart from all others: deep, abrupt, poorly accessible canyons. John Wesley Powell perhaps described them best:

> The Virgen, Kanab, Paria, Escalante, Fremont, San Rafael, Price, and Uinta on the west, the Grand, White, Yampa, San Juan, and Colorado Chiquito on the east, have also cut for themselves such narrow winding gorges, or deep canyons. Every river entering these has cut another canyon; every lateral creek has cut a canyon; every brook runs in a canyon; every rill born of a shower and born again of a shower and living only during these showers has cut for itself a canyon; so that the whole upper portion of the basin of the Colorado is traversed by a labyrinth of these deep gorges.[13]

Through the heart of the arid Canyon Country flow many rivers and streams, some originating in snowmelt in far-off mountains, others in springs literally gushing from sandstone walls. Cottonwoods, willows, watercress, and maidenhair fern line their bottoms. Visitors sometimes compare these stream-side oases to a garden in the desert, a Shangri-La, a Lost Eden. But in the end the inaccessibility of the canyons trumps their riparian security.

Almost all of these streams are cut off from the surrounding arid landscape by cliffs from ten to several thousand feet high, forming canyons as narrow as ten inches and as broad as fifteen miles. Access to the water at the bottom by means other than by foot is difficult if not impossible in most places. The farther into the web of drainage visitors go, the deeper and more inaccessible the canyon bottoms become. Thus we have another irony: this desert has water in abundance, but it has long been unusable for settlers and travelers. Furthermore, the canyons dictate that travel in the region cannot follow straight lines. In contrast to more utilitarian landscapes in the temperate eastern or northwestern United States, where rivers have long served as natural highways, active erosion and flood deposits in the canyons of the Colorado system have created hundreds of rapids (although very few true waterfalls), making large-scale commercial barge transport impossible.

Quick travel by land is equally difficult. From its high plateau peripheries (for example, along Highway 12 on Boulder Mountain looking southeast along the Kaiparowits Plateau to Navajo Mountain), visitors may gaze across the Canyon Country's seemingly endless expanses and broad horizons and almost be fooled into thinking that it is a wide and uniform plain. Not so. Many have attempted to cut directly across the Canyon Country, following the straightest line on a map, but quickly ran into an impassable canyon, forcing them to detour miles upstream to its head. There they encounter yet another canyon, forcing another detour, and another, and so forth.

As visitors approach the larger rivers—the Green, the Colorado, the San Juan—the added challenge of finding a crossing to reach a route down the canyon walls arises. For example, at the Colorado River's most easily accessible point in the Canyon Country—Lee's Ferry, Arizona—currents are swift and deep, making crossing hazardous. This problem of the canyons has thus dictated that most major historical routes through the region avoid the Canyon Country completely or traverse its peripheries. Indeed, a human history of this region is difficult to construct because it has long been a place to avoid, not to settle. Nonetheless, the desire for a linear, ordered landscape, spurred on by the presence of great rivers in the region, has continuously enticed many into the canyons.

This combination of aridity, large rivers, and deep canyons has not only shaped the exploration and settlement of the region; it has created a landscape that has provoked not just revulsion through the centuries but more recently scientific curiosity and reverential intrigue. The erosional processes of the rivers and their tributaries have exposed millions of years of sedimentary strata in the canyons, and aridity has minimized the cliffside vegetation that characterizes similar plateau regions in Appalachia and the Pacific Northwest. Here geology is stripped naked, for easier observation than in more temperate climates.

Furthermore, beyond such empirical observation and study, the red cliffs on talus pedestals, the isolated spires, and the sculpted slot canyons of this stark landscape prompt a deep aesthetic, even sacred, sense in many. This reverential fascination with the Canyon Country landscape is much more difficult to describe than the aforementioned processes of exploration, settlement, and exploitation. The towering cliffs set in the harsh desert epitomize the horrific beauty of philosopher Edmund Burke's "sublime" landscape. According to Burke's *Philosophical Enquiry into the Origins of Our Ideas of the Sublime and the Beautiful* (1757), sublime landscapes such as towering mountains and waterfalls instill in humans feelings not only of awe but of terror and dread at the landform's inhospitable nature. "Astonishment...is the effect of the sublime in its highest degree; the inferior effects are admiration, reverence, and respect."[14] Sublimity is not necessarily beautiful either. The beautiful is characterized by being small-scale, cultivated, and "smooth and polished," as opposed to the sublime's large scale of intimidating, sometimes horrific, wilderness grandeur.[15]

Edward Abbey, the writer most associated with the Canyon Country, described this sublimity (without using the word) the first time he laid eyes upon the region in the 1950s. Approaching the Canyon Country from the southeast over the top of Comb Ridge, he wrote:

> I hesitate, even now, to call that scene beautiful. To most Americans, to most Europeans, natural beauty means the sylvan—pastoral and green, something productive and pleasant and fruitful—pastures with tame cows, a flowing stream with trout, a cottage or a cabin, a field of corn, a bit of forest, in the background a nice snow-capped mountain range. At a comfortable distance. But from Comb Wash you don't see anything like that. What you see from Comb Wash is mostly red rock, warped and folded and corroded and eroded in various ways, all eccentric,

with a number of maroon buttes, purple mesas, blue plateaus, and gray dome-shaped mountains in the far-off west. Except for the thin track of road, switchbacking down into the wash a thousand feet below our lookout point, and from there climbing up the other side and disappearing over the huge red blister in the earth's surface, we could see no sign of human life. Nor any sign of life, except a few acid-green cottonwoods in the canyon below. In the silence and the heat and the glare we gazed upon a seared wasteland, a sinister and savage desolation. And found it infinitely fascinating.[16]

This study includes many people who encountered the Canyon Country with a similar combination of repulsion and fascination. Some, especially early visitors, were simply disgusted because the region was so alien to their preconceived notions of both beauty and utility. Later, beginning with John Newberry in 1859 and flourishing with the surveys of John Wesley Powell in the 1870s, visitors would marvel at the region precisely for this same alien otherness. But it was rare for even the most excited and enthusiastic explorer to describe the entire Canyon Country with the adjective "beautiful."

Borders and Boundaries

Given the distinctive nature of the Canyon Country, we might assume that it has clear boundaries and that mapping out the region for this study is straightforward. This is not entirely the case, however. The Canyon Country lies within political, topographical, and social boundaries that do not always coincide with one another. The U.S. Southwest, of which some consider the Canyon Country a part, is itself a politically designated portion of a huge transnational desert region that includes the northern half of Mexico as well. With the exception of the California-Arizona state line along the lower Colorado and the Texas-Mexico line along the Rio Grande, most state and national borders in the U.S. Southwest follow imaginary grid-based lines of longitude and latitude. The linear dominates political maps much more here than it does in regions farther east (see fig. 0.1).[17]

Many definitions and names in the Canyon Country implicitly follow similarly invented contrivances. Whenever we call the region "southeast Utah" or

0.1. Location of the Canyon Country within United States political boundaries, the Colorado Plateau, and the Arid Southwest United States.

the "Four Corners Region" we establish a reliance upon linear political borders that have no link to natural features. On a smaller scale, state and county-level chambers of commerce and tourism boards have divided the Canyon Country into several subregions to promote tourism: "Castle Country" in the north, "Color Country" in the west, and "Canyon Lands" in the southeast. All of these divisions are along county lines, which for the most part follow latitudinal divisions running east-west and more natural mountain ridge lines and riverways running north-south.[18] But even these naturally determined boundaries can be problematic—the terrain on both sides of the Green River near its confluence with the Colorado is essentially the same geologically and scenically. What difference does it make that it is called "Color Country" to the west and "Canyon Lands" to the east?

The imposition of these rigid, linear boundaries is a symptom of Euro-Christian and American society's inability to come to terms with the Canyon Country. It is a metaphor for the compulsion to turn Bad Land to Good Land. Thus I avoid using any definition or classification of the Canyon Country in relation to these political boundaries, except for points of reference. Of the many labels used for this region, "Four Corners Region" is perhaps the least in touch with the geographical and environmental character of the land. Naturally occurring lines of drainage, aridity, and topography define the Canyon Country much more effectively, but even these have their ambiguities in places.

The area's most clearly defined border is in the west, where a chain of 10,500-foot plateaus runs north-south through the center of Utah and northern Arizona. These high, well-watered plateaus—the Wasatch, Thousand Lake, Awapa, Aquarius, Paunsaugunt, Markagunt, and Kaibab—have long given shelter and security to Mormon settlements huddled along the edges of the Canyon Country desert.[19] The north-northeast border of the Canyon Country is similarly well defined: the crumbly but imposing Book Cliffs of the Tavaputs Plateau, extending from Price, Utah, over 200 miles to Grand Junction, Colorado, are broken only by the canyons of the Price and the Green Rivers.

The Canyon Country's eastern and southern borders are less clear. Near the upper Colorado's (formerly Grand River's) eastern entrance into Utah, the La Sals, a laccolithic mountain range nearly 13,000 feet high, gradually fade southward into the Great Sage Plain, a mile-high bench that runs roughly north-south along the Utah-Colorado border and is itself bounded farther east by the west slope of the Rocky Mountains. The Canyon Country's southern boundaries are its most ambiguous. South of the San Juan River the terrain gradually gives way to the flatter, less broken, but equally arid deserts of Monument Valley, the Little Colorado, and the Navajo Reservation. Farther west along the Utah-Arizona border, the Echo Cliffs and Vermillion Cliffs separate the southwestern boundaries of the Canyon Country from the Grand Canyon region, before ultimately terminating at the Kaibab Plateau in the far west (see fig. 0.2).

This summary of the Canyon Country's peripheries is well established in the region's literature and encompasses most of the regions that epitomize its combination of aridity, rivers, and canyons.[20] Several areas that certainly fit the appearance of the Canyon Country actually fall outside these geographic boundaries, however, such as Colorado National Monument, Dinosaur National Monument, Zion National Park, and, most importantly, the Grand Canyon. For the most part their stories are different from the story of the Canyon Country, so I treat them only peripherally here. While the Zion area and the adjacent towns of "Utah's Dixie" in southwest Utah are geologically and scenically similar to the Canyon Country, they were never as remote from population centers and transportation routes. Compared to

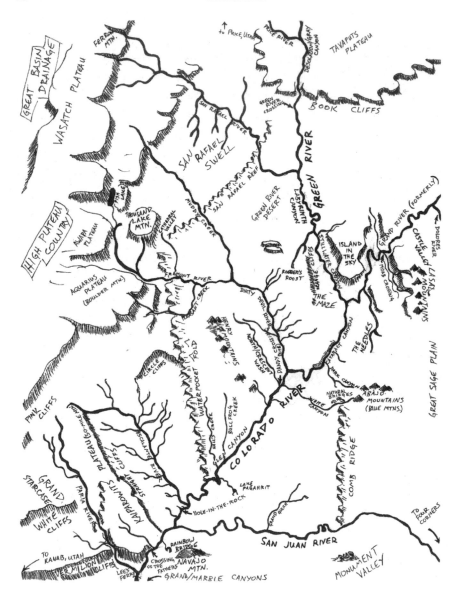

0.2. Nonhuman features of the Canyon Country, circa 1900. (Map by author; not to exact scale)

Glen Canyon, the Dirty Devil Gorge, or the San Rafael Swell, Zion Canyon is quite short in length, though not height. The Grand Canyon, in contrast, is so dramatically inhospitable and huge that it never tempted the same sorts of exploration, settlement, and agricultural exploitation that the Canyon Country did.

Perhaps a more relevant and less frustrating means of mapping the Canyon Country's boundaries rests upon the region's very resistance to settlement through the last few centuries. On a map of the region (such as the map of Mormon settlement in chapter 7), locate the town of Price in the north. Draw a line from Price southwest through the towns of Castle Valley (Castle Dale, Ferron, Emery), continuing through Torrey and Boulder before trending west again through Escalante, Cannonville, and Tropic and then south along the present route of Highway 89 through Orderville and Kanab. From Kanab take the line southeast across the Arizona line to Page and Kayenta then back into Utah through Mexican Hat and Bluff, before turning north through Blanding, Monticello, Moab, and Green River and finally northwest to return to Price.

This line around the Canyon Country touches every long-standing community examined here, with one exception. It is an oblong oval dictating the limits of arable and irrigable land within the Canyon Country. All of these towns along the circled periphery of the Canyon Country were established near mountains, providing the water, soil, and timber necessary for settlement. While a dozen or so communities were founded within this circle, away from the security of the high plateaus, Hanksville is the only one that remains today—more because of its necessity as a refueling-resupply station for travelers than for its self-sustaining agricultural assets. In other words, we can map the Canyon Country according to its very ability to hinder settlement.

Like settlement, transportation routes also have long avoided the region, as a quick glance at a map of modern highways through the area shows. With the exception of Interstate 70, which cuts through and over the San Rafael Swell in the northern Canyon Country, all other high-speed federal highways (U.S. 89, 191, 6) run along the periphery of the region. Those state highways that enter the heart of the area (such as routes 24, 12, and 95) wind through canyons and over ridges, requiring patience and a willingness to trade speed for scenery. Only one road, SR 95, bridges the Colorado within the region— and it was not paved and bridged until 1976. There is no quick land route to get from one side of the Canyon Country to the other, and there never has been. Thus this study pays a significant amount of attention to people who passed through the peripheries of the Canyon Country, looked in with disgust, awe, or perhaps Burke's sublime terror, and left.

The very nature of this desert labyrinth has made it a sort of no-man's-land, a frontier between different peoples and often a neutral meeting place for them. The Canyon Country has been the Far North for Ancestral Puebloans, Spaniards, and Navajos. It has been the Far West for Colorado miners and Utes. It has been the Far Southeast for Mormons and Shoshones. But it has actually been "home" to relatively few. The rivers and canyons have both brought peoples together and separated them. Even for Mormons, who managed to push a few settlements across and beyond the Canyon Country, the region was a harsh dividing line that required compromises and improvisation away from orthodox ways of life. Settlements such as Monticello and Bluff on the far side of the area were forced to do away with many of their traditional "Mormon" means of agrarian sustenance.

Historian Jared Farmer has written that Glen Canyon, the now-submerged heart of the Canyon Country, embodied a contradiction: it was "a periphery that acted like a center."[21] From a cultural point of view this is true. From a geographical, geological, or aesthetic perspective, however, we could just as easily say that the Canyon Country is a center that behaves like a periphery. It is a concentration of perceived Bad Land, a maze of canyons flowing into one another to form a major hydraulic artery of the United States, but it has nonetheless long divided different peoples and ways of life from one another. It has rarely accommodated its visitors. They in turn have rarely accepted it on its own complex terms as they established their straight lines across the crooked landscape.

1

Inventing Teguayo

OLD WORLD CHRISTIANS AND NEW WORLD DESERTS

On November 7, 1776, Fray Silvestre Vélez de Escalante made his way down steep slickrock toward the river far below, carefully edging his feet into the steps carved into the sandstone. He was descending into what Americans would later name Glen Canyon, and the river would later become the Colorado. Escalante's Spanish predecessors called it the Tizón or Buena Esperanza. To him it was simply El Río Grande. Throughout his expedition's last few months of wandering, the river and its surrounding country had been a barrier.[1]

Nonetheless, the crossing proceeded without mishap. The late-autumn sun reflecting off the sandstone cliffs warmed the party, the river's current was slow, and the horses managed to cross the entire channel without swimming. Escalante was no doubt glad finally to have crossed El Río Grande. He would soon reach familiar ground at the Hopi Pueblos and be home in Santa Fe a week or so later. His party had spent the last two weeks searching for a place along the river that would allow access down through the canyon walls to a shallow crossing, only to be turned back repeatedly at dead ends such as "Salsipuedes" (get out if you can).[2]

Escalante was certainly fatigued and frustrated with the Canyon Country region by the time he crossed the river. He and his superior, Fray Francisco

Atanasio Domínguez, were supposed to have found a new, easy route from Santa Fe to recently colonized Monterey, California, without the harsh desert or violent Indian tribes of more southern routes. According to centuries of accumulated geographical speculation that had preceded him, Escalante should have entered a region in the far north called "Teguayo," where he would find lush grasslands, fertile and floatable river corridors, and perhaps even a strait of salt water that would lead him easily across the interior of the continent to Monterey. Furthermore, he was supposed to have found a great inland lake, a northern counterpart to the Aztec civilization's Lake Texcoco in central Mexico, homeland of another Indian civilization awaiting conversion. Instead he was returning unsuccessfully to New Mexico, picking his way through a labyrinth of canyons and relying as he always had upon Indian trails that were the antithesis of his wishful geography of straight lines.

It is easy to cast the supposed failure of Escalante and Domínguez in the dichotomized mold of hope versus experience. They expected to find something very good and instead discovered the opposite. In a way this view contains the ingredients of the clichéd stereotype of all Spanish explorers: false reports of the mythical and fantastic (El Dorado in the Amazon, the Fountain of Youth in Florida, the Seven Cities of Gold in New Mexico), the resultant expeditions sent to find these new lands, and the inevitable failure of the explorers to locate anything valuable. This is "quixotic" defined.

The problem with this view is that the Escalante expedition did confirm some "mythical" expectations. A great inland lake that supported a sizable population did in fact exist: Lake Timpanogos (today's Utah Lake) and the Laguna Ute Indians. The expedition's cartographer, Don Bernardo de Miera y Pacheco, even went so far as to say that of all New Spain's regions Lake Timpanogos alone was "capable of maintaining a settlement with as many people as Mexico City."[3] While Utah Valley's current population of around 500,000 is nowhere near Mexico City's 21 million, Miera's optimism is still understandable; this was unquestionably Good Land. But en route to this fabled Valley of Timpanogos the expedition had also encountered and endured the ultimate Bad Land in the Canyon Country. Miera had nothing positive to say about this region at all:

[It] is made uninhabitable because the river runs through a tremendous canyon between very high and steep red cliffs. Indeed, not even the heathens live on this river for a distance of more than five leagues on either side, because of its extreme sterility, the terrain being rough and broken, and the canyon extending downstream through all the country.[4]

The new land of Teguayo had thus shown the expedition both the best and the worst of geographical expectations—Good Land and Bad Land. Furthermore, there is another important yet oft-overlooked aspect of the Domínguez-Escalante expedition—the imagery of the Old Testament. The party had passed through the howling wilderness of Exodus to find the Promised Land, or even the Edenic garden of Genesis, completing a familiar Judeo-Christian narrative of trial and then redemption, environmental and spiritual. To Escalante this trial narrative was particularly profound.

The expectations and hopes for Teguayo of Domínguez and Escalante, which ultimately came to clash with the imperfect realities of the Canyon Country, were the result of over two hundred and fifty years of geographical speculation about the interior of the North American continent. This speculation, originating far from the gritty deserts and muddy rivers of the Canyon Country, was heavily influenced by biblical themes and worldviews. The stories of Spanish Catholics' unfolding collage of Good Lands and Bad Lands, with Indians ripe for conversion and the hope for a divinely created anthropocentric landscape that could both punish and reward in the New World, are a logical introduction to later Euro-Christian cultures' own profound misunderstandings of the Canyon Country.

GOOD LAND: NEW WORLD EDENS

The biblical journey through a desert wilderness of trial to a promised land of hope and redemption exemplifies the strictly dualistic prism through which the Judeo-Christian mind has long viewed land in a tradition extending back well before the Age of Exploration. With Columbus's discovery of a New World in the West, however, European explorers, intellectuals, and theologians had the perfect opportunity to apply polarized concepts of Good Land and Bad Land, gardens and deserts, and civilization and savagery to a newly perceived "Virgin Land." The expectations and perspectives of the Domínguez-Escalante expedition, and of most later Euro-Christian incursions into the Canyon Country, built upon this tradition both intellectually and spiritually.

At the root of these ideas was the notion that the entire world used to be in an Edenic condition. Only with Adam and Eve's transgression did deserts appear, along with the resultant savagery and harsh wilderness that accompanied them. Reclaiming this Edenic state and achieving its former innocence and state of grace remained deeply ingrained in Christianity's spread through Europe and beyond.[5] This myth would be at the vanguard of European colonialism, as new lands came under varying degrees of Euro-Christian incorporation. In a sense this is why the Canyon Country is so important. In terms of aridity, broken terrain, and remoteness it was the most nonproductive and therefore the most "fallen" landscape, the most difficult to reclaim and redeem.

Most know that Christopher Columbus's encounter with the New World was shaped by his desire to find a quick route to the riches of the East Asia, thereby giving Spain and Christianity an advantage in global commerce and proselytizing. These mistaken geographies and the optimistic desire for direct, linear routes between commercial centers would reemerge in the Canyon Country of Escalante and Domínguez. But the link between Columbus's vision of discovery and later encounters with the Canyon Country runs deeper than simple misconceptions. Columbus held a view of westward-moving destiny that placed the beginning of the human historical narrative in an eastern Eden and moved west toward the End of the World.

To thinkers of Columbus's world, which was much more medieval than Renaissance in intellectual terms, this Eden still very much existed on earth. Thomas Aquinas had written much earlier that "[even if] men have explored the entire habitable world and not yet found paradise," it was quite possible that this Eden had been "shut off by mountains, or seas, or torrid regions which cannot be crossed, so that people who have written about topography make no mention of it."[6] To Columbus the Western Hemisphere had indeed been shut off until the final days of the earth, at which time he was destined to open it to Christian expansion. Given that the earth was spherical and "far east" was now synonymous with "far west," the progression of humanity had come full circle, back to Eden. To quote John Phelan: "The New World Was the End of the World," the logical conclusion of the human narrative.[7]

Furthermore, the idea of balanced, complementary opposites would come to be very important to the views of Columbus and his successors on the New World. Eden could be the location of the "New Jerusalem," the establishment of which would herald the return of Jesus. Dante Alighieri had stressed this balance in the "Purgatorio" section of his *Divine Comedy*, with the "Earthly Paradise" as a polar counterpart to the Old World Jerusalem. This geography not only put the Earthly Paradise in opposing balance with Jerusalem but stressed a balance of water and land on the globe, with the world evenly divided between a hemisphere of earth and a hemisphere of water. Finally, and perhaps most important to Columbus's conception two centuries later, Dante's earth was not a perfect sphere. Rather, the Earthly Paradise was raised from the general topography of the rest of the earth; it was a little closer to heaven, giving the earth the oblong shape of a pear.[8]

These were the ideas that Columbus brought to the New World, especially on his third voyage (1498), which took him to the mainland of what was to become Venezuela, at the mouth of the Orinoco River. According to accounts of this voyage written fifty years later, Columbus felt a sense of profundity as his ships ascended the Orinoco. Though farther south than he had ever been before, he noticed "fresh breezes which come from the springs and rivers and their waters, which produce temperateness and mildness," and extensive forests so intrinsically good that "even if there were nothing of profit other than these beautiful lands…they would still have to be greatly esteemed." This could only mean one thing—Columbus was ascending to the lofty heights of the Earthly Paradise. "As they went to the west the mild weather grew more calm and moderate, and he felt that the sea was rising and the ships were being gently lifted up to heaven…The farther the ships go to the west, the more they are lifted."[9]

If the cool temperatures were not enough proof for Columbus that he was approaching Eden, the very presence and scale of the Río Orinoco was. While not quite the size of the Amazon, the Orinoco drains a significant portion of the world's largest rainforest and certainly dwarfed any other river that Columbus had ever encountered in Europe. It was common biblical knowledge at this time that the Garden of Eden was the earth's master water source, with its superior elevation and huge spring feeding the world's four major rivers: the Nile, Tigris, Euphrates, and Ganges. While the Book of Genesis said nothing about the Orinoco, this huge amount of freshwater simply had to be significant to earth's master watershed, perhaps flowing into one of the four major rivers "through its cataracts below the earth and the sea."[10] Had he continued farther up the river, Columbus was certain that he would have found a huge inland lake, with all the earth's major rivers flowing outward and downward, like the spokes of a wheel. This would be the hub for global maritime travel and commerce, with all continents interconnected. Here was the order of a divinely utilitarian, anthropocentric geography—Good Land.

Realizing the profundity of this evidence regarding his approach to Eden, Columbus came to a dramatic conclusion: the earth was not round. Rather, this new hemisphere was "like half of a pear with a tall stem, or like a woman's nipple on a round ball," with Eden at the tip of the stem or the nipple, albeit "very far from where he currently was." Columbus's later chronicler Bartolomé de Las Casas would write that this idea went "against all the common knowledge of astrologers and philosophers." But it is in fact quite similar to Dante's worldview of an earthly paradise, separated from the "known" world, situated high and close to heaven, and a polar opposite to Old Jerusalem.[11]

But what does Christopher Columbus sailing up a South American jungle river have to do with a southern Utah desert? As this work shows, no other explorer, settler, or missionary who would encounter this New World (except Joseph Smith)—be it in the Amazon or the Canyon Country—would be so bold as Columbus, saying: "I have found the Garden of Eden!" But the imposition of Euro-Christian models and expectations of the earth's geography and the belief that all land would simply work for the good of colonists would persist in more subtle variations as later Europeans approached the Canyon Country, both intellectually and geographically. Columbus's hopes and faith for a Good Land set the stage for Euro-Christianity's rough introductions to Bad Land.

INDIANS OF EDEN

An essential point in the invention of words such as "wilderness" and "desert," both of which imply uninhabited land, is the equating of non-Euro-Christians with the landscape and nothing more. Terms such as "savagery" and "wilderness" become interchangeable and ultimately imply that a region devoid of European civilization is truly uninhabited.[12] Columbus and later proponents of the medieval mysticism that equated the New World with Eden did not use the terms "savagery" and "wilderness," and certainly not the negatively charged "desert." Christian geographical theorists and their successors were completely unprepared to conceive of a broken, arid region such as the Canyon Country; they were hoping for precisely its opposite. In contrast to terms such as "desert" or "wilderness," a new term for the human element of the geographical Eden deserves attention: "innocence."

The hope for converting the inhabitants of the Americas rested upon their dwelling in a state of Edenic innocence. This optimistic European view stressed that, while Indians were naïve and knew nothing of Christianity, they were also free from the evils of secular Europe: lust, violence, greed, thievery. These empty vessels, these *tabulae rasae*, needed only to be injected with a "pure" Christianity free of secular blemishes to become perfect inhabitants of the Earthly Paradise. In 1493, well before Columbus placed Eden on the Orinoco, the papal bull *Inter Cetera II* based its description of the West Indian Tainos on Columbus's earliest reports, saying that "they go about naked and do not eat meat," implying a pre-Fall, childlike innocence.[13] Columbus brought skin color into the picture, writing that the inhabitants near his supposed Eden on the Orinoco were "rather more white than others that had been seen in the Indies" and hinting at notions of a skin-based purity that Mormon settlers brought to the American desert centuries later (see chapter 6).[14] Quite simply, good people lived in Good Land.

Following the conquest of the Aztec Empire in 1519, it became clear to Franciscans such as Gerónimo de Mendieta that a unique opportunity had presented itself. Even more than the Tainos of the Caribbean, Mexico had a huge number of Indians presumably just waiting for conversion. True, they were savages and idolaters; but they were not heretical like Muslims, Jews, or most of all the emerging Protestants of Mendieta's mid-sixteenth century, all of whom had presumably been exposed to Christ's word and then rejected it. The Indians possessed an innate childlike goodness, a "meekness, gentleness, simplicity of heart, humility, obedience, patience, and contentment with poverty." They were "human beings reduced to the most simple and essential denominator of humanness…[they] possessed natural reason, and they were capable of receiving grace; but they lacked all those superfluous emotions and desires which had always led men of other races (the Europeans) into committing sin."[15]

This "Indians as innocents" idea is a perfect extension of Columbus's vision of an uncorrupted New World Eden and its simplistic naked and vegetarian childlike inhabitants. The combined overlying themes of the land and people of this New World were simple: the new Good Land would be cool, high, green, and well watered, with a large lake at its summit, close to heaven. The discovery of this Earthly Paradise would be one of the final steps in Christianity's westward journey to the Apocalypse. Its inhabitants would be innocent, naked, and inherently virtuous beings who needed only a Franciscan version of pure Christianity. This conversion again would be one of the final steps in the westward journey to the Apocalypse.

This vision was obviously overflowing with optimism bordering on the naïve and was most popular with theologians and theorists who were quite displaced from the reality of land and Indian encounters in the New World. *Inter Cetera II* was obviously composed from the comfort of Rome, and Mendieta was writing in New Spain's metropolis: Mexico City.[16] Furthermore, the very idea of "The New World as the End of the World" was a minority view even among missionaries in the Americas, tied to the Spiritual Franciscans, a medieval sectarian movement that had emphasized the poverty of Christ, the corruption of the world, and a "monastic-apocalyptic wilderness theology."[17] In the end Mendieta lamented that this vision was the last gasp of medieval mysticism in the New World. The opportunity to build the City of God in the Americas had ultimately failed with the arrival of secular European corruption in the latter half of the sixteenth century.[18]

This is just as well. As Spain's empire began to focus less upon conquest and incorporation and more upon consolidation in the latter half of the 1500s, more "scientific" minds began observing the New World with a sophistication that surpassed the polarized medieval mysticism of Columbus or Mendieta. Empiricism increasingly began viewing new environments not as Good Land or Bad Land but rather as dynamic landscapes of their own.

Incorporation into the Euro-Christian mind would not come from merely converting Indians or from tranquil Edens simply awaiting discovery but from the large-scale transformation of the New World into a new Europe through human ingenuity and agency.[19]

On the peripheries of Spain's empire, however, religious dualities superseded empiricism; medieval mysticism trumped the Renaissance. As Spain gradually pushed farther north from Mexico City into arid lands that were more akin to the howling wilderness of Exodus than the verdant Garden of Genesis, new versions of trial and redemption presented themselves to explorers. If lush Edenic virgin paradises nurtured innocent and pure Indians, then the arid and fallen deserts of the North likely harbored fallen, savage barbarians; bad people lived in Bad Land. The sense of destiny in converting both peoples and land remained strong and even grew as good Christians encountered Bad Land in the North, and the ever-present hope of Good Land beyond the desert persisted.

BAD LAND: NEW WORLD DESERTS

The desert was the Old Testament antithesis of the Garden of Eden in every possible way: the garden was a water source, the desert was dry; the garden was shaded and cool, the desert was burned and desiccated; the garden was an ordered, pyramidal rise to heaven, the desert was a convoluted maze of broken rock and crooked arroyos; the garden was balanced, the desert was asymmetrical; the garden was virgin and nurturing, the desert was fallen and deadly. Nonetheless, the desert wilderness had a position in Christian myth and history as a place not only of "moral waste" but also of potential paradisiacal bliss. It was fallen but could be redeemed. The desert was also a valuable place of trial and spiritual rejuvenation, even of cultural identity—as in the Israelites' forty-year wilderness ordeal or Christ's forty-day battle with Satan.[20] The Judeo-Christian tradition was rooted in aridity.

One of the earliest people to take this idea of the desert as a place of reflection and contemplation to the New World was the venerable Gregorio López (1542–96), a Spaniard who came to the Americas in 1562 simply to subject himself to spiritual ordeal in the aridity of northern Mexico. His biographer, Francisco de Losa, compared him to Abraham, writing that God had brought him to the New World at the age of twenty "both to try his faith and obedience, and to conduct him into the Desert and there speak to him in his heart."[21] A contemporary of Mendieta, López similarly represented a modification of medieval mysticism, fit for the Americas. But the common ground between the two men ends here. Rather than focus upon grand ideas of Indian conversion or upon the inherent innocence, goodness, and virtue of the New World and its indigenous peoples, López valued the New World precisely because it was a spiritual wasteland, an anti-Eden.

Like Mendieta, López also saw the value of the New World, particularly the desert, as a place to escape the corruption of secular European society. Having traveled from Mexico City to Zacatecas, a rough silver mining town on Spain's northern frontier, López finalized his decision to retreat into the solitude of the desert after he witnessed a fatal sword fight between two miners. To López, this fight was a manifestation of European corruption, which had now even tainted the virgin land of the New World. Thus he rejected the corrupt greed implicitly tied to the search for precious metals, exchanging it for a wild state of nature among the Chichimec Indians, "whose cruelty in those times was much feared by the Spaniards."[22] For the next three years, López lived in a crude hut, subsisting on cornmeal, water, and self-flagellation.

What López did not do was just as important. He obviously did not attend Mass during these three years of his hermitage, which elicited charges of being a "Lutheran Heretick" from the occasional passing Spanish slaver and even drew the attention of the Holy Inquisition.[23] More importantly, he appears to have had no interest in the Chichimecas as potential Christians and made no attempts at converting them. These were certainly not Mendieta's Edenic innocents. López's desert and its inhabitants were valuable to him only on the most personal and introspective level. The desert was a place for internal reflection, trial, and communication with God but not for obligatory proselytizing.

This makes López an anomaly as our narrative extends northward across increasingly harsher, more anti-Edenic deserts. The major Spanish Catholic speculators on what existed in the interior Canyon Country would be missionaries, who had motives and optimism involving both the conversion of Indians and the transforming of Bad Land into Good, of deserts into gardens.

Increasingly, the metaphor of the unredeemed world as a desert wilderness and Christianity as the cultivated garden would come into play, obligating explorers and geographical theorists to view deserts as something to improve in an Isaic redemption process.[24] It would be hundreds of years before people would once again intrinsically value a howling wilderness for the very fact that it was a terrible wasteland.

CORONADO AND THE GREAT RIVER OF THE NORTH

As Spanish attempts at exploration, colonization, and conversion gradually extended northwest from Mexico City through the sixteenth, seventeenth, and first half of the eighteenth century it is unlikely that any Euro-Christians did more than brush against the southern fringes of the Canyon Country. Nonetheless, expectations of exactly what lay beyond the northern frontier began to take shape. Beginning in the mid-1500s, these hopes centered around the ever-elusive Northwest Passage (Spaniards called it the Strait of Anián) a navigable waterway through the North American interior that would manifest Columbus's hopes of a western ship route to the Orient.[25] On the more regional scale, these same hopes eventually created Teguayo, the high roof of the continent somewhere south of Anián. Here lay Lake Copala, a mythical homeland of the Aztecs, the source of the major rivers of Spain's northern frontier, and a variation of Columbus's master water source in Eden.[26]

This promising region, which lay exactly within the Canyon Country, did not receive the definitive name "Teguayo" until the late 1600s.[27] But the Spanish idea of Teguayo, which one historian has called "a compound of Aztec myth, Coronado's Seven Cities, and information supplied by Indians," extended back at least to the 1540s.[28] The curiosity of its gradual invention is that Spaniards drew so selectively upon the most hopeful and optimistic elements of secondhand Indian reports that Teguayo ultimately became a region completely opposite to the Canyon Country's true nature. The idea of Good Land superimposed itself over a veritable Bad Land.

Furthermore, while the expectations of the literal Garden of Eden that characterized Columbus's voyages were not present, the similarities between the master lake at the tip of a pear-shaped hemisphere feeding the world's rivers and an inland civilized lake feeding the continent's rivers are striking.

Both reflected hope, order, and an ease of linear passage across the continent. The vision of a transcontinental water network in which all of North America's rivers originated at a common lake source sprang from the same desire for a divinely created geography of balance and symmetry that created an earthly paradise at the apex of a global watershed.

As many different European explorers began to map the east and west coasts of North America through the sixteenth and seventeenth centuries, they discerned that at least superficially the shape and drainage of the continent had a logical symmetry. Florida had its counterpoint in Baja California; the Gulf of Mexico in the Sea of Cortez; the St. Lawrence River in the Columbia River; and the Mississippi in the Colorado. It is not difficult to see why explorers could assume that this symmetrical geography—"Pyramidal Height-of-Land" in the words of John Logan Allen—culminated in one common water source.[29] Of particular interest here is the river that would become the Colorado, the master stream that drains the entire Canyon Country and along with its tributaries carves the gorges that give the region its name. The first Euro-Christians to encounter this river and speculate about its upper reaches were members of Francisco Vázquez de Coronado's 1540–42 expedition into the interior West of North America.

The story of Coronado is well known and stands in popular memory as one of the prime examples of a conquistador following the promise of riches toward failure in an utter wasteland. Acting upon reports of a mythical Seven Cities of Gold, one of which had been seen on a previous journey by his guide Fray Marcos de Niza, Coronado organized a force of some two thousand soldiers. Most of these soldiers were themselves Nahuatl-speaking Indians from central Mexico, who harbored their own origin myths of seven caves near a great lake from which their ancestors had emerged to migrate south to Tenochtitlán (Mexico City).[30] Coronado found no rich civilizations, only the Pueblo Indians of what was to become northern New Mexico and later the Wichitas of what was to become central Kansas. After suffering a head injury in a fall from his horse, Coronado returned to Mexico with his army, physically incapacitated and financially ruined.[31]

Despite the undertones of the mythical Aztec homeland, which would later become inextricably associated with Teguayo, the Great Basin, and the

Canyon Country, Coronado was not terribly concerned with the region that lay to his north and west. The magical and elusive place-name for his search was not Teguayo but rather Cíbola (present-day New Mexico) and later Quivira (Oklahoma and Kansas). Nonetheless, two reconnaissance parties to the Colorado River compiled information and perceptions of what lay to the northwest. In July 1540 Don Pedro de Tovar left the main army from Cíbola, traveling as far west as the Hopi Mesas of present-day Arizona, which he called Tusayan. Here the Indians gave him "word of a large river" several days' journey away, where "there were marvelous peoples with large bodies."[32] Based upon these reports, a larger party under Captain García López de Cárdenas approached this river the following month. They traveled about twenty days beyond the Hopis, gradually climbing out of the hot summer desert and ascending the 6,000-foot Kaibab Plateau, where they noted increasingly colder temperatures. Finally they arrived at "las barrancas"—the rims of the Colorado's Grand Canyon.[33]

Although Cárdenas reached the canyon rim near what the National Park Service today calls "Grand View Point," he was evidently unimpressed by a view that we consider beautiful today.[34] But he did become the first Euro-Christian to notice the Canyon Country's prime dilemma—a bountiful river perversely set thousands of feet below the surrounding desert, cut off by cliffs so huge that they distorted the river's very scale. Although the party's Indian guides insisted that the river was "half a league wide," Cárdenas assumed that the ribbon of water he viewed was much smaller and sent his three "most agile" men to descend into the canyon. They returned unsuccessful, having not even scrambled a third of the way into the gorge. Assumptions of size and scale within the canyon turned out to be as fluid and fleeting as mirages. Even without reaching the river, the three agile men realized that it was much greater than the assumed "six feet across." They reported that rocks that had originally seemed to be "the height of a man" were actually larger than the church tower of Seville. In summarizing the group's attempt at reaching the river, the expedition's chronicler Pedro de Castañeda wrote that "what from above seemed easy was not, but rather very rugged and rough." These words would epitomize the Canyon Country experience of visitors for centuries to come.[35]

Cárdenas did not speculate about the source or the mouth of this great river. While he and his party gazed into the depths of the Grand Canyon, however, others were simultaneously exploring the lower reaches of the river. Coronado had originally sent Melchior Díaz to rendezvous with a resupply company that was sailing up the river from the Sea of Cortez. The two groups never met, although by late September Díaz had come within fifteen leagues of the river's mouth, noting its great width of nearly half a league. Confirming the Tusayan Hopis' report to Tovar about the inhabitants of the river, Díaz also made note of the "gigantic" size of the Yuma Indians in the lower valley. Finally, he bestowed a European name upon the river: "Tizón." This name, a Spanish word for "firebrand," referred to the torches that the Yumas carried to warm themselves "because of the great cold."[36]

It is curious that the lower Colorado valley inhabitants were experiencing "great cold" in early autumn, although this was the time of the Little Ice Age between the fourteenth and nineteenth centuries when colder weather prevailed.[37] Nonetheless, the name Tizón stuck, and subsequent geographers easily connected Díaz's wide, slow river with Cárdenas's perplexing and inaccessible stream. The Spanish Empire now had a Great River of the Northwest to counterbalance the Mississippi, which Hernando de Soto had explored the previous year. Beyond this, however, Díaz did little with the Colorado/Tizón. The Yumas were appearing increasingly unfriendly to the Spaniards. After torturing and killing an Indian informant who told them of an impending attack, the Spanish intruders quickly returned to their main party. Coronado himself likewise cared little for what the Tizón meant. What lay to the north of the Grand Canyon and the Hopi Mesas concerned him much less than the promise of "Gran Quivira," which would lead his party northeast onto the Great Plains. Coronado's expeditions had identified the river that flowed out of the Canyon Country and even reached one of its most stupendous canyons, but they learned nothing of what lay beyond or farther upstream. Aztec myth and legend notwithstanding, the region that would become Teguayo would wait.

The Good Hope of the Unknown

Coronado's failure was by no means the end of a lingering search for riches beyond the Spanish Empire's northern fringes. Rumors from Indians provided indirect confirmation that there was still something out there. Within the first decade of New Mexico's 1598 settlement, the colony's governor, Juan de Oñate, made several exploratory trips, both toward Coronado's Quivira in the east and to the Hopi villages and San Francisco Mountains in the west. In the autumn and early winter of 1604, amid settlers deserting the colony, rising charges of misconduct, and his failure to find any fabled wealth, Oñate made yet another trip west. This time he journeyed to the banks of the lower Tizón in a desperate final attempt to get any report of riches and secure his quickly falling status in the empire.[38]

Although this expedition went nowhere near the Canyon Country, its Franciscan chronicler, Francisco Escobar, compiled a variety of Indian reports about the river upstream and the land surrounding it. In collecting this indirect information, Escobar provided the earliest written descriptions of what actually lay in the Canyon Country. His descriptions mention nothing of desert, broken country, or the Euro-Christian concept of Bad Land—quite the opposite. But Escobar nonetheless tempered his diary, which he would deliver the following year to the viceroy in Mexico City, with a healthy amount of skepticism and sobriety about these reports of Good Land. This skepticism was certainly not becoming in a Franciscan desiring royal support for the exploration and evangelization of the region.

Through October, November, and December of 1604 the Oñate expedition moved slowly across what was to become central Arizona, following the drainage of the Bill Williams Fork of the Colorado River. In contrast to the frigid weather that Díaz had encountered over a half-century earlier in this region, Escobar noted that the area had "a different climate, for it does not snow and has no matter of cold...although it was midwinter." Reaching the Tizón well above the point at which Díaz had reached it over sixty years earlier, the party gave it a new name: Río Buena Esperanza (River of Good Hope).[39]

What "good hope" did this river hold? Escobar learned of a lake "nine or ten days' journey away," in the interior of the continent, both from the Amacava (Mohave) Indians and a few days later from a Bahacecha chief named Otata. But Escobar never connected it to the Lake Copala of mythical and rich Aztec origins. And while Otata did stress that the inhabitants of this far-off lake wore jewelry of forged metals, Escobar did not automatically assume that these metals were gold or silver. In the midst of Oñate's yearning for riches to save his colony, the extent of Escobar's optimism about valuable metals was that "[the Indians] almost convinced me beyond doubt that there are both yellow and white metals in the country, although it is not certain whether or not the yellow may be gold and the white silver, for of this I have some very grave doubts."[40] Perhaps drawing upon the well-known experiences of Coronado, sent by the Pueblo Indians off into the grasslands of Quivira in search of nonexistent wealth, Escobar likely knew that it was very much in the Indians' interest to lead Spaniards away from their villages with reports of precious metals.

In addition to the good hope of wealth, Escobar harbored doubts about the very environment of the upper river basin as the Indians described it. The chief Otata "and many others" painted an enticing picture of Good Land on the upper reaches of the river:

> On the river of Buena Esperanza, toward its source, there are many buffalo, and very large deer, who wander amongst them. And they say that from a point of six days from the source to the mouth, which is where it enters the sea on the Port of Conversion, it was thirty days [in other words, thirty-six days from source to sea], the entire distance being settled by people who plant maize like the Amacava. This being the case, as the Indians testify, wherever the buffalo lives there can be no lack of grass, and the country must be colder. And thus it seems to me, saving a better judgment, that the exploration could be better made by land and by sea from the source of the River Buena Esperanza, for since the Indians say there are so many buffalo, there must be grass for us for the horses and even for farms. The Indians gave us to understand, also, that the maize was better and grew higher, and that the calabashes were better. And there would be the same convenience for making the exploration by water, for the Indians declare that the river rises near the sea, although there is no more reason to believe them in this than in other matters of which they told us.[41]

Cooler temperatures, agriculture, abundant game, and easy travel by water—here was a perfect land waiting Spanish incorporation, not to mention the conversion of countless souls to Christianity. But all that Escobar could conclude was that he had "no reason to believe" these descriptions. Even the allusion to a transcontinental waterway, a northwest passage, and the "Strait of Anián" extending across the continent, which future geographical theorists would embrace, evoked cautionary qualifying statements from Escobar. While the Indian reports implied a navigable flat-water route up the Buena Esperanza, Escobar made clear that "I have not seen what obstacles there may be."[42]

Today we know what these "obstacles" were. Instead of a cool, grassy, and flat river valley extending for a distance of thirty days' travel up to the continental divide, the "Good Hope" of the river was this: less than a week's travel upstream would have taken Escobar, Oñate, and their party to the enclosed lava and sandstone cliffs of Black and Boulder Canyons. Following the river as it turned east, they would slowly have struggled up rivers with increasingly swift currents and obligatory crossings. Beyond this, they would have reached the Grand Wash Cliffs, which mark the western terminus of the Grand Canyon. From there they faced nearly three hundred miles of impassable rapids, falls, and cliffs dropping directly into the river without banks before reaching the "ribbon" of water that Cárdenas had gazed at a half-century earlier from a plateau rim one mile above. Upstream from this point were Marble, Glen, and Cataract Canyons and the broken maze of the Canyon Country desert extending for hundreds of miles in all directions. At no point in nearly one thousand miles would they have encountered open pastures, buffalo herds, or anything more than the smallest of maize gardens. Escobar did not describe the Bad Land of the Canyon Country at all in his report, but his cautionary statements hint at what lay upstream on this River of Good Hope.

Escobar's restraint would not carry on to his successors, however. A few years later, in 1612, cartographer Claes Jansezoon Visscher drafted a map of the New World from the comfort of his Amsterdam studio. In the area of the Canyon Country he placed Coronado's lost seven cities of Cíbola. Near these cities was an unnamed lake, with a river flowing out of it to the Colorado. Clearly the riches of these cities were easily accessible; perhaps Coronado simply had not been trying hard enough to reach them.[43]

Visscher's map was not published until 1641. But New Mexico Franciscan Jerónimo Zárate y Salmerón did not need a map to paint a more hopeful version of Escobar's cautionary narrative. Like Escobar, Salmerón had experienced the northern frontier of New Spain directly—from 1618 to 1626 he had served as missionary to Pueblo Indians at Jémez, southwest of Santa Fe.[44] Despite this firsthand experience with the landscape and its peoples, Salmerón left his greatest mark in his 1626 *Relaciones*, a geographical and historical synthesis of New Spain's northern frontier based much more on previous reports than on direct personal experience. As part of this attempt to impress the imagined potential of this region upon his superiors in Mexico City and Madrid, Salmerón transformed Escobar's restrained account into a work of optimistic boosterism.

The *Relaciones* begins with a brief and skewed account of Coronado's expedition, with the obvious objective of showing the potential for riches, settlement, and conversion that Coronado had passed up. Stating erroneously (perhaps as an optimistic nod to the potential of Teguayo) that the party traveled northwest from the Río Grande Pueblos to Quivira, Salmerón ignored the party's disappointment and loss on the Great Plains, stating that they had found a "very highly populated city surrounded by a wall and gates," although the men "did not enter it because they were so few." Modestly, Salmerón hinted at the riches of this city by simply declaring: "I do not dare to state here the great riches of this city." He concluded his narrative of expedition by attacking Coronado himself, blaming the expedition's failure not on a lack of riches but on Coronado's wish to return home to his new wife, which prompted him to fake his head injury in the horse accident. The expedition failed because of poor leadership. All that the Spanish Crown needed to do to obtain these riches was to mount another expedition, this time led by "a captain that is fit for such discoveries, a Christian and unselfish, zealous in God's law, and wanting to enrich the royal treasury."[45]

After this indictment of Coronado, Salmerón laid out a grand plan for exploring the interior of the continent and Quivira via a series of imagined ocean inlets and navigable rivers stretching from the St. Lawrence to the Columbia and beyond. Then he came to the pinnacle of his *Relaciones*— a master lake at the apex of the continent, connecting all rivers as surely as Columbus's Edenic lake in the Amazon fed the Nile, Euphrates, and Orinoco. Here Salmerón's interpretation of Escobar and Oñate's expedition approaches the fantastic. Bolton noted these obvious embellishments to Escobar's narrative and assumed that the added details came from additional eyewitness accounts of the expedition to which Escobar had no access.[46] This may be so, but it is equally plausible that Salmerón's own hopes of riches in the Far North shaped this part of his *Relaciones*, just as they did his distortions of the Coronado expedition.

Nonetheless, Salmerón's version of the Oñate expedition to the lower Colorado is significant. Like Escobar, he emphasized the slowness of the river's current, writing that "it is as gentle as the Guadalquiver."[47] More importantly, Escobar's unnamed inland lake has a connection to the mythical Copala in Salmerón's condensed version of one Captain Gerónimo Márquez's upriver reconnaissance to meet the Amacava (Mohave) Indians:

> Here was where they had the first news of the Laguna de Copala, from where, it is presumed, the first Mexicans who settled New Spain left. In glowing words, they described this lagoon and its lands and its shores as very settled. And one Indian said "Copall" very clearly. Captain Márquez told me that these Indians, on hearing a Mexican Indian, the servant of a soldier, speak, one of them asked, "Where is this man from? Is he perhaps from Copala?"[48]

This exchange finally offered proof of the mythical connection of the Far North to an ancestral civilization of the Aztecs. It was not difficult for Salmerón to assume that this civilization on Lake Copala must also possess great wealth in precious metals, just as its descendants in Tenochtitlán had. The linguistic connection also shows the real ancestral link between Utes of the northern Great Basin and the Mexican Indians; today linguists and anthropologists classify the language family of both as "Uto-Aztecan." The Chicano movement of the 1970s constantly referenced its ancestral homeland of "Aztlán," somewhere in the American West.[49] Salmerón himself cited evidence of this ancient southward migration, linking the Indians' movement to the prehistoric ruins and ditches north of the Hopi villages. "Many centuries ago a great number of people had passed through there, who had come out of the Laguna de Copala…traveling to the south."[50]

Salmerón emphasized that approaching this rich new land would be simple and straightforward. Again, drawing upon Escobar's reports of a river route north into the continental interior, he made the case for a direct route from Mexico City to Copala. Instead of taking the existing route to Santa Fe via El Paso and the Río del Norte (today's Río Grande), it would be more direct to move north from farther west, through Sonora to the Hopi villages, thereby hitting the Río Buena Esperanza.[51] In describing this route, Salmerón said nothing of the difficult desert terrain of Sonora and present-day southern Arizona, let alone the Grand Canyon of the Colorado, which the route would have intersected. What mattered was that this route offered a straight line of travel; geography was merely an afterthought.

The present-day Colorado River, however, was not a direct highway to Lake Copala even from Salmerón's optimistic perspective. While the great river did presumably continue eastward and upstream into Quivira, providing an inland passage to the St. Lawrence, Copala was more elusive. Reaching it would require actually crossing the Buena Esperanza and surmounting a divide into yet another major river system.[52] This route would take one through the land of an unpacified tribe of Indians to the north: "Apaches de Nabaju"—Navajos.[53] After passing through their land the traveler would encounter "a very large river that flows into this lagoon [Lake Copala]. The river is all that is needed for a guide, and all the land was level with good pastures and fields, between the north and the northwest."[54]

Here is an echo of the level, easily traveled river valleys of Escobar's report and another description of the Canyon Country that portrays a land completely opposite in character. Topography aside, if we assume that the idea of Copala is based upon Indian reports of the Utes and present-day Utah Lake, the description of crossing the Colorado, crossing a divide to descend into another river, and following that river to the lake is roughly parallel to Escalante and Domínguez's route the following century, which crossed the upper drainages of the Colorado, crested the Wasatch divide, and descended the Spanish Fork River to Utah Lake. But beyond this very little about this route was easy: the river was not all that was "needed for a guide" and certainly did not follow "good pastures and fields."

In altering Escobar's restrained and cautionary report, Salmerón's complex geography established several important precedents that would persist well into nineteenth-century geography via Escalante, Domínguez, Alexander von Humboldt, Meriwether Lewis, and William Clark. According to this view, in the interior of the North American continent lay a series of both saltwater straits and freshwater rivers, with master lakes connecting them to one another. All of these waterways were geographically symmetrical and navigable. Pastoral and agricultural land lined the river valleys. Nowhere in this geographical layout did mountains, canyons, rapids, or deserts have a place; the Bad Land of the Canyon Country was nonexistent, regardless of Cárdenas's horror at the Grand Canyon and Escobar's warnings of vague and unnamed obstacles.

TEGUAYO NAMED

A quarter-century after Salmerón penned this grand vision of the untapped wealth and promise of North America, another Franciscan also began compiling information about what lay beyond the northern frontier of New Spain. From 1650 to 1660 Fray Alonso de Posada traveled as a missionary to various New Mexican pueblos. For four years after that he was the overseer of the Custodia de la Conversión de San Pablo del Nuevo México, a position that allowed him to collect reports on the land from all missionaries under his direction.[55] Like Salmerón, Posada did little exploration himself beyond the New Mexican frontier and waited until he had returned to Mexico City to pen his promotional report of 1686. Although he never explicitly said so, the desire to repopulate the colony after the calamitous Pueblo Revolt of 1680 almost certainly shaped his promotionalism. Most importantly, the grandiosity of his continental perspective surpassed even that of his predecessor Salmerón.

Posada's report was most concerned with Quivira and the eastern portion of the northern frontier, particularly with making the case for an overland route from Florida through the lush grasslands of the southern plains to New Mexico. In perhaps the greatest geographical invention since the Strait of Anián, Posada constructed the Sierras Nevadas, a major mountain range running west-to-east along the northern edge of Quivira, from the Sierra Blanca (the present-day southern Rockies), through present-day Kansas, across the Mississippi, and all the way to the Appalachians. The reasons why Indians or missionaries would have told Posada of this nonexistent range are less important than his reasons for believing it. From a practical stance, a mountain

range such as these Sierras Nevadas would protect his proposed Florida–
New Mexico route from French or English interference. This was even more
important than it would have been for Salmerón. By 1673 the French Jesuit
Jacques Marquette had descended the Mississippi River, coming dangerously
near the mythical Quivira. Upon conversing with Indians near the mouth
of the Missouri River, Marquette developed his own vision of a inland lake,
"small and deep," which logically connected the Mississippi drainage westward to the "Vermillion Sea" (Sea of Cortez) by way of an unnamed but obviously great river.[56]

Posada no doubt recognized the apparent importance of these imagined
mountains in keeping the French out of Quivira and Teguayo, writing that
"they can have been an impediment so that the foreign settlements could
not have spread into the land of the interior."[57] Furthermore, these Sierras
Nevadas somehow offered a balance, the aforementioned "Pyramidal Height-
of-Land," to the continent's layout. Mountains did not fit into Escobar's or
Salmerón's idea of Good Land, but to Posada they could serve a beneficial
purpose. The Sierras Nevadas implied a God-given order in Posada's image of
the continent. But Posada applied an even greater geographical invention farther west, in the region with which we are most concerned. Assigning Lake
Copala to the region of Teguayo, a greater country and worthy counterpart to
Quivira, Posada took the mythical idea of Aztec origins to near Edenic levels.

Although Salmerón had touted the existence of two great civilizations in
the north—Copala in the west and Quivira in the east—he had never fully
explained how they were connected to one another. His Río Buena Esperanza
originated in Quivira and connected to the St. Lawrence, another unnamed
river flowed into Lake Copala, and somehow the Strait of Anián arched over
all of this, terminating to the southwest in the Sea of Cortez. To Posada, Anián
would become the northern centerpiece of Teguayo, serving as a Beringian-
style bottleneck for all southbound Indian migrations. Thus Teguayo was not
simply the homeland of the Aztecs but of all Indians in the Americas to the
south. It was the New World Eden.

> [The Aztec tradition] states that from that region came not only the
> Mexican Indians, who were the last, but also all the rest of the nations

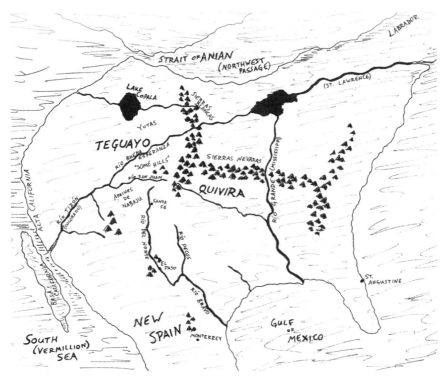

1.1. North America according to Alonso de Posada's written description in 1686. The Canyon Country is labeled as "Some Hills," just south of Teguayo. (Map by author)

which in different times were settling in these lands and kingdoms of New Spain. They mean that this applies to Guatemala and all the rest of the kingdoms and provinces of Peru and those which are contiguous on the mainland because in early times when men were spreading themselves throughout the world and lacked large boats, only through that region did they have facilities to enter with ease through the Straight of Danian [Anián].[58]

Given the evidence about the Bering Strait migrations of ancestral Native Americans, Posada's ideas were not inaccurate, just misplaced. But in locating Lake Copala just south of Anián, Posada hoped to secure the place of a great inland lake as the centerpiece of a transcontinental waterway and a Pyramidal Height-of-Land (see fig. 1.1). The imagined Copala was truly at the crossroads of the continent. Long after the Strait of Anián faded from the imagined geography of the interior West, the presence of a lake would continue to tantalize the hope of a waterway across the continent.

Like his intellectual predecessors, however, Posada was either unaware of the quintessential Bad Land of the Canyon Country or chose to ignore it. He did add very slightly to Salmerón's route description through Navajo land to Copala, noting correctly that the present-day San Juan and Colorado Rivers served as that tribe's northern boundary. Beyond this crossing, "one then enters some hills," which served as the boundary between the Utes and Navajos.[59]

Thus any Spanish mind that chose to regard the Canyon Country at all viewed it as just "some hills." Perhaps the Indian reports of these hills hinted at something that went beyond Posada's Euro-Christian mindset. Rather than simply assuming that Indians would not tell Europeans of deserts, box canyons, cliffs, and impassable rivers, perhaps it makes more sense to believe that their worldview lacked the polarized Judeo-Christian dichotomies between Good and Bad Land, between Eden and the wilderness, that had so shaped the views of European explorers in the New World. By the close of the seventeenth century the Christian mind had constructed an optimistic mythology of what exactly lay in the interior of the continent, to the far northwest of Santa Fe and beyond the political and intellectual frontiers of Christendom. But the true anti-Edenic nature of the Canyon Country remained obscured and perhaps incomprehensible.

2

Encountering Teguayo

THE PARTIAL LEGACIES OF RIVERA AND ESCALANTE

Throughout the eighteenth century, from the gradual repopulation of New Mexico after the 1680 Pueblo Revolt to the 1776 journey of Domínguez and Escalante, the Canyon Country remained little more than a blank space on imperial maps—perhaps with a lake to its north, a straight river running through it en route to the Sea of Cortez, and the name "Teguayo" superimposed on what was still very much *terra incognita* to the European mind. In the absence of documented firsthand accounts of the region, Spaniards understood it to be Good Land: well watered and pastured, culminating at the inland lake that held the key to transcontinental water transport. The visions of Salmerón and Posada were alive; the skepticism of Escobar lay dormant.

Although this Good Land was still associated with Edenic, utopian imagery of a virgin land and virgin peoples awaiting the blessing of the Spanish cross and Crown, geographical theorists by this time had no need to support their vision with Columbus-style millenarianism and mysticism. For the time being Enlightenment beliefs in the inherent goodness of humans and nature that would later come to full fruition with Thomas Jefferson's ideas of a transcontinental Yeoman Democracy overlapped with Catholic missionaries' hopes for more innocent Indian converts in the far north of Teguayo.[1] Geographical optimists could now make the case for Good Land by way of reason—deductively through assumptions of continental symmetry and Pyramidal Height-of-Land and inductively through reports by Indians. But neither faith nor reason would ultimately be compatible with the cliffs, canyons, and deserts that underlay the idea of Teguayo.[2]

Perhaps, then, it is fitting that the Rivera expedition, the first known party to document its entrance into the Canyon Country, was pursuing pragmatic, capitalistic goals and not searching for any grand confirmation of a divinely inspired geography. Domínguez and Escalante's idealistic vision for a route from New Mexico to California via Teguayo later drew support from top-down conjecture by Posada, Escobar, and Salmerón. But their practical goals—which trails to take, which rivers to cross, which Indians to seek—lay in a much messier frontier world of slave trading, prospecting, and semilegal intertwined relations of Indians, Spaniards, and Bad Lands.

Rivera: An Instrument of Empire

Juan María Antonio de Rivera was a prospector and a trader, not a Franciscan. He wrote in a script more befitting a peninsular Spaniard than a provincial New Mexican, though he probably had lived in Santa Fe as early as the 1730s.[3] Beyond this, we know relatively little of his life before 1765, when he made two forays toward Canyon Country and ultimately reached the upper Colorado River near present-day Moab, Utah.

In the spring of 1765 an unnamed Ute from the north brought a chunk of silver ore to a trade fair in Taos. Piquing Rivera's interest, the Indian told him that a certain chief named "Cuero de Lobo" (Wolf Skin) knew where to find more of the mineral. On July 6 Rivera, four companions, and a *genízaro* interpreter procured the services of an old Indian woman who claimed to know the whereabouts of this elusive Cuero de Lobo.[4] Two days later another Ute guide attempted to murder the woman, claiming that she was going to lead the party astray into a harsh wilderness.[5] At its outset, then, this story resembles the narrative of Coronado's expedition, with feuding Indians of ambiguous loyalties leading the Spaniards deeper into the unknown, toward wealth, death, or both. In Rivera's story, Cuero de Lobo danced like a shadowy mirage always just on the horizon, beckoning the men nearer and nearer to Teguayo.

The party made its way northwest, past a boulder bearing the image of the Virgin of Guadalupe, and across the San Juan River. It passed by a ruined city that later Americans would call Mesa Verde, a "pueblo in a canyon so expansive and large that it would appear to be two times larger than the village of Santa Fe."[6] Knowing from their guides that they were approaching an increasingly fallen and corrupted land, the sight of this once great but now fallen city added to the ominous and uncertain feeling of Rivera and his companions.

Three days later, on a lively mountain river that Rivera called Río Dolores (River of Sorrows), a lengthy conversation with a Moache chief called "El Chino" confirmed the party's fears of the unknown.

> Chief Chino spoke, beginning the conversation…asking why were the Spaniards traveling through such badlands?…to which we responded that we were looking for a Ute named Cuero de Lobo, that it was said that he was with the Paiutes, and that we desired to find where there was a great river, that is called the Tizón. They replied, that the said river was far away and was through bad country without foliage or water, that there were many sand dunes that would tire out the horses, and that we would burn up from the sun along the trail.[7]

In giving the name "Tizón" to his intended destination, which actually did flow into the river that Melchior Díaz had encountered and named Tizón over two hundred years earlier, Rivera shows that he must have been somewhat familiar with the body of geographical speculation that made up the Spanish image of the far north. We do not know if he had read the reports of Salmerón or Posada directly. It is more likely that he would have heard rumors spawned by the reports around Abiquiú and Taos among Indian slave traders and prospectors. In any case the name "Tizón" invoked Salmerón's old reports of lush valleys, Indian gardens, and bison herds that supposedly lined the river's length from source to sea. El Chino's tales of Bad Land had no place in the existing Spanish image of Teguayo or the Tizón. This conflicting information must have deeply troubled Rivera.

Heat stroke, aridity, and deep sand—El Chino was certainly describing a July walk in the Canyon Country. But his description of a complete antithesis to the expected Good Land of Teguayo went further. Even if Rivera and his companions were to succeed in reaching and crossing the Tizón, they would come across a cavern guarded by a monster "which cuts up in pieces anyone who comes or goes without giving it a skin." Should Rivera pass by this obstacle, he would then come to a "huge ditch" that was crossable only by precarious wicker baskets and finally come upon "barbarian white men dressed in iron suits…and their women have on their arms iron rings."[8]

We could easily dismiss this as simply yet another example of Indians telling sensational and fantastic myths to European explorers. Tales of monsters in unknown lands arrived in Europe on the heels of Columbus's first voyage, with late fifteenth-century publicists writing of Amazons, Cyclopes, and the like.[9] The promise of a lost or remote white civilization, a metaphor for a garden of virtue and order beyond the chaotic wilderness, was also well established in the mythical view of the New World by this time. Columbus wrote of inhabitants along the Orinoco getting whiter as he approached Eden, Coronado's Seven Cities were said to have been established by seven exiled Portuguese bishops who were fleeing the Moorish invasion of Iberia, and Salmerón wrote of white bearded people, perhaps Russians, who lived along the fabled Strait of Anián as it passed through North America.[10] Later Mormon missionaries similarly sought out and speculated about lost tribes of white-skinned "Nephites" in the American Southwest who had somehow escaped their God's curse of red skin and savagery.[11]

But what of El Chino's "huge ditch" that was beyond the river crossing and the skin-greedy monster? For the first time since Cárdenas encountered the Grand Canyon over two centuries before, this was a cogent though brief description of the Canyon Country's namesake gorges. The two-word description "huge ditch" again posed an opposite to the expected wide, fertile river valleys of Teguayo's Good Land. We do not know what specific canyon El Chino may have been describing. One Rivera expert has written that it must be the Grand Canyon, which is the largest "ditch" in the region. But no prominent Indian trails led directly from the upper Colorado near Rivera to the Grand Canyon. The Black Canyon of the Gunnison River has also been mentioned as a possibility, but this gorge was much too close to Rivera's camp on the Dolores and on the near side of the Colorado.[12] Beyond the Colorado River crossing at Moab to the north and west, however, lie a number of "huge ditches," such as the San Rafael River's Little Grand Canyon, Eagle Canyon, Coal Wash, and Desolation or Labyrinth Canyons on the Green River. El Chino's tales of monsters were fantastic, even horrific, but his "huge ditch" was certainly real.

None of this was what the Spaniards wanted to hear. El Chino's tales were enough to halt Rivera, who began considering a prompt return to New Mexico. Two days after meeting El Chino the Spaniards did finally encounter the elusive Cuero de Lobo, who led them to the supposed silver source. In an anticlimactic moment Rivera found that the fabled ore was more likely to be lead than silver. They took a few samples back to New Mexico. The ore probably did not amount to much, as the record says little else about it.[13]

Later that year Rivera retraced his steps to the Dolores and beyond. The promise of minerals alone was probably not enough to prompt his return to the far northwest. But the promise of Teguayo, even if its location was now pushed beyond the howling wilderness of El Chino's tales, would draw him back. Unlike his first foray toward the Canyon Country (a small-scale, illegal quest for riches) this one was directly ordered by New Mexican governor Tomás Vélez Cachupín. Its objective was to secure Indian relations and establish exactly how this new land in the north and its borders related to the rising clash of empires across North America.[14] Specifically, how close was Teguayo to British holdings on the continent? Characteristically in this era of the Spanish Bourbon Reforms, in which the increased royal power attempted to establish a stronger and more standardized presence in colonies worldwide, Rivera was now an instrument for imperial expansion.

To keep news of the true objectives of his expedition from reaching rival European powers via Indian channels, Governor Cachupín's orders instructed Rivera to continue the charade of searching for minerals. Presumably prospectors and traders would seem unremarkable to Indians.[15] Rivera's true objective as charged by the governor, however, was a direct continuation of Salmerón's and Posada's continental visions. He was to find El Chino's crossing of the Tizón, locate the "large ditch," and "find if the Tizón River has its origin in the Great Lake Copala that the Pueblo Indians call Taguallo [Teguayo]…and if it is surrounded by many large Pueblos, according to ancient and modern reports."[16]

Around October 1, 1765, with the same men but with a new purpose, Rivera headed north. Now that he had official backing, he made much more

detailed observations of mountains, water sources, and pasturage. He also
continued to pay attention to Indian reports of what was to come, pressing cautiously into land of an increasingly broken nature, but more determined than before. By October 10 the party was camped in a barren region
somewhere between the Abajo and La Sal Mountains, perhaps at the head
of Indian Creek Canyon.[17] Nearby Tabeguache Utes repeated the stories of
danger and monsters ahead, and it was only with great difficulty that Rivera
procured a young guide for his final push to the Tizón. Five days later they
climbed out of the canyon, passed by the southern flank of the La Sal Mountains, and followed a "pretty little river" (probably the cool waters of Mill
Creek) to what we today call the Colorado River in Moab Valley.[18]

But was this the great River of the West, the Tizón, the Buena Esperanza,
the path to Lake Copala and Teguayo, the missing piece in a transcontinental
waterway? Despite their young Tabeguache guide's insistence that it was "the
big river," Rivera could not believe that this was what he had been seeking. His
disappointment was confirmed the next day when he traveled upstream to
find a confluence where "nine small rivers join together."[19] This being October
and the Colorado being fed by snowmelt, the stream may have been shallow,
narrow, and thoroughly unimpressive to Rivera, who very likely had formed
expectations based upon the navigable Guadalquivir and Tagus Rivers of
Spain. This simply could not be the Great River of Lake Copala and Teguayo.

Rivera took his frustrations out on his young guide, admonishing him
that this river:

> was not the Río del Tison for which we searched and that he had failed
> us in his quest…He replied, somewhat reserved, that there was no
> other river larger than that one and that that was the one for which
> we searched, that he had brought us there because he had heard from
> his people that farther downstream one cannot cross because it is
> wider than the eye can see and there comes [sic] together all of the Rio
> Grandes which we had crossed.[20]

In a way the guide was correct, although Utes and Navajos more familiar with the terrain of the Canyon Country would have spoken of inaccessible canyons rather than an uncrossably wide river. Until the construction

of bridges and reservoirs beginning in the 1920s, no easy crossing of the Colorado River existed for over 500 miles between Moab Crossing and Pierce's Ferry, well beyond the mouth of the Grand Canyon.[21]

Despite this disappointment, the idea of Lake Copala, the literal and metaphorical roof of North America, persisted. Rivera's young guide insisted that this river was the only and greatest one in the region but also gave a promising hint of the mythical lake civilization that had tantalized Spaniards for centuries and that Escalante would encounter eleven years later in present-day Utah Valley. Beyond the great river, the guide said, at the foot of a "small mountain," lived "people more numerous than stones."[22] This was enough to keep the myth of Teguayo alive, along with its undertones as a lake-based homeland to the Aztec people.

Two days after the disappointing realization of a puny Tizón, five Saguagana Utes visited Rivera's camp on the river. This tribe apparently had fled into the howling wilderness after taking part in the Pueblo Revolt of 1680, having feared retribution by Spaniards for over eighty years. Rivera thought little of the Saguaganas and gave them the label *gandules*, a colloquial Spanish word meaning "shiftless" or "lazy."[23] Instigating a tradition that many later observers of desert Indians would follow, Rivera saw them as an inferior people in an inferior land. "Higher" Indian tribes such as Utes or Navajos rode their horses in and out of the Bad Land. Only the lowly—Saguaganas, Paiutes, and Gosiutes—actually made their homes there. Later explorers such as John C. Frémont and F. V. Hayden would describe them as "most degraded" and "digger" Indians.[24]

After discussing the nature of the country both below and beyond the river with the Saguaganas, Rivera reluctantly concluded that he was not being deceived and decided to turn back to Santa Fe for the second time. Although the Saguaganas invited him to continue across the river and Rivera must have realized that he had reached a very significant bottleneck in Indian trade routes between New Mexico and the elusive Teguayo, he was clearly ready to return home, Cachupín's orders be damned. This was Bad Land, his men were tired, and his horses were losing shoes.

Returning south, and leaving the Canyon Country, Rivera made note of the arid landscape. "We descended to the south through big valleys of very sandy terrain although with some pear cactus." It was *pinta serpanino mineral por que no tienen pastos*—winding, painted, multilayered minerals, exposed because the ground was denuded of vegetation.[25] This is a classic Canyon Country vista, what American geologists would later name the Chinle Formation, a rainbow-hued conglomeration of clays, shales, and sandstones. Although Rivera collected some rock samples from this *pinta serpanino*, falling back from the mythical to the pragmatic, they would yield no wealth (although this same Chinle Formation would prove to be very rich in uranium in the 1910s). Thus Juan Antonio María de Rivera left the far north for a second time much the same as he had the first time: disgusted, disappointed, and perhaps even frightened. His journal gave no hint of any sort of agricultural, mineral, or religious promise in the region.[26]

In a way, then, Rivera's second expedition, and the first direct Spanish encounter with the Canyon Country, was double-edged. The supposed role of the Tizón/Colorado as the Great River of the Far North ended. Rivera correctly concluded that the shrunken river he found did indeed empty into the Sea of Cortez and that it did not originate in a great inland lake as previously assumed.[27] This was another small step—neither the first nor the last—in exchanging the mythical and the unknown for something quantifiable and not terribly impressive in Rivera's eyes. In this sense Rivera's conclusion was as significant as Lewis and Clark's later discovery that no easy water route from the Missouri to the Columbia existed. The Tizón ceased to be a Great River of the North for Spain. Now it was a smaller, less impressive river of the desert wilderness. No longer a path or highway, it was now a confirmed boundary between the known and the mythical.

But Rivera also kept alive the vision of Teguayo and the Far North of the Spanish frontier beyond the Tizón. Armed with descriptions of the Timpanogos Utes around Utah Lake, he reinforced the existence of Lake Copala and its civilization. As Domínguez and Escalante's subsequent journey and its accompanying map would make perfectly clear, the negation of the Tizón-Colorado as a Great River of the Far North only prompted the Spanish invention of a more linear, logical, and naïvely optimistic waterway from Copala to the Pacific: the San Buenaventura.

DOMÍNGUEZ AND ESCALANTE: THE LAST OF THE MENDICANTS
Much changed in northern New Spain in the ten years following Rivera's

journey into the Canyon Country. In 1767 Carlos III expelled the Jesuit Order from all Spanish colonies, seizing its schools, hospitals, ranches, and mission holdings.[28] This was one of the most profound of the secularizing Bourbon Reforms, which two years earlier had indirectly prompted Governor Cachupín to employ the trader Rivera in exploring New Spain's far northern fringes. If the Franciscan Order was a product of medieval mysticism and millenarianism, the Jesuits were a product of the Renaissance, specifically the Counter-Reformation of the early 1500s. In contrast to the Franciscans, who took vows of poverty, these highly educated "spiritual storm troopers" built a veritable empire within the Spanish Empire (as well as French and Portuguese Empires), successfully incorporating Indian missions into global commerce and becoming very wealthy.[29]

Given the differing ideologies, backgrounds, and objectives of the Jesuits and the Franciscans, it is worthwhile to speculate how the Spanish consciousness regarding Teguayo would have been different had Jesuits done most of the geographical theorizing about the region. Had the order not been expelled, it is possible that Jesuits from Baja California and Pimería Alta (modern-day southern Arizona), following the legacies of explorers such as Eusebio Francisco Kino, would actually have entered the Canyon Country and perhaps have described its complexities with the same detail that Kino had applied to the deserts of Baja California.[30] But ultimately the thrust toward Teguayo emanated northwestward from Franciscan-dominated New Mexico.

In 1769, two years after the expulsion of the Jesuits, Spain began by sea the colonization of Alta California, perhaps the most quintessentially "Good Land" in North America. This venture was tied directly to the vacuum left by the Jesuits. Gaspar de Portolá, the head of the exploratory expedition, had recently overseen the expulsion of the order from Baja California, and the missionization of this new region was carried out by Franciscans under Fray Junípero Serra, a self-flagellating throwback to the medieval mysticism of Mendieta or even Gregorio López. Despite their zealotry, or perhaps because of it, secularized Spanish policy exploited Franciscans such as Serra by this time and certainly later desert ascetics such as Francisco Garcés, Silvestre Vélez de Escalante, and Francisco Atanasio Domínguez as a means of securing New Spain's northern fringes.[31] Missionaries hoped to convert Indians of Teguayo, providing allies against the British to the north, and eventually set the stage for expansion and population into the Good Land of the continent's interior.

The colonization of Alta California brought about the culmination of the optimistic Spanish view of the interior West. Teguayo and the Canyon Country were no longer a hinterland beyond all Christian civilization. Now they were between two Spanish colonies: New Mexico and California. In 1774 Juan Bautista de Anza and Fray Francisco Garcés found a reasonably direct route from Sonora to the Los Angeles basin via the lower Colorado River. Two years later Anza repeated this journey with 240 settlers and founded San Francisco.[32] But this route traversed terrible deserts and passed Indian tribes not always friendly to Spaniards: in other words, Bad Land and Bad People. As Escalante wrote of the southern route, it had "more than one hundred leagues of impassable road, there being for a large part much rock and most of it pebble and flint, and water and pasture is scarce."[33] The rumored Good Land of Teguayo promised a better alternative: well-watered river valleys emerging from Lake Copala, a cooler, more temperate climate, and a more direct line between Santa Fe and Monterey, California.

Underlying all of these expectations was the ever-present promise of a receptive society of innocents in Teguayo, though by this point not even missionaries such as Escalante were evoking blatantly Edenic imagery. In contrast with the Yumas and Mohaves along the southern route, corrupted by aridity, the northern region was sure to hold virtuous Indians waiting to be infused with Christianity. Furthermore, in a letter to New Mexico governor Pedro Fermín de Mendinueta making the case for this northern route, Escalante repeated the promise of lost white civilizations beyond the Tizón that would surely aid in both converting the Indians and strengthening the northern frontier. Expectations for an equally benevolent geography also appeared in Escalante's letter, as he mentioned the possibility of travel by "straight lines"—in other words, Good Land and Good People.[34]

Ironically, then, the 1776 expedition of Domínguez and Escalante, which for the Canyon Country was the culmination of the centuries-old Franciscan view of innocence, destiny, and conversion in the hinterlands, was inextricably tied to the previous tumultuous decade of the Spanish Empire's consolidation. For all the friars' emphasis in their writings on the intrinsic, unselfish,

and simple God-serving nature of their expedition, they were ultimately acting as pawns for the rising secular bureaucracy of New Spain in finding a
route to the new colony of California.

Because individual state histories place high emphasis on the "first" whites
to cross modern state boundaries, the basic narrative of the 1776 Domínguez-
Escalante expedition is well known to any student who has taken a fourth-
grade Utah history class, although those wishing to squabble about who was
first in Utah should probably give that credit to Rivera on a technicality.[35]
Leaving Santa Fe on July 29, 1776, the two friars and perhaps ten companions took Rivera's general route to the Dolores River Canyon. Rather than go
toward the Moab crossing, however, they trended toward the northeast and
the Gunnison River before reaching the Colorado well above present-day
Grand Junction. From here they traveled across high mountains to the White
River and then the Green River in the Uinta Basin, before climbing into the
high country, where the east-west oriented Uinta Mountains meet the north-
south running Wasatch. They dropped into Utah Valley from Spanish Fork
Canyon, along present-day U.S. Highway 6. After preaching to the Laguna
Utes there, they went south, roughly following the course of today's I-15 to the
location of Hurricane, Utah. They turned east along the Utah-Arizona border,
first to Lee's Ferry and then to a Ute ford in Glen Canyon (see the beginning
of the first chapter). After this final river crossing, they reached the familiar—
though not particularly friendly—Hopi villages on November 17 and were
back in Santa Fe by January 2, 1777.

The details and subtleties of this expedition go beyond their course, however. Tension between the friars and the laypeople who accompanied them
rose quickly regarding trade with Indians, slavery, weapons, and eventually
the route that the expedition was to take. The friars were young (Escalante
was in his mid-twenties, Domínguez his early thirties) and idealistic. While
both had experience with the messy realities of proselytizing to Indians (notably Escalante with the Hopis) their vision of Teguayo and the Far North was
steeped in the optimistic reports of Posada and Salmerón. In letters proposing the expedition to his superiors, Escalante stressed not only the familiar
mythical elements of Teguayo but also a very positive view of the Indians that
he hoped to encounter. No matter how "hostile" or "savage" the Indians of

this new land might be, he wrote, their conversion could not be forced; their acceptance of the Gospel would have to be completely "free and voluntary." The friars would have to avoid "the indiscreet ardor with which others have tried to convert Indians and infidels with the sword."[36] Regardless of whatever imperial goals their explorations might fulfill, the friars saw their mission as a very simple one: "God's greater glory and the spreading of the faith." They would have "no other destination than the one which God would grant us; nor did this tempt us to any worldly purpose whatsoever."[37]

But not all of the party were young and idealistic Franciscans. Most others were hardscrabble frontiersmen, Indian fighters, prospectors, and slave traders. Some were also much older than the friars. The expedition's cartographer, Don Bernardo Miera y Pacheco, had experience in the hinterlands going back at least to a 1747 military expedition to the Gila River, longer than Escalante had been alive.[38] Translator Andrés Muñiz and his brother Lucrecio were *genízaros* who had made at least two forays into the region. Andrés even claimed to have accompanied Rivera on his first journey in 1765.[39] These men, who according to Escalante would be the chief inciters and dissenters during the expedition, did not care about the inherent value of innocent Indians or about converting them. They wanted furs, slaves, information about precious minerals, and a quick route to California.

Domínguez and Escalante had drawn their ideas from the well-documented, highly speculative writings of previous Franciscans. Miera and Muñiz were drawing theirs from a legacy of oral accounts circulating among fellow traders and from firsthand experience north of New Mexico. There, on the northern frontiers of New Spain, blankets, weapons, and Paiute slaves passed through the porous boundary between Utes and Spaniards, as both groups attempted to survive in a complex peripheral colonial economy. The objectives of the friars and the laypeople were at odds with one another and very nearly destroyed the expedition. The friars would beg Miera and Muñiz "not to engage in commerce, so that the infidels might understand that another motive higher than this one brought us through these parts."[40] At the heart of this dispute lay a conflict that would come to dominate future views of the Canyon Country even today, although in a very different form: the reverential versus the utilitarian. To Miera and Muñiz, the friars were naïvely idealistic;

to Domínguez and Escalante, the two laymen were greedy, self-serving, and bad Christians.[41]

Tensions surfaced within weeks of the party's departure from Santa Fe. With Muñiz and local Tabeguache Utes as guides, the party descended into the canyon system of the Dolores River, which runs northward along today's Utah-Colorado border. While this area is not within the boundaries of the Canyon Country's core, its winding canyons and red rock cliffs still share some characteristics with the heart of the Canyon Country to the west. Escalante made note of this, writing of one canyon's "many turns for seven leagues," only traveling a straight line of "four or five [leagues] at most."[42] His hopes for a direct line of travel were beginning to crumble around the edges, but at the time this seemed only a slight inconvenience to the friars. They did not exhibit horror or disgust at the landscape, certainly not as they would later while crossing the more broken landscape of Glen Canyon. Escalante wrote about the Dolores River canyon's "pleasing scenery of rocky cliffs" in the earliest recorded hint of an aesthetic appreciation for the region. The canyons were not yet overwhelming the party, and this was not yet Bad Land.[43]

Hinting at rising tensions between the religious and the secular, Escalante named this complex region "El Laberinto de Miera" (Miera's labyrinth). Throughout this broken country, Miera annoyed the friars by riding ahead of the others and often losing them. Later the friars would find out that Miera and Andres Muñiz had begun secretly trading goods and weapons to the Tabeguache and Sabuagana Utes in this region, contrary to their orders.[44] Furthermore, Muñiz was beginning to show his ineptitude as a guide in this area. Although he had traveled (or claimed to have traveled) in the area with Rivera's first expedition in 1765, he lacked the large-scale geographical vision of Rivera. Guiding the party northeast from the Dolores labyrinth to the Río de San Francisco Xavier (today's Gunnison River), Muñiz told them erroneously that this was the great Tizón.[45]

The major curiosity of the party's journey to the Great Basin is that it took a huge northeastern detour along the west slope of the Rocky Mountains. Despite the presence of Muñiz and their knowledge of Rivera's foray, the Domínguez-Escalante expedition completely avoided the Moab crossing of the Colorado River.[46] Although this in a way affirmed the Canyon Country's role as a place to avoid, it also abandoned Escalante's desired "straight line" to Teguayo, one of his justifications for the trip to Governor Mendinueta. The route that Rivera had taken to the Colorado River was a preexisting Indian trail, the major route for trade with the Laguna Utes of the Great Basin. Though arid, it was open and direct for most of its length.[47]

Instead of taking this direct line, which would have been familiar to the Tabeguache guides if not to Muñiz, the expedition contrived a difficult route through the Dolores and Gunnison Canyons. On several occasions it encountered trail junctions and consciously turned to the northeast, away from both the Canyon Country and Teguayo. Escalante never gave a clear explanation for this diversion from the linear, despite his earlier emphasis on direct lines of travel. Perhaps the party, both laypeople and the friars, were thinking of Rivera's cautionary tale of abandonment, sorcerers, monsters, and Bad Land. Furthermore, although Muñiz had accompanied Rivera on part of the route, he did not have direct knowledge of the route to the Moab crossing, only of the Gunnison-Dolores region.

Geographically speaking, once the party entered the Dolores system of "Miera's Labyrinth," the ridges and canyons forced it to trend to the northeast, away from Rivera's route. Later, as the party members proceeded northward after crossing the upper Colorado, the Tavaputs Plateau and Desolation Canyon system of the Green River continued to prevent them from heading west, forcing them still farther north until they could cross the Green River in the open country of the Uinta Basin. But their chosen route was not a complete failure. Although not direct or open, it avoided the lower deserts of Rivera's route. Water was not an issue. Throughout their northward journey along the western slope of the Rockies, Escalante was impressed with the land, which was "very moist and has good lands for farming without irrigation."[48]

It is also possible that their Indian guides were trying to get the party lost, or worse. Ever-present just over the mountains from this northeastern route were the Comanches, who at this time were at war with Ute-speaking peoples and would likely kill the group. Although the Spaniards' Ute guides warned of this danger, they also took the party dangerously close to the Comanche-Ute boundary.[49] Furthermore, in the large-scale scope of trade and empire, Escalante was aware that Indians suspicious of Spanish motives would not see this expedition as a simple search for a route to California. Well aware of intertribal communication networks to the south and west, Escalante actually worried that news of Francisco Garcés's explorations south of the Grand Canyon would reach the Utes via the Havasupai, Hopi, and Paiute Indians, leading all tribes to conclude that some sort of large-scale invasion was brewing.[50] Of course, this apprehension was more real than even Escalante himself could believe. Despite Escalante and Domínguez's faith that they were simply undertaking a benign and unarmed missionary effort, they were effectively agents for Bourbon Spain and for its planned incorporation of Teguayo and its peoples into a Euro-Christian framework. Powerful equestrian Indian tribes that controlled trade routes had no interest in an increased Spanish understanding of the interior West and certainly not in missionaries who might protest their slave trade.

All of this plays into the uneasy conflicts and contradictions that surely were flooding the minds of Escalante and Domínguez as they journeyed north and then west toward the Laguna Utes and Timpanogos Lake in today's Utah Valley. They knew that they were approaching a great people near a lake and had faith that Copala and the possible ancestors of the Aztecs were near. By staying in the Good Land of the mountains they also had avoided the howling wildernesses and monsters of Rivera's report. Keeping in line with the equation of fallen lands and fallen inhabitants, they had likewise encountered no "bad" Indians. Rather, both land and Indians were fertile ground for European agriculture and Christianity. As the friars drew nearer to the Promised Land of the Lagunas, they emphasized more and more the receptiveness of the Indians to Christianity and the suitability of the land for irrigation and farming.[51]

But at the same time these Franciscans had to keep the corruption of secular society away from these innocent lands and peoples. Just as Gerónimo de Mendieta had lamented Europe's ruining of the New World Eden in Mexico and Gregorio López had seen corruption in secular mining culture, Domínguez and Escalante saw the evils of trade and mining manifest in their companions Miera and Muñiz. Notably, Escalante never mentioned mineral potential at all in his assessments of this land, whether out of an ascetic disdain for valuable metals or out of a fear of possible Indian enslavement in mines. His emphasis was on the agrarian, the organic, and the renewable. Mormon settlers in the same region would carry similar views a century later.

Considering the two centuries of mythical background concerning Teguayo and Copala, Escalante's account of the expedition's entrance into Utah Valley was neither a culmination nor a defeat—somewhere between Cortés's glorious entry into Tenochtitlán and Coronado's crushing realization that there was no Quivira. Emerging from Spanish Fork Canyon into Utah valley must have been a pleasant end to the circuitous canyon, but its Indian residents had also set series of fires to the dried autumn grasses as a warning to the intruders. The friars named the valley "La Vega del Dulcísimo Nombre de Jesús" (Plain of the Most Sweet Name of Jesus) and emphasized that the Laguna (Lake) Utes were much more ripe for conversion than any tribes encountered earlier, but Escalante definitely gave no hints that this was the conclusion in a grand search for an inland Eden.[52]

Indeed, if we remember the imagined role of Lake Copala as a great liquid hub of the continent's rivers (connecting the Missouri, the Río Grande, the Columbia, and the Colorado as Jacques Marquette had thought or even as Lewis and Clark would later envision), the descent of Domínguez and Escalante into the Great Basin represented the antithesis of a Pyramidal Height-of-Land. Utah Lake was beautiful and surrounded by fertile land— Miera would go on to write of its potential as the new metropolis of New Spain—but it led to nowhere. More troubling, the larger body of water, the Great Salt Lake just to the north, was an inverted pyramid: a sink, not an apex. Instead of being the center for a neo-Aztec civilization, the saline desolation of the Great Salt Lake was a natural frontier between the Utes and the Shoshones (called Comanches by Escalante), inhabited only by untrustworthy "bewitchers" who were neutral at best.[53]

Perhaps the friars' missionary zeal and self-supposed altruism helped them cope with their disappointing loss of the mythical Teguayo. After all, they still had the promise of "perhaps some other nation heretofore unknown which may always have been living in the region north of El Río Grande." Although the party did not personally visit the Great Salt Lake, reports of a huge body of salt water fit the old legend of an ocean strait somewhere north of Lake Copala.[54] Furthermore, several days after leaving the Lagunas with promises of a return and further baptism, another part of the Teguayo myth emerged into reality. Near today's Sevier Lake the party met a tribe of bearded Paiutes, who "more resemble Spaniards than they do all other Indians known in America until now."[55] Here were the white bearded folk of Posada's and Rivera's reports. To the friars, they were the archetype of Edenic innocence:

> They replied very joyfully that we must come back with the other padres, that they would do whatsoever we taught them and ordered them to do—the chief adding that then, if we so wished and deemed it more advantageous, they would go to live with the Lagunas...Scarcely did they see us depart when all—following their chief, who started first—burst out crying copious tears, so that even when we were quite a distance away we kept hearing the tender laments of these unfortunate little sheep of Christ, lost along the way simply for not having the light.[56]

Teguayo might still exist, and in the meantime the friars could be content in the simple fact that they had reached the Lagunas and the bearded Paiutes solely for the glory of God.[57]

In the midst of all this missionary zeal, however, the lay members of the expedition remained eager to continue seeking the ultimate goal—a quick route to Monterey. The Lagunas and bearded Paiutes had rightly told the party that a route directly west across the Great Basin would cross a harsh, arid desert, which prompted them to turn directly south in search of some sort of waterway that would lead them across this Bad Land. As the October days grew colder and shorter, the party continued moving south, well beyond the latitude of Monterey. At this point Miera and Muñiz were annoyed that the friars were still more concerned with preaching to new Indian tribes than with reaching California. In fact Escalante's journal implies that the friars' main motive in moving south was reaching the promising Cosnina (Havasupai) Indians, whose oasis village in the bottom of the Grand Canyon had been reached by their fellow Franciscan Francisco Garcés a few years before.[58]

As always, the friars' motives offered no commercial potential, and the secular members of the expedition grew "unbearably irksome" at the Franciscans' willingness passively to put all matters of the journey into God's hands.[59] Escalante had no tolerance for this un-Christian dissent, writing:

Many times before leaving La Villa of Santa Fe we had reminded each
and every one of our companions that in this journey we had no other
destination than the one which God would grant us; nor did this tempt
us to any worldly purpose whatsoever; and that whosoever tried either
to trade with the infidels or to follow out his private notions by not
keeping before him the sole aim of this undertaking, which had been
and is God's greater glory and the spreading of the faith, had better not
go in our company.[60]

Tensions finally exploded on October 11, near present-day Cedar City, Utah,
with the friars appearing increasingly apathetic about reaching California.
Miera, speaking for most of the party, demanded an immediate turn to the
west, away from the beckoning paradise of the Cosninas. The friars, in an
ultimate submission to divine will, proposed a casting of lots to determine
the direction as well as future leadership of the expedition. Apparently, God
was still with the Franciscans: the lots fell in their favor and the entire party
begrudgingly continued south.[61]

We know today that if the lots had fallen in Miera's favor they would have
embarked across increasingly worse deserts toward Death Valley, a dangerous route. But they very quickly learned that no escape route would be easy
from their location at the intersection of the Great Basin, Colorado Plateau,
and Mojave Desert. Near the future location of Toquerville along the Virgin
River in southwestern Utah, Escalante joyfully made note of the local Indians' charming gardens, "both on account of the hope it gave us of being able
to provide ourselves with familiar provisions far ahead, and more importantly because it furnished evidence of these peoples' practice of agriculture—and to find all this in an advanced stage for reducing [them] to civil
ways of living."[62]

This was to be the party's last encounter with agrarian people in a Good
Land, however. Indians informed the friars that the Cosninas were unreach-
able from this point, cut off by the mile-deep gorge of the Grand Canyon.
Now both Monterey and the Cosninas were out of the question. Autumn
made a move back north risky; the party was very much in retreat. The
only way to return to Santa Fe from this point was to turn directly east. The

topography of this desert was funneling the expedition back toward the Bad Land that it had been avoiding all along: the Canyon Country. Escalante's narrative of the party's journey to the Lagunas and the light-skinned bearded Utes of the Great Basin may have evoked imagery of an ascent to some sort of promised land or earthly paradise. But his account of their retreat back to New Mexico was more a descent into the inferno, through the worst land they had ever seen.

Heading east across what would later be called the Arizona Strip, the party was hemmed in by the Vermilion Cliffs on the north and the Colorado River gorges of Grand and Marble Canyons on the south. Food and water were scarce, and soon the expedition members were reduced to eating prickly pears and horse meat. The Canyon Country paradox of abundant yet inaccessible water taunted the group, and Escalante noted with disgust that the nearby Colorado ran "very deep inside a canyon, so that even if the land were good the river is of no help for farming near it."[63] The local Shivwits Indians had no gardens from which to feed the Spaniards, and their ability to survive in the desert upon grubs and cacti failed to impress Escalante. Miera by this time had stopped protesting the route, as he had become so sick and weakened "that he could barely talk."[64] He also had certainly had enough of the Franciscans' religion by this point and on one occasion actually sought out a magical cure for his illness through "idolatries" of a Kaibab Paiute shaman, much to the horror of the friars.[65]

The low point of the entire expedition—in terms of both spirits and elevation—came on October 26, when it finally reached the Colorado, which at this point Escalante called "El Río Grande de los Cosninas."[66] This point at the Colorado's junction with the Paria River, at what would later become Lee's Ferry, is the easiest access to the river in over five hundred miles between Moab and Pierce's Ferry, Nevada. But other than offering accessibility, this spot gave no hope to the friars, for the Colorado did not conform to any of their assumptions of rivers as natural highways. Immediately upstream were the cliffs and quicksand of Glen Canyon; downstream were the rapids and even greater cliffs of the Marble and Grand Canyons. Most disappointingly, even at this low-water stage of late October, the Colorado was a deep, raging torrent. Two swimmers were sent across but, "despite their prowess, were barely able to reach the other side."[67] For a dozen weakened Spaniards to cross the river with horses was out of the question. With an infernal desert at their backs, a raging river ahead, and "mesas and hogbacks" on either side, it appeared that the party was trapped or, in later Canyon Country parlance, "boxed in."[68] The friars cynically named this place "San Benito de Salsipuedes" (get out if you can).[69]

Although Escalante barely hints at it in his journal, it is possible to infer that the situation would not have seemed quite so dire to the Indians in the area. Trade across the Colorado by Utes, Paiutes, and Navajos was well established at this time, extending as far from the river as the Hopis to the south and the Lagunas to the north. To cross the Colorado in the Canyon Country, Utes did not let the open land funnel their trails to areas like Salsipuedes. Rather, they knew of the most shallow section of the river, a ford several dozen miles upstream. Escalante had heard of this ford prior to being boxed in at Salsipuedes, and his guides had told him that "the entire river was very deep except at the ford." But only after seeing the true ferocity of the Colorado's currents did he realize how unique and essential this alternate crossing point would be. Unfortunately, it would be also very difficult to reach.[70]

By grace of God, or perhaps geological weakness, the Muñiz brothers found a faint path climbing 1,700 feet up a cliff between the junction of the Colorado and the Paria. After a week of staring at an uncrossable river, the party members ascended out of Salsipuedes.[71] In another week, after picking their way through sandstone ridges and slots and occasionally stumbling across Indian trails, they finally reached the salvation of the ford, which they named "La Purísima Concepción de la Virgen Santísima" (Immaculate Conception of the Most Holy Virgin).[72] Ironically, in contrast to the easy access of Salsipuedes, this ford was surrounded by miles of slickrock, and the party had to carve footholds in the sandstone in order to descend. Upon crossing the Colorado, all members of the party were overjoyed, shooting their muskets in the air. The largest obstacle of this Bad Land was past, and within a month they would be back in the familiar territory of New Mexico.

In retrospect, Escalante justified to himself that if they had obtained Indian guides for this section they would not have "made detours, wasted time from so many days spent in a small area, and suffered hunger and thirst."[73] All he could do was fall back on his faith. He had not reached California and had very nearly perished, but in the end he could be content that he had personally overcome his own trial in the desert and reached his own Promised Land garden in Utah Valley, even if it had not amounted to Teguayo or Copala. "God doubtless disposed that we obtained no guide, either as merciful chastisement for our faults or so that we could acquire some knowledge of the peoples living hereabouts."[74]

THE RIVERS OF TEGUAYO

Every member of the Domínguez-Escalante expedition agreed on one thing: they had traveled through Bad Land to reach Good Land and returned by way of the worst land of all. The valley of the Laguna Utes, while no longer the lofty Teguayo envisioned by Salmerón or Posada, was fertile. Its land was brimming with potential for European agriculture and its people were full of potential for European religion. The Canyon Country was the opposite—its land infertile and its people subhuman at best. To take the parallels between landscape and inhabitants further, while the Colorado certainly held necessary water for irrigation, it was simply too far removed from potential mesa-top farmlands to be beneficial. Likewise, Escalante and Domínguez no doubt saw that the Shivwits or Kaibab Paiutes of the Canyon Country possessed souls, but some essence of the desert still kept them removed from the Christian-Agrarian ideal exemplified by the Lagunas or the bearded Paiutes. To the friars, a people's potential for conversion was directly related to the fertility of the surrounding landscapes.

Beyond this dichotomy of good and bad peoples and lands, however, the secular and religious members of the expedition could agree on nothing. The friars were disgusted by Muñiz's trading, by Miera's acceptance of Indian medicine to treat his illness, and most of all by their stubborn refusal to acknowledge that this expedition was for any but the most holy of purposes. Muñiz and Miera were fed up with the friars' bumbling about in search of souls, with their ineptitude in making decisions about the route, and most of all with their constant assertions that this expedition was only for the most sacred of purposes.

In the end the friars were satisfied that they had merely visited many new lands and Indian peoples—the mission had been intrinsically valuable. The secular members were disgusted at opportunities lost by the party's failure to reach Monterey and blamed the friars for hindering what could have been a profitable venture. These opposing reverential and utilitarian attitudes both profoundly shaped the ways in which Escalante and Miera would interpret the Canyon Country's geographical layout. Before the expedition Escalante had steeped himself in reports of the fantastic in Teguayo, but he ended the expedition with an acceptance of the geographical realities of this new land. Miera, in contrast, continued to let optimistic promise shape his perceptions. In an ironic twist, the secularly pragmatic would be sucked into false hopes much more than the religiously idealistic were. Nothing shows this more than the way that each man pieced together the rivers of the Canyon Country—Escalante in his journal, and Miera in his 1777 map.

The oldest and most basic component of the Teguayo myth, tied to Columbus's visions of a master lake in Eden feeding the world's rivers, is the top-down logic of water flow across the continent. At the apex of Teguayo had to be a lake that connected all of western North America's rivers, from the Mississippi to the Columbia, into one fluid network. Given that Europeans formed their expectations based upon observations of the coastal mouths of rivers, it is logical that they would construct a geography in which, say, the Columbia River of Oregon, the American River of California, and the Colorado would all have a common source at Lake Copala. Furthermore, one river had to be the Great River of the Far North, providing easy passage from the continental interior directly to the Pacific. Rivera realized this in 1765 when he eliminated the upper Colorado (or Tizón) as any sort of great river leading from Copala—it was simply too small to fit the vision.

Escalante was equally unimpressed with the upper Colorado/Tizón when he crossed it on September 5, 1776. He said little of it, apart from naming it the "San Rafael" and designating it a mere tributary to the great Río Grande de los Cosninas that would later thwart the expedition at Salsipuedes and flow through the Grand Canyon.[75] For Escalante, the true promise of a great, westward-flowing river came nine days later, when the party crossed the Río San Buenaventura (today's Green River). Escalante would write that this new river was "the most copious one we have come by, and the same one which Fray Alonso de Posada…relates in his report as separating the Yuta nation from the Comanche."[76] The San Buenaventura was clearly an important route and boundary, with plenty of historical backing.

Essential to this idea of the San Buenaventura as a route to California was its westward course. In reality the Green River flows almost directly south to its confluence with the Colorado in Canyonlands National Park. At the point of Escalante's crossing in the Uinta Basin, however, it veers temporarily west. By linking it to a border between the Utes in the south and Comanches (Shoshones) in the north, Escalante further emphasized a westward course. He truly wanted this to be a new river system, completely separate from the Colorado, which he knew flowed uselessly into an impassable canyon. Escalante yearned to keep the Green and Colorado systems separate from one another, writing in his journal that the San Buenaventura "comes together with the San Clemente [White River], but we do not know if it does with the preceding ones [the Colorado, Dolores, and Gunnison]."[77]

But this desire for a great, westward flowing river had logical problems. Escalante's guides to Lake Timpanogos convinced him to detour away from the San Buenaventura, although he did not indicate the reason. Furthermore, as the party members traveled south from Utah Lake, they crossed the west-flowing Sevier River and speculated that this was once again the San Buenaventura on its course to the Pacific. At this point Escalante made a curious comment in his journal: "this river...appears to be the San Buenaventura, but we doubt that this can be so since here it carries much less water than when we crossed it [further east and thus upstream]."[78] Two days later Indians told him that the Sevier entered a lake to the west and that from there it continued on to California.[79] This was only partially correct. The Sevier ends in Sevier Lake, which like the Great Salt Lake has no outlet. However, when gazing west from near Highway 50 it is almost possible to be convinced that this lake does have an outlet, flowing through mountain breaks, beyond the Great Basin desert's western horizon and toward California.

Escalante's journal, which neither explicitly affirms nor denies the flowing of the San Buenaventura to the Pacific, hints at his conflict. While he truly wanted the easy route to the west that an open river would provide, a confirmation of all the speculations about Teguayo that he had read, he continued to rely on Indian guides and trails that avoided following the river. He could speculate about a river to California, or even about the Great Salt Lake as an inlet of the Pacific, but he could not bring himself to act upon and follow these speculations. This restraint likely saved the party's lives.[80] By the

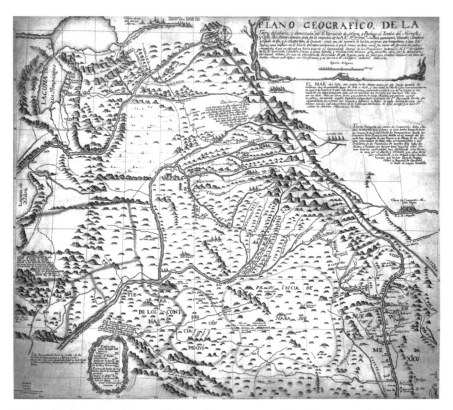

2.1. Don Bernardo de Miera y Pacheco's map, 1777 version. (Courtesy of the Earth Sciences and Map Library, University of California, Berkeley)

end of the expedition Escalante had come to terms with its failures as well as an imperfect geography that was more a savage test from God than a verdant paradise. Teguayo was dead, but Escalante's faith remained.

Miera could not be content, however. His missed opportunities at trading and prospecting screamed for a land that continued to entice and promise. This would show in his map of the Great Basin and the Canyon Country. Miera was an excellent artist and mapmaker (a disgusted Escalante wrote that "only for this [cartography] do I consider him useful") and his map was the most lasting legacy of the entire expedition (figs. 2.1 and 2.2).[81] As historical geographer Richard Francaviglia writes, Miera's map "marked the first time that those who actually *experienced the region* began to make maps of it."[82]

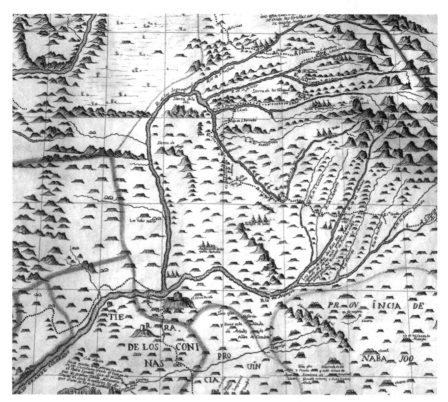

2.2. Detail of the Miera map, showing approximate area of the Canyon Country. The expedition's crossing of the Colorado River is seen in the lower left, along the dotted line. (Courtesy of the Earth Sciences and Map Library, University of California, Berkeley)

Few if any subsequent explorers and trappers of the United States would read Escalante's journal, but Miera's map influenced many, especially Alexander von Humboldt's widely circulated 1809 map of New Spain, as the next chapter shows.[83]

Perhaps due to optimistic yearning, perhaps out of spite for Escalante, however, Miera's map contains several features that are nothing less than a blatant rejection of Escalante's precautions regarding the course of the San Buenaventura. Miera shows the Río de San Buenaventura emptying into the Sevier and then into a lake, with an open end stretching west into *terra incognita*, toward California. There simply had to be a viable waterway to

California in Miera's imagination. After enduring the wandering of the expedition to find a ford in the canyons of the river, Miera was thoroughly disgusted with the region of the Colorado River and wanted his Great River of the West to have nothing to do with the Canyon Country's "extreme sterility" and "rough and broken" terrain.[84] Quite simply, nothing could be gained if the San Buenaventura emptied into the Colorado's wasteful canyons, flowing away from California.

Historians of exploration in the region that is today the American Southwest have long given a brief nod to the Domínguez-Escalante expedition's "opening" of the interior West—or New Spain's Far Northwest. In some ways the expedition fits American history's stereotype of quaint and naïvely idealistic Franciscans who preceded the great wave of rational U.S. government–sponsored explorer-scientists in the nineteenth century. They signaled the last gasp of a vision in which missionaries and explorers held Teguayo as a Promised Land, an Eden, a domain of innocent Indians and millenarian destiny. Or did they? As the following chapters show, the Mormons who attempted to incorporate the Canyon Country into their worldview in the mid- to late 1800s brought an ideology to the land and its inhabitants that was similar to that of the millenarian Franciscans: Escalante, Domínguez, Posada, Salmerón, Escobar, and even Mendieta and Columbus.

But in the immediately coming decades the image of the Canyon Country would take on a strikingly secular guise in which capitalistic trade, transport, and market expansion—not redemption, conversion, and reverence—were the catchphrases. Within four years of his excursion, and barely past the age of thirty, Escalante would be dead of an unknown illness. Few if any explorers of the new nations of the United States and Mexico would ever be familiar with his journal's rich store of information.[85] But all later explorers, geographers, and traders would be familiar with the contents of Miera's map. Miera's ideological successors, not Escalante's, would be at the forefront of future exploration in the Canyon Country.

3
Old Spanish Trails and Trappers' Tales

THE DAWN OF CANYON COUNTRY COMMERCE

Don Bernardo Miera y Pacheco's map was important. Much more than any of Escalante's sentiments, it was a signal of things to come in the Canyon Country. Each man's geographical vision—Escalante's written, Miera's drawn—acknowledged and consolidated the presence of a very Bad Land en route to Teguayo. But beyond this their views were completely opposed. Certainly by the end of the expedition, and probably from its inception, Escalante saw Teguayo's people—and by extension Teguayo—as an end unto themselves: intrinsically valuable for agrarian redemption and a harvesting of souls with no overt need for straight lines or direct travel (*Para Teguayo*). Miera, however, remained loyal throughout and after the expedition to its original imperialist and secular goals of commerce, mineral extraction, and above all the straight lines of a benevolent transcontinental landscape (*Por Teguayo*).

Those who immediately followed the Domínguez-Escalante expedition's rough route across the Canyon Country to the Promised Lands of Lake Timpanogos or California were not millenarians, desert ascetics, or missionaries; they were trappers, horse thieves, weapons smugglers, and slave traders, concerned with moving as quickly as possible between the markets of New Mexico and California. Mapmakers, who with the exception of Miera still drew from indirect reports, reflected these mercantilist, utilitarian objectives. The first four decades of the nineteenth century very much promised to fulfill Miera's goals for commerce in the Far North.

During this time the linearity of political boundaries, parallels, and meridians also gradually began to impose itself upon North America's most non-linear landscape. The traders passing stealthily through the Canyon Country along the "Old Spanish Trail" represented a diversity of identities: Ute, Navajo, Paiute, Spanish, Mexican, American, French, Catholic, Protestant. It mattered little to them that the Canyon Country became Mexico's Far North in 1821, the United States' interior West in 1848, and even briefly the far southeastern part of the Mormon state of Deseret in 1849. But as both "official" and "unofficial" explorers of the United States began to encounter the Canyon Country in the 1850s, attempting to assimilate it into a larger American state, it became increasingly clear the region would not accommodate straight lines or political boundaries easily.

Cartographic Ripples and False Rivers

For all of the grandiose speculation by Franciscans such as Posada and Salmerón concerning what exactly made up Teguayo, maps depicting the region prior to Miera's were remarkably restrained. For the most part they simply labeled Teguayo, perhaps added the elusive Lake Copala somewhere safely beyond Europeans' imaginative grasp, and left it at that. A 1755 map produced in Paris, "Carte de L'Amérique Septentrionale," was typical of such works: Teguayo was simply a blank spot, with the added qualifier that "one does not have any certain knowledge" of the region.[1]

After Domínguez and Escalante's roundabout loop through the region, Teguayo was much more than a blank spot. It was a tangled topography of canyons, rivers, mountains, and lakes—some Bad Land, some Good Land, and all laid out in meticulous detail by Miera. In the years following 1776 at least seven versions of Miera's map circulated throughout European and American intellectual circles.[2] This new rationalized vision of North America's interior must have excited all who saw it: both explorers such as William Clark and Zebulon Pike and more broad-thinking aristocrat-scientists such as Alexander von Humboldt and even Thomas Jefferson. The map was a product not of Indian reports or even tales by lowly traders but of enlightened, direct, firsthand experience. It simply had to be completely accurate.

We cannot simply view Miera's map as an abrupt shift from an idealized view of land to a rationalized one, however. As shown in chapter 2, mythical elements of Teguayo persisted in Miera's Río San Buenaventura, a synthesis of what we call today the Green, Sevier, and Humboldt Rivers, which flowed west across the Great Basin to California. Escalante ultimately rejected the existence of a large river providing safe passage across the Great Basin, but by the early 1800s his narrative seemed an outdated relic. The detail, logic, and beauty of Miera's map were a much more perfect introduction to what William Goetzmann has termed the "Second Great Age of Discovery": post-Enlightenment science, reason, and eventually romanticism brought North America's last subarctic blank spot—the interior West—into the Euro-Christian consciousness.[3]

Most maps depicting the region in the early nineteenth century built upon Miera's legacy. None gave serious attention to the Canyon Country—which, after all, Miera had dismissed in disgust. But nearly all focused upon the optimistic mythical elements of Teguayo as an Aztec homeland with a bountiful lake and a California-bound river. Perhaps the most important direct descendant of Miera's legacy was Alexander von Humboldt's 1809 "Carte generale du Royaume de la Nouvelle Espagne" (see fig. 3.1). Humboldt, a German explorer, naturalist, and cartographer, was one of the finest scientific minds of the late 1700s and early 1800s and a logical link between the Enlightenment and Charles Darwin. He traveled from the volcanoes of Peru to the steppes of Siberia, and the sophistication of his observations and interpretations of these new parts of the natural world influenced generations of future explorers of the interior American West, including John Wesley Powell and Clarence King. Had he personally seen the Canyon Country, Humboldt would have explored and tried to rationalize its objective complexity and subjective beauty more thoroughly than any other geographical theorist of his time.[4]

Unfortunately, however, Humboldt never saw the region. His map had all the limitations and errors of Miera's original as well as a few of his own. Indeed, Humboldt likely knew that his map was incomplete, later regretting that he "could only give a very imperfect map of Mexico" (of which the

3.1. Detail of an 1809 version of Alexander von Humboldt's "Carte generale du Royaume de la Nouvelle Espagne," showing the Canyon Country and Eastern Great Basin. (Courtesy of the David Rumsey Map Collection, www.davidrumsey.com)

Canyon Country was a part).[5] Giving credit to the Domínguez-Escalante expedition, albeit with inaccurate names and dates, Humboldt used Miera's names for all of the Colorado's major tributaries: Dolores, San Rafael, Nabajoa.[6] He also followed Miera's reference to the upper Colorado as the Río Zaguananas, showing that even by this time the stream that we today designate as the headwaters of the Colorado had no particular significance as a master stream. Likewise his placement of the Navajo, Tabeguache, Hopi, and Havasupai Indians fits with Escalante's writings and Miera's cartography.[7]

More importantly, Humboldt propagated the San Buenaventura as the Great River of the West and, like Miera, molded it out of the Green and Sevier Rivers. After passing through the flats of today's Sevier Lake, labeled "Valle Salado" (Salt Valley), Humboldt's San Buenaventura flows into an open bay, toward the promise of California. Upon the image of this body of water Humboldt wrote that the "western limits of this salt lake [Sevier Lake] are unknown," leaving its potential as a western route open-ended. Further reinforcing the idea of a logical, Pyramidal Height-of-Land, Humboldt installed in the region of the Great Salt Lake another great unnamed river, flowing northward from Lake Timpanogos and off the map, perhaps beckoning toward the Columbia River, which Lewis and Clark had explored a few years earlier.

The San Buenaventura was a symbol of the mythical Teguayo and of whatever promise the region still held in the minds of Miera or Humboldt. This great river avoided the Canyon Country completely. It simply had to—the Canyon Country was confirmed as Bad Land by this time. Although Miera cared little for the "rough and broken" country of the Colorado River's canyons, he did not want to leave the region as blank *terra incognita*.[8] Thus he filled the Canyon Country in with images of uniform mesas and mountains, with only one unnamed Indian village south of the Abajo Mountains. This negated any open-ended promise of Good Land. Conveniently, in his original version Miera even laid a chart of the map's Indian tribes over the top of the most unfamiliar, broken portion of the Canyon Country, quite literally covering up his incomplete knowledge.[9]

Humboldt added to this ambiguous vision of the Canyon Country. On the banks of the Río Nabajoa (today's San Juan River), on the Navajo-Ute frontier, appear these words: "First abode of the Azteques come from Aztlan in 1160. Tradition uncertain." The legend of Teguayo as a mythical homeland, of course, was nothing new—it extended back at least to Escobar's account from the early 1600s. But the mythical homeland had long existed on the shores of Lake Copala, which by the early 1800s had morphed into Lake Timpanogos, with its civilized and orderly Laguna Utes: Good People in a Good Land. So why did Humboldt transport the Aztec homeland into the Bad Land of the Canyon Country? It is not clear. The only part of Miera's map that may have influenced Humboldt to do so was a very small note in the same area mentioning great ruins of some old civilization, around today's Mesa Verde National Park.[10]

This minor note about an "uncertain" tradition and lost mythical home-lands hints at much to come in the Canyon Country. The great ruins at Mesa Verde, Canyon de Chelly, and Chaco Canyon, as well as dozens of smaller sites throughout the canyons, are today inextricably linked to the intrigue and perplexity of the Canyon Country, as well as to myths of its once nurtur-ing environment and present hostility to human incursion. Of course, Rivera and earlier geographers had given brief mention to lost white tribes in the region. As later chapters show, Mormon folk traditions regarding white Indi-ans and even ancient dwelling places of *Book of Mormon* figures would later arise with the Canyon Country as their chosen backdrop. At the root of all these "uncertain traditions" was the idea that this fallen land had not always been this way: it had once been a Good Land that nurtured nascent civiliza-tions, like Eden itself.[11]

For the moment, however, these Ozymandian myths of fallen civilizations and ancestral homelands would have to wait, taking a back seat to Hum-boldt's and Miera's pinnacle of promise: the San Buenaventura. William Clark's "Master Map" of the American West, published in 1810 on Humboldt's heels, included the San Buenaventura and also gave a name to Humboldt's vague, north-flowing river: the Multnomah.[12] It is not surprising that Clark would have taken this idea of Pyramidal Height-of-Land and interconnected rivers even further than Humboldt did; after all, his famous 1804–5 expedi-tion with Meriwether Lewis rested upon Thomas Jefferson's assumption that there was an easy transcontinental passage from the headwaters of the Mis-souri to the Columbia.

Miera's mythical San Buenaventura persisted well into the 1820s and 1830s with maps such as Anthony Finley's 1827 *New American Atlas*.[13] With this information in mind, trappers and traders now entered the interior West with the assumption that a Great River of the West leading to the Pacific was located there. Upon viewing the Great Salt Lake in 1828, Peter Skene Ogden wrote that there "must be a large river" in this "barren country."[14] Pas-sage to California may also have played into Gen. William Ashley's near-fatal decision to descend the Green River (which trappers by this point called the Seeds-ke-dee) in 1825, although caching supplies for his fur company was another motivation. Instead of finding California, Ashley's party wrecked its boats in the canyons of Flaming Gorge and present-day Dinosaur National Monument.[15]

It took the brilliant 1827 explorations of Jedediah Smith and confirmation by the formal, government-sponsored 1844 expedition of John C. Frémont to put to rest the idea of an easy water route across the West to California and finally cement the dreary existence of the Great Basin. But even as late as 1848 overlanders like William Manly were attempting simply to float down the Green River, west to California gold fields. Like Ashley, Manly's party wrecked boats and lost gear in the rapids of Flaming Gorge and Lodore Canyon.[16] Finally, after meeting with the Utes in the Uinta Basin, the party opted to leave the river. Ute warlord Wakara was "astonished" as to why they "were going down the river when we wanted to get west" and even drew maps in the sand to illustrate the "awful bad canyon" of the Bad Land that awaited them in the Canyon Country if they continued.[17] Unfortunately, Wakara was not available to warn Manly away from another Bad Land later in his journey to California: many of his party would later die in Death Valley.

Despite expert assertions by Wakara, Smith, and Frémont that the Green River did not flow to California, explorers and settlers still persisted in the need to have a water route to the West. At last they informally designated the present-day Humboldt River of northern Nevada as the real successor of the mythical San Buenaventura, Multnomah, or Seeds-ke-dee. When the Humboldt actually flows, both its source and mouth are entirely within the Great Basin desert; it has no outlet. But at least it provided a sporadic 300-mile highway for western migration for a portion of the journey, a drastically diminished Great River of the West.[18]

THE OLD SPANISH TRAIL: COMMERCE THROUGH THE CANYON COUNTRY

Even during the heyday of the San Buenaventura's promise during the early 1800s, the Canyon Country played only a small part in the construction of a benevolent interior West. Most still knew that it was Bad Land and something to avoid, just as the San Buenaventura's imagined course did. Few cartographers attached much significance to the middle reaches of the Colorado as it flowed through Glen and Grand Canyons. They knew that it was inaccessible and surrounded by barren desert on all sides. Still, the Canyon Country happened to lie under the most obvious straight line between Santa Fe and California. The legacy of Miera's commercial vision prompted traders and trappers, if not cartographers and state-supported explorers, into the canyons.

Just as the secular traders and prospectors preceding Escalante and Domínguez (including Miera) kept few records of their perceptions of the Canyon Country, the merchants who succeeded them in the early 1800s left little in the way of geographic speculation or grand theories about the region's relevance to the rest of their world. We do know that by the early 1820s traders had pieced together sections of Domínguez and Escalante's route to form a circuitous series of routes between New Mexico and California, across what was by this time Mexico's far northern frontier. New Mexicans, Americans, and Indians—legitimate traders and illegal smugglers—moved horses from California to New Mexico, blankets from New Mexico to California, furs from remote rivers to towns, and Indian slaves from the desert to "civilization."

Today we call the route by which they traveled the "Old Spanish Trail." In reality it was neither old nor necessarily Spanish, nor even a coherent single trail.[19] Contrary to our popular image of "explorers" making grand pushes across previously unknown country, the Old Spanish Trail developed just as the rest of Christian Europe's understanding of the continental interior had—by way of gradual incursions, ebbs and flows of understanding, which followed Indian reports and trails every step of the way. In fact Ute and Navajo traders from the Canyon Country had "discovered" Spanish New Mexico long before any Spaniards had approached Teguayo. As noted in chapter 2, Spanish traders probably knew of routes to the upper Colorado River even before Rivera's time. Although Escalante would never fulfill his promise to return and bring the Laguna Utes into the fold of Christianity, by 1800 Spanish traders were making occasional trips to trade with them on the shores of Lake Timpanogos. Traffic in guns, furs, horses, and Indian slaves thrived—Escalante would have been horrified.

Few of these trading forays were well documented. In 1805 a seventy-year-old *genízaro* interpreter named Manuel Mestas traveled from New Mexico to the Laguna Utes to recover stolen horses. Because the 1,200-mile round-trip journey took barely one month, Mestas must have had a deep familiarity with the region that likely even predated Domínguez and Escalante. Given his speed, which averaged a nearly incredible forty miles a day, he could not have taken the roundabout route that the friars had taken through the well-watered western Rockies. He would have followed a direct line, probably along Rivera's route to present-day Moab, and then cut across even worse desert to the northwest en route to Spanish Fork Canyon. Mestas must have known the Canyon Country well, but he tells us nothing of it.[20]

Eight years after Mestas's trip to the Lagunas, seven traders led by Mauricio Arze and Lagos García also reached Lake Timpanogos before turning south to the Sevier River and then east to the Colorado. In fact they may have coined our modern name for the Sevier River, which they called the "Río Sebero" rather than using Miera's name "Río de Santa Isabel" or assuming that it was a part of the San Buenaventura. The group almost certainly used the same Ute Ford that had proved to be Domínguez and Escalante's salvation but mentioned nothing of it or the rest of their route. They may not have mentioned the route because it was so familiar to traders by this time.[21] Terrain, whether good or bad, did not concern Arze or García as much as the resources that they obtained from this region in illegal trade: twelve Paiute slaves and 109 fur pelts.[22]

In 1821 the Canyon Country ceased to be New Spain's far northern periphery and became part of Mexico, although this probably mattered little to traders on the northern frontier. Significantly, Mexico enforced trading restrictions even less than Spain had, and the idea of connecting New Mexico to California through the lower Colorado desert to the south and the Canyon Country to the north gained new momentum.[23]

By this time Hispanic and Indian traders had definitely pieced together some sort of understanding of the region's intricacies. The main points were something like this: between Santa Fe and the Laguna Utes was a complex of deserts, rivers, and canyons that impeded travel. Travelers could conservatively avoid this Bad Land by cutting well to the northeast and then turning directly west, staying near the well-watered Rocky and Uinta Mountains the whole time but wasting valuable time and dealing with snow and cold in the spring, winter, and fall. Or, if they were more aggressive, confident, and quick, travelers could trend nearer the Bad Land, following Rivera's old route from the San Juan north past the Abajo and La Sal Mountains to reach the Colorado at Moab crossing and a few days later the Green en route to Price and Spanish Fork Canyon.[24] Finally, if they were very confident and river levels were low and temperatures cool, they could cut directly across the worst of the Bad Land, picking unobvious Indian trails in and out of sandstone domes and slot canyons, crossing first the San Juan and then the Colorado at the Ute Ford where Escalante had crossed. Under no circumstances should traders be tempted to follow either of these rivers, despite what they promised.

If some sort of watershed moment in which this conglomeration of knowledge about the Canyon Country came together to form a route between California and Santa Fe ever occurred, it was with Antonio Armijo's caravan of over thirty men, which left Abiquiú in early November 1829. With a load of wool blankets, products of New Mexico's sizable sheep industry, they forded the Colorado at the Ute Ford in early December and reached San Gabriel, California, nearly three months later. Armijo traded the blankets for livestock and returned to New Mexico in early April.[25]

Like his predecessors, Armijo mentioned little of the topography that he experienced—he was more concerned with his woolen merchandise, which certainly made him quite a bit of money. From Abiquiú he traveled by way of Mesa Verde and the Mancos River region before reaching a group of Navajos living on the San Juan River, near today's Four Corners. After securing a guide in exchange for eleven mares, the caravan followed the wide, shallow San Juan for nearly a hundred miles before veering north through the complex canyons leading to the Colorado River and the Ute Ford. Noting this significant crossing point, the party "repaired the upgrade of the canyon, the same one which had been worked by the padres," and Armijo even noted finding inscriptions left by Domínguez and Escalante. From this point it was relatively easier going across the Arizona Strip and Virgin River country to California.[26]

This route, tracing in reverse Escalante's return to New Mexico half a century earlier, took nearly three months. Armijo's return trip to Abiquiú by an unspecified route took only forty days, however, "because their route was straighter and better known, and they were not hindered by the terrain or the mountains."[27] But beyond this his route and his descriptions are hazy. Even the official governor's report to Mexico City lamented Armijo's lack of useful insight concerning the Far North:

> The *empresarios*, although they are known to be courageous, rugged, and eager to discover new lands, are lacking in instruction and literature, by means of which they would have been able to note the various products that the territory of the Mexican Republic possesses in this region; and they are only able to say that there exist suitable locations for establishing new villages, and that in the hills there appear variously colored rocks or veins resembling minerals, some of the said hills having the shape of elevated *bufas* without forest or grass land, streaked with veins or rock strata.[28]

What was the "instruction and literature" that Armijo and his companions lacked? Grandiose visions of Teguayo or education regarding mineral development? The unnamed author of this report clearly believed that this great land of promise and "hills" to the north deserved exploration by someone more enlightened than mere traders. But a visit to the Canyon Country by someone versed in this "instruction and literature" would have to wait.[29]

THE TRAPPERS

The southwestern fur trade, which was roughly concurrent with the Old Spanish Trail's trading heyday, also brought many Europeans and Americans into the Canyon Country. As mentioned earlier, trapper William Ashley had attempted unsuccessfully to float the Green River to its presumed mouth in California before capsizing far to the north of the Canyon Country in 1825. More importantly, if we are to believe his story, in the spring of 1826 James Ohio Pattie crossed the entire region from southwest to northeast by following the Colorado River's canyon rims the entire way.

Of course, Pattie's route involves problems. The very nature of the Canyon Country confounds not only river-level travel but also travel along the tops of the cliffs that line the region's waterways. Every tributary that enters the Colorado River has its own cliffs hundreds of feet high, forcing detours that may very well lead to more side-canyons and tributaries. Pattie's narrative of this route says little of this problem and is more concerned with daring exploits against "savage" Indians and the deaths of his companions than with describing the country. This is as close as his narrative comes to describing the Canyon Country:

> On the 28th [of March], we reached a point on the river where the mountains shut in so close upon its shores, that we were compelled to climb a mountain, and travel along the acclivity, the river still in sight, and at an immense depth beneath us. Through this whole distance, which we judged to be, as the river meanders, 100 leagues, we had snow from a foot to eighteen inches deep. The river bluffs on the opposite shore were never more than a mile from us. It is, perhaps this very long and formidable range of mountains, which has caused, that this country of the Red River, has not been more explored, at least by American people.[30]

This description is indeed vague, and it is probably true, as Frank Waters writes, that "Pattie was gifted with little powers of observation."[31] Pattie could have been describing the Grand Canyon (as most historians have assumed, because it is the most dramatic and well known of the Colorado's canyons), Glen Canyon, or Cataract Canyon, but it is unlikely that these last two canyons would have been blanketed with snow as he described in late March. Furthermore, he repeatedly mentioned "mountains," and not desert canyons; by the 1820s most American explorers were making distinctions between high country and deserts and would not have labeled the Colorado Country as "mountainous."

Most importantly, Pattie's descriptions of the country that they reached both before and after the Canyon Country simply do not make sense. Pattie wrote of "an abundance of the finest lands" on the downstream end of the region that does not exist along the lower Colorado. He also described what seems to have been the confluence of the Green and the Colorado as a "clear, beautiful stream" and made no mention of the two rivers' wide, muddy character. Later, as he approached the upper Colorado's mountain source, he mentioned "the chief village of the Nabahoes," which would have been nowhere in this vicinity.[32]

But clearly Pattie was aware that this was Bad Land, even if his whole narrative was simply an exaggerated account of Indian fighting in a region that he may never have seen. At the very least his observation that "these horrid mountains, which so cage it [the Colorado] up, as to deprive all human beings of the ability to descend to its banks, and make use of its waters" seems uniquely suited to the Canyon Country.[33] Pattie shared this lamentation at a bountiful river's inaccessibility with Rivera, Escalante, and Miera.

If we continue reading Pattie's narrative, however, we also find a more intangible side of his overarching view of Bad Land. James Ohio Pattie may have been the first Protestant, proto-Turnerian American to enter the Canyon Country and certainly saw the region from the perspective of Jacksonian America.[34] A year after his trip along the length of the Colorado, Pattie and his father, Sylvester, crossed the desert again, this time across the lower Colorado to San Diego, California. This journey, which nearly dehydrated them, only strengthened Pattie's general revulsion at the sheer uselessness of all deserts. Upon reaching San Diego, the two Patties were arrested for trespassing in Mexico without passports. Here his narrative became one of rugged individualists under fire by a Mexican general; democracy versus despotism; Protestantism versus Catholicism; white versus brown.

Confined in his eight-by-ten foot cell, with his father dying next door, Pattie began to reminisce as if his desert experience had been an extension of American freedom (never mind that the actual region belonged to Mexico at this time). "Liberty is dear to everyone, but doubly dear to one, who had been from infancy accustomed to free range, and to be guided by his own will. Put a man, who has ranged the prairies, and exalted in the wilderness, as I have for years, in a prison, to let him have a full taste of the blessings of freedom, and the horrors of shackles and confinement." At least in retrospect, Pattie preferred Indian attacks, starvation, and dehydration to imprisonment. In fact he would fantasize about meeting the tyrannical Mexican general on his own turf, "together in the wild woods, and I armed with my rifle."[35] Bad Land, then, tempered Pattie into his own heroic self-image, as its hostility drew the ascetic Escalante closer to his God. This was a step toward our own romanticized but conflicting "love-hate" relationship with the Canyon Country, which intrigues us in many ways precisely because of its hostility.

Slightly less dramatic but definitely more well-grounded than Pattie's narrative is a brief mention of the Colorado River Canyon in Warren Ferris's *Life in the Rocky Mountains*. Ferris, a clerk for John Jacob Astor's American Fur Company, traveled the interior West a few years after Pattie (1830–35). His narrative was not published until 1843–44 as a serial in *Western Literary Messenger* magazine, well over a decade after Pattie had exposed the Bad Land of the Colorado to the American public. Unlike Pattie, Ferris had never seen or even claimed to have seen the Canyon Country—he probably never got nearer to the region than the Green River in the Uinta Basin (present-day northeastern Utah). Nonetheless, Ferris's brief description epitomizes the negative view of Euro-Christianity toward the desert, and his language speaks to raw horror more than to beauty or even Burke's notion of the sublime. This was the worst land of all: "even to those, who have seen and for years been familiar with the mightiest productions of nature, [the region] presents a scene from which they recoil in terror."[36]

It is unclear whether Ferris is referring to the Canyon Country or to what we call the Grand Canyon proper; he made no distinction between the two regions. He describes a "great gorge" as beginning "a short distance below the junction of the Green and the Grand rivers," which would indicate the Canyon Country. But the rest of his description centers upon one canyon, not a complex series, which hints at the Grand Canyon. In any case it is not terribly important which specific part of the Colorado River Ferris is describing. It is clear that he intended to give a general description of the horrific nature of the entire Colorado River region.

Ferris drew upon familiar elements of horror and paradox reaching back to Cárdenas in the mid-1500s. Just as Cárdenas had invoked the size of Seville's tallest churches 300 years earlier for comparison with the stature of the Grand Canyon's boulders, Ferris invited his readers to consider the size and fury of Niagara Falls, which he claimed the Colorado dwarfed. Also like Cárdenas, Ferris emphasized the way in which the huge scale of these canyons distorted perspectives:

> Gaze upon the frowning hills, and burning sands, with which you are
> to suppose yourself half surrounded; and you will certainly attempt to

descend to the lovely scene beneath, and perhaps may resolve to step over the brook, and recline yourself in the shade of a cluster of willows; alas!, if you succeed, how sadly will you be disappointed. The little brook will gradually enlarge itself as you descend, until it becomes a mighty river, three hundred yards wide; the bushes will increase in size, and stature, until they become giant cottonwoods.[37]

The desert Canyon Country tempts Ferris's hypothetical reader into a false sense of security and familiarity with rough comparisons to pastoral scenes of verdure, for which an eastern traveler in the region would no doubt be starving. But it is not as it seems: the river is not nurturing, and any verdure is a mirage distorted not by heat but by sheer distance and scale.

The relatively unknown and little-studied Warren Ferris was quite astute in observation and compilation of geographic perceptions, even if some were composed from secondhand information. In addition to his insightful description of the Colorado's canyons, he also compiled a map of his travels in 1836 that completely avoided the allure of the San Buenaventura myth. Ferris's map, unfortunately little used by explorers, rightly showed the Great Salt Lake and Sevier Lake as parts of a Great Basin, rather than as draining to California. His rivers and canyons in the Southwest were complex and intricate drainages, unconnected to any sort of coherence such as Pyramidal Height-of-Land or easy routes between population centers. It is clear that Ferris took a utilitarian view of rivers in terms of trapping and not in terms of the transcontinental transportation for which Miera, Clark, and Humboldt were yearning.[38]

To Ferris, a trapper thinking about the location of beaver, waterways were of paramount importance. His map of the West was more concerned with drainages than with any other topographical feature. The drainages of the Canyon Country, which he described with such horror, are pushed well into the lower right-hand periphery of his map for good reason. Like all his predecessors who had written of the Canyon Country, Ferris acknowledged its most fundamental and ever-present paradox: in this desert the life-giving rivers were shut off by canyon walls. In order to pass safely across this region, travelers had to avoid the rivers.

At least one trapper ignored this bit of wisdom. Many of today's Canyon Country river-runners know his name: "Denis Julien" left at least five inscriptions carved into the cliffs along the Green and Colorado Rivers in Desolation, Labyrinth, Stillwater, and Cataract Canyons. A Frenchman, probably from New Orleans, Julien spent most of his life trading and traveling along the rivers of the upper Mississippi drainage. By 1800 he was married and had a family with his Indian wife in St. Louis. By 1827 he was in Taos. By 1831 he had begun working for fellow Frenchman Antoine Robideaux trapping in the Uinta Basin, where he left the first of his rock carvings. Five years later, in May 1836, he was working a trap line along the Green River in present-day Canyonlands National Park.[39]

Beyond this we know little. It is likely that Julien was making his way slowly upstream: two of his inscriptions give dates indicating that it took him from May 3 to May 16 to travel the approximately twenty miles from Hell Roaring Canyon to Bowknot Bend. He may have had a small sailboat, as one inscription indicates. Less detailed inscriptions show that he may have ranged along the river corridor as far downstream as Glen Canyon and as far upstream as Desolation Canyon. He may even have camped one night in 1844 in present-day Arches National Park, where he left another inscription.[40]

Beyond Julien's compulsion to leave his mark on the desert sandstone, however, we can only speculate. Some historians believe that he drowned in the rapids of flood-swollen Cataract Canyon; others believe that he made his way to California, where he lived out the autumn years of his life.[41] But we know nothing of Julien's perception of the Canyon Country, even though he must have known the region intimately. We do not know what Julien was thinking as he slowly followed the Green River's eddies upstream: whether he was basing his travels upon Indian reports, hearsay from the rendezvous campfire, or a simple desire for more beaver pelts. Julien's story, or lack thereof, typifies the overarching dilemma of the Canyon Country's history throughout the decades of the Old Spanish Trail and the fur trade: those who knew the region best tell us the least about it.

This would supposedly change in the 1850s, after the 1848 Treaty of Guadalupe-Hidalgo ceded the Canyon Country from Mexico to the United States. If mercantilism and geography were to progress beyond the shady and informal knowledge of Manuel Mestas or Denis Julien, it was clear that educated sci-entist-explorers would need to see the Canyon Country for themselves. The United States' most irrational region still needed incorporation, straight lines, and above all improvement. But this process would be rough.

4

United States Explorers

DISGUST, INTRIGUE, AND MAKING SENSE OF AN AMERICAN DESERT

*The erosion of the mountains occurs on a grandiose scale,
and can be recognized easily since no marked vegetation hides
the destruction. Nature seems to be in a devastating process only,
without developing simultaneous activity.*

—DR. JAMES SCHIEL, on the Green River Desert, 1853

GUNNISON'S AUTUMN

The desert was unusually cold and wet in October 1853. Streambeds were caved in and undercut by excess runoff. The waterlogged gray clays that stretched between the Grand and Green Rivers bogged down the heavy wagons. Captain John William Gunnison's expedition was surveying a railroad route along the 38th parallel of what was in 1848 the western United States of America. They were not the first party to pass this way. Gunnison's second-in-command, Lt. E. G. Beckwith, noted that for miles they had been following a series of "Old Spanish Trails," up to twenty parallel paths of horse-prints and wagon tracks imprinted on the fragile crust of the badlands. "Though seldom used of later years," these tracks were "still very distinct."[1] Along canyon walls the party also noticed petroglyphs: images chipped into the rock by Indians,

Mexicans, and an unknown "American Captain" who had preceded them.[2] This vanguard of United States exploration was by no means the first party of non-Indians in the Canyon Country. The desert preserved many traces of their predecessors.

Color and paradox surrounded the party on all sides. Distant clouds blended their whiteness into the snowcapped peaks of the La Sals, Abajos, and yet-to-be-named Henry Mountains on the horizon. In turn these snowy peaks blended into sterile white alkali flats in the foreground. Gray, red, and blue shales formed crumbling towers "resembling ruins of immense churches and dwellings." Occasionally Beckwith looked to the horizon from atop a ridge and called the vast expanse of land a "plain," but he could not have been more wrong.[3] As the party moved farther into this region, from the wide valley of the Grand River to the Green River crossing and into what we today call the San Rafael Swell, the "plain" became a veritable labyrinth of canyons. Beckwith called this broken landscape simply "Rock Hills"—understated, perhaps, but succinct.[4]

Beckwith sometimes broke from this somber tone to marvel at elements of the Canyon Country that he perceived as beautiful:

> Desolate as is the country over which we have just passed, and around us, the view is still one of the most beautiful and pleasing I remember to have seen. As we approached the river yesterday, the ridges on either side of its banks to the west appeared broken into a thousand forms— columns, shafts, temples, buildings, and ruined cities could be seen, or imagined, from the high points along our route.[5]

Beckwith was able to find romantic solace in this landscape; James Schiel, a German who served as the party's doctor and geologist, could not. Despite his assumed role as a scientist, applying logic and objectivity to the terrain, Schiel's utter disgust at the San Rafael Swell echoed throughout his written report. Like Beckwith, Schiel compared the terrain to architectural forms, usually gothic. He also realized, probably for the first time in this region, that aridity compounded the effects of erosion upon the landscape. Because of a lack of plants and loamy organic soils, the desert floor absorbed little precipitation. Sporadic but violent rains ran over the shales, clays, and sand-stones, forming rivulets then streams then rivers, all the while carving and carrying away sediment toward sea level. This lack of vegetation also stripped the country naked, allowing detailed observation of erosional forces and geological layers that would have been impossible in more temperate climates.[6]

Above all, erosion and aridity emphasized Schiel's journal's overarching theme of a fallen and decaying landscape. To Schiel, Canyon Country rain was not nourishing but destructive and degrading. Nearly a century earlier Juan María Antonio de Rivera had observed the abandoned ruins of Mesa Verde and noted that this was a landscape of decline, abandoned by humans and left to crumble. Schiel came to the same conclusion through observation not of abandoned structures but of the landscape itself. Geology alone was sufficient for his case:

> Deep gullies and ravines cut into the mountain and give it the appear-ance of half destroyed, colossal fortifications. In view of the desolate nature of the countryside this is not without interest, and if one consid-ers the fantastic formations on the other side of the river, the churches, temples, houses, and towers, one cannot avoid the impression that at one time evil spirits had lived here and had found death in a struggle of extermination. For Indian Country is extermination country.[7]

This was a landscape of death, and more so because of the scattered bands of Paiutes that the expedition encountered. Schiel wondered, with more dis-gust than admiration, at "how these people could find enough to eat in such a sterile country."[8] In a tradition extending back through the centuries, he equated Bad Indians with Bad Land. This was an awful wilderness.

More contributed to the expedition's pessimism than just Bad Land, how-ever. The search for a 38th parallel railroad route was more political than prag-matic. Gunnison had been through the area before, while surveying the Great Salt Lake area under Howard Stansbury in 1849, and personally believed that a railroad there would never be practical. Though the route was the most direct line of travel between East and West, it passed through much more broken terrain than proposed routes to the north or the south. Gunnison was

probably aware that secretary of war Jefferson Davis had organized the expedition through the Canyon County in part simply to prove wrong his political rival Thomas Hart Benton, who was a strong advocate of the 38th parallel
route. His superiors wanted him to fail.[9]

Furthermore, for all of Schiel's hyperbole, some members of the party
were indeed en route to "extermination country." They knew that newly
arrived Mormon settlers were at war with Indians farther west but had been
assured that they would pass through the Canyon Country in peace.[10] But
tragically, after passing up the gorge of the San Rafael River and ascending
the 11,000-foot Wasatch Plateau, Gunnison descended into the valley of the
Sevier River to his death in a massacre by Pahvant Utes.[11]

The Gunnison-Beckwith expedition was not of particularly great significance to the Canyon Country. Schiel's geological (and even aesthetic) observations were shallow in comparison to those of others who would follow him
in the next few decades, such as John S. Newberry, John Wesley Powell, and
Clarence Dutton. And Beckwith's approach to understanding the region was
for the most part the same as that of his Old Spanish Trail predecessors—he
marveled at the Canyon Country's broken, forbidding nature while skirting
its peripheries but wisely avoided its worst parts. The only trace of optimism
or boosterism that he showed about the region's potential was a brief allusion to the possibility of building a railroad through the San Rafael Gorge,
an idea that he certainly never promoted or pursued.[12]

The doomed Gunnison, however, marked the beginning of the United
States' impending attempts at incorporating the Canyon Country. While this
new nation was in no way exceptional in viewing the desert as broken, fallen,
or in need of improvement, the means by which it explored the region were
something new. The surveying and construction of railroads, of course, represented the ultimate in travel by straight lines—if the Bad Land contained no
natural transcontinental waterway such as Spain or even earlier Americans
had sought, then industry and technology were the logical solutions. Despite
Beckwith's rejection of the railroad route, the Canyon Country was no different than the rest of the United States in the eyes of future engineers and
entrepreneurs. Just as in the temperate East, railroads could cross canyons
by bridges and could parallel the entrenched rivers by tunnels and blasting,

gaining access to the Colorado's precious water, which had eluded so many past travelers. Land would conform to technology, not vice versa. While for the most part this is a story of later decades, as the final chapter shows, the railroad survey of Gunnison represents a small initial step in this direction.

In designating scientists and engineers specifically as explorers, the United States no longer had to be content with semimythical reports from supposedly dim-witted foreign traders, naïvely idealistic missionaries, or, worst of all, Indians. Successors to Gunnison, Beckwith, and Schiel were post-Humboldt, post-Darwin geologists, naturalists, astronomers, cartographers, and even artists and aesthetes. As always at the root of all these explorations was the incorporation of the Canyon Country into something useful for the rest of the nation. But for the most part the Canyon Country remained as illogical and confounding to science as it had been to religion and commerce.

On the broad, continental scale United States exploration through the nineteenth century was not a simple, uniform movement of optimism from the Good Lands of the east to the Bad Lands of the interior West. Early government explorers approached arid and even semiarid regions with cautionary pessimism; the hope of Lewis and Clark for a benevolent transcontinental waterway was balanced by Zebulon Pike's and Stephen Long's disappointment at the "Great American Desert." In crossing the southern Plains of Texas and Oklahoma on his 1807 illegal foray into New Spain, Pike gave only a brief nod to the by now familiar promise of a "grand reservoir" at the head of the Río Grande before lamenting the utter waste of the entire region.[13] The southern plains were North America's own version of the Sahara, he wrote, completely devoid of even "a speck of vegetable matter."[14]

Subsequent promoters of the arid West—and even modern historians— have chided Pike for his pessimism. After all, he was not even in the most arid or broken region of North America—the southern plains were not the Mojave Desert or Death Valley, and certainly not the Canyon Country. Perhaps, however, Pike was more accurate in his description than any of his successors could have known. We now know that the water source of the southern plains, the Ogallala Aquifer, is a nonrenewable resource. Similarly, the earliest "official" U.S. explorers to visit the Canyon Country, the Macomb expedition, exhibited Pike-like disgust or disregard for the region's uselessness and likewise would not be remembered well by later explorers because of these viewpoints.

In tracing "official" United States explorations in and around the Canyon Country, we find a clear movement from outright disgust, to uneasy intrigue, to unbridled fascination. Many explorers of the 1850s—Schiel, John C. Frémont, John Macomb—saw absolutely nothing redeeming about the Canyon Country. But these exploration parties often included individuals with more complicated views of the region. Beckwith had no problem calling portions of the Green River Desert "beautiful," and later John Newberry was enthralled at how the entire region exposed geological layers for study in ways that more forested, humid environments in the East never could. These attitudes laid the groundwork for John Wesley Powell's in-depth surveys of the 1870s, which saw in the Canyon Country an unprecedented, unparalleled combination of romantic beauty and geological data.

FRÉMONT'S WINTER

The cold, rainy weather in the San Rafael Swell had been annoying to the doomed Gunnison expedition, but it would only get worse as the fall of 1853 turned to winter and yet another railroad survey followed closely on Gunnison's trail. Celebrity government explorer Colonel John C. Frémont felt jilted. Perhaps because of his antislavery leanings, his court-martial during the U.S.-Mexican War, or the failure of his last expedition of 1848–49 due to starvation, hypothermia, and cannibalism in Colorado's San Juan Mountains, Secretary of War Davis had passed Frémont over for the 38th parallel survey in favor of Gunnison. In response to this snub, Frémont mounted his own privately funded survey with the help of his father-in-law, Senator Benton.

This was Frémont's final expedition through the West and unfortunately the one we know the least about. Frémont was obviously concerned with visual documentation. He brought along photographer Solomon Nunes Carvalho and cartographer-artist F. W. von Egloffstein. But Frémont did not want written records. Desiring a monopoly on any publishable memoirs in the future, he allowed no journals on the expedition and even fired one expedition member at an early stage for attempting to keep one. Because Frémont never published memoirs of this expedition, our only written view of this winter disaster is through Carvalho's covertly kept personal diary.[15]

Frémont's broad plans for the route were simple: cross the Continental Divide in Colorado and roughly follow Gunnison's route through the Canyon Country, over the Wasatch Plateau, and into the Great Basin. Though taking the same route, he planned to upstage Gunnison in several ways. First, Frémont intentionally planned a winter expedition, thereby proving the feasibility of a year-round railroad route in a way that the doomed Gunnison could never have achieved.[16] Apparently the winter tragedy of 1848–49 had taught Frémont little.

Perhaps more important, however, was Frémont's intention to visually document the arid West by new means: through the lens of the camera. Carvalho was one of the nation's leading innovators in daguerreotype photography, a method in which light-sensitive copper plates were directly exposed to their subjects, to become images without the use of negatives. Because these plates were the finished products, the only way to reproduce copies was to hire an artist physically to engrave a lithograph copy. Frémont and Carvalho, however, both chose this method over the more mass-produced wet plate method in anticipation of harsh weather conditions, worrying that the liquid chemicals in wet plate photography would freeze. Given the harsh temperatures that the party would encounter, these concerns were certainly justified.[17]

Despite his hope to capture the West's vast landscapes and panoramas, Carvalho's photography failed to document the expedition accurately. Although he continued to take pictures throughout the brutal winter, he ultimately found that the tiny daguerreotype images were best suited for close indoor portraits, not Canyon Country vistas.[18] Unfortunately, we will never know today how good or bad his images of the region were; they were all destroyed in a fire in the 1870s. Carvalho's covert writings alone would prove to be the most accurate, long-lasting record of Frémont's final expedition.

The party was fortunate to encounter low snow levels as it crossed the Continental Divide in December, descending the west slope of the Rockies into the Gunnison River valley. Very quickly, however, things began to fall apart. Carvalho had never been in remote areas before, and his journal recounts events as the party entered the Canyon Country with unfolding horror. First, as they were passing through the Grand River Valley near present-day Grand Junction, Colorado, a horse and a mule fell to their deaths off an embankment. Then, running low on food, members of the party killed and ate a supposedly stray horse, prompting a tense standoff with the animal's enraged Ute owners. A few days later, with food dwindling on the banks of the Green River, Frémont gathered the party members to swear collectively that they would not resort to cannibalism in the coming weeks. The men swore their oaths and then plunged into the icy river crossing. To celebrate the crossing the men bought an unknown, nutty, grass-seed flour from local Indians and ate it along with another horse.[19]

Given these dire circumstances, we may forgive Carvalho for being light on geographic details. Like nearly everyone else who followed this portion of the Old Spanish Trail, he noted that the country was "barren and sterile to a degree."[20] Frémont's desire for a direct route across this region that followed riverways may have convinced him to divert south from Gunnison's route and into the heart of the San Rafael Swell. In addition to experiencing much harsher weather than Gunnison, Frémont went deeper into the Bad Land.

We can gather only this from Carvalho concerning the route: upon crossing the Green River, the party members immediately began following another smaller tributary, the San Rafael River. They followed the river upstream, thinking of how well it would accommodate a railroad grade as it approached the uplift of the San Rafael Reef's thousand-foot walls. At this point the river enters a series of narrows, the Upper and Lower Black Boxes, in which tan Permian-era sandstone walls form canyons hundreds of feet deep and as narrow as a few dozen feet. Carvalho mentioned nothing of the cavernous Black Boxes or of the frigid waterfalls within them that would have halted progress, so we can only assume that the party bypassed them to the north. He noted that they returned to the small river through a "fertile, although unknown valley" enclosed by "high sandstone mountains," probably the San Rafael's junction with Buckhorn Wash.[21]

Beyond the San Rafael River, through January, the party members struggled southwestward, away from the river, through more canyons, more desert, and more cold, miserable weather. They were approaching the flanks of Thousand Lake Plateau by way of what we today call the Moroni Slopes and Cathedral

Valley, since Carvalho tells of finding "some volcanic rocks," which are not present in the drainage of the San Rafael river.[22] Here cold and hunger killed party member Oliver Fuller.[23] In a final desperate attempt to get out of this Bad Land, the members of the party turned directly west, dropped all unnecessary supplies, pushed over the 10,500-foot crest of Thousand Lake Mountain, and reached their salvation at the Mormon village of Parowan.

The fifth Frémont expedition was in such a desperate situation that the record says little except that they were most definitely going through some truly Bad Land. But the expedition members were dismissive, even contemptuous, of the region, which is important in showing how explorers still regarded the Canyon Country at this time. Frémont already had a marked disdain for all things arid, and this expedition certainly capped his disgust.[24] Finished with the West, and especially with the Canyon Country, the celebrity explorer would move into politics, running as the Republican Party's first presidential candidate in 1856. After his rough introduction to the arid west, Carvalho traveled north to Salt Lake City. There he would meet Brigham Young, the Mormon Moses, and the final portion of his *Incidents of Travel and Adventure* offers a unique Hebraic perspective on the Mormons in their New Jerusalem.[25] Egloffstein's map of the expedition's route turned out to be quite inaccurate, but he would go on to find work with the 1857 J. C. Ives expedition exploring the lower Colorado up to the mouth of the Grand Canyon. By this time, no doubt tainted with contempt for desert rivers and canyons, Egloffstein's engravings from the Ives expedition depicted exaggerated, nightmarish scenes of a turbulent Colorado crashing through subterranean canyons, perhaps confirming his recurring terror of the region.[26]

NEWBERRY'S SUMMER

Egloffstein and the rest of the Ives expedition to the lower Grand Canyon never came close to the Canyon Country in 1857. The expedition's leader declared that their party was the first and doubtless last "party of whites to visit this profitless locality." However, one member of this expedition, Dr. John Strong Newberry, somehow managed to see scientific value in this broken and terrible landscape.[27] Utility and productivity aside, this topography stripped bare was invaluable to the scientist as evidence of uplift, erosion, and, above all, vast geologic time. Two years later Newberry would find these values in the Canyon Country.

Like the Ives expedition, the 1859 expedition of Captain John N. Macomb was tied to the new presence of Mormon settlers on the Great Salt Lake. Rather than search out railroad routes as Gunnison or Frémont had, these expeditions under the U.S. Army Topographical Corps intended to find as many trails into the Mormon territory as possible. These potential trails were all the more important given the eruption of the short-lived "Mormon War," in which troops under Albert Sidney Johnston invaded the new Great Basin Theocracy and Mormon settlers at Mountain Meadows to the southwest massacred over 120 Arkansas emigrants. The rising federal power of the United States required knowledge of the nature of the Bad Land that made up Mormondom's southeastern frontier.[28]

In the summer of 1859 the party members left Santa Fe, crested the San Juan Mountains, and descended into the desert (see fig. 4.1). They were not avoiding broken terrain. Unlike Gunnison or Frémont, they had the explicit goal of seeking out perhaps the heart of the Canyon Country—the elusive confluence of the Green and Grand Rivers, the head of the great Colorado.[29] Macomb's brief summary of the expedition was very much in the tradition of Frémont or Schiel—expressing disgust. Given that he viewed the land as a terrible, uninhabitable wilderness, Macomb mentioned Indians only once, despite hints that the party constantly sought them out for topographical advice. Macomb much preferred to emphasize the now abandoned pueblos of the region over its still-existent Paiutes. Like Schiel, he also saw a landscape of decline, a once-glorious place now in ruin. But unlike earlier Spanish missionaries or his Mormon contemporaries, who harbored obligations of restoring Eden both literally and metaphorically, Macomb saw no need to improve the Canyon Country or transform this wasteland.

Mentioning the Old Spanish Trail, which by this time had already entered the realm of myth, Macomb wrote that it was "much talked of as having been the route of commerce between California and New Mexico in the days of old Spanish Rule [actually recent Mexican rule], but it seems to have been superceded [*sic*] by the routes to the north and south of it, which have been opened by modern enterprise." To Macomb, the Old Spanish Trail symbolized

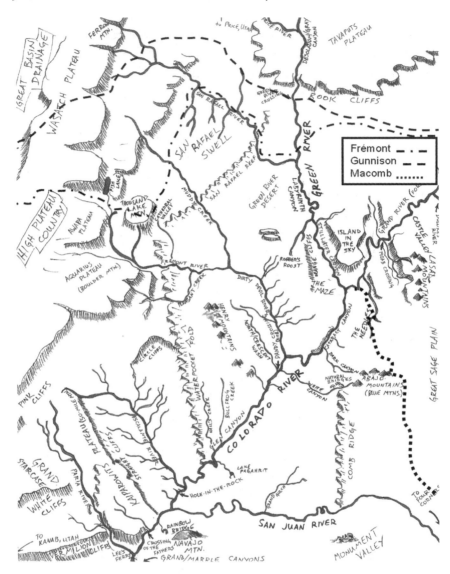

4.1. The routes of Gunnison (1853: dashed line), Frémont (1853–54: dotted and dashed line), and Macomb (1859: dotted line) through the Canyon Country.
(Map by author)

the United States' view of the entire Spanish Empire: clunky and archaic, an outdated route through a useless land. "Modern enterprise" would do well to avoid the unredeemable Canyon Country. In probably his most oft-quoted condemnation of the area, Macomb summarized: "I cannot conceive of a more worthless and impractical region than the one we now found ourselves in. I doubt not there are repetitions and *varieties* of it for hundreds of miles down the great Colorado."[30]

Unlike the Mormon scouts and settlers who were already beginning to enter the Canyon Country by this point, Macomb saw absolutely no potential or need to settle and improve this wasteland. He cited the extinct civilization of the cliff-dwellers, writing that "it requires no effort of the imagination to fancy that they may have starved or frozen to death; for the winters are severe, and fuel is very scarce."[31] Furthermore, in one of his rare nods to an existing Indian culture of the region, Macomb noted that the Navajos living along the San Juan River had not attempted to cultivate the river area, despite its fertile soil and "abundant water for irrigation."[32] Macomb was not criticizing the Navajos for this; he was actually complimenting them for also recognizing the uselessness of this country. This was quite different from concurrent and future Mormon attitudes or even from John Wesley Powell's later arguments for efficiently harnessing and conserving what little water existed in the region. As later chapters concerning the Mormon drive to irrigate all lands show, future settlers would have done well to adopt some of Macomb's skepticism toward desert rivers.

Given Macomb's view of this region, which certainly was a dismissible Great American Desert in the tradition of Pike, Long, Frémont, and Ives, it is not surprising that he would have been perplexed at Dr. Newberry's "particularly zealous and energetic" examination of the country.[33] While Newberry's account of the expedition is not free from descriptions of some misery and hardship (after all, he was crossing a desert in August), he also showed a sense of aesthetics, wonder, and enthusiasm that no observer had yet applied to the Canyon Country. It is worthwhile to examine Newberry's reminiscence of the party's first view of the Canyon Country, from the crest of Mesa Verde:

> Here we were to leave the lofty Sierras of the Rocky Mountain system, which had so long looked down on our camps and marches, the picturesque scenery of the foothills, their flowery valleys, and sparkling streams, the grateful shade of their noble forests, and take our weary

ways across the arid expanse of the great western plateau; a region whose
dreary monotony is only broken by frightful chasms, where alone the
weary traveler finds shelter from the burning heat of the cloudless sun,
and where he seeks too often in vain a cooling draught that shall slake
his thirst. To us, however, as well as to all the civilized world, it was a
terra incognita, and was viewed with eager interest, both as the scene of
our future explorations and as the possible repository of truth which we
might gather and add to the sum total of human knowledge.[34]

This description is as complex as the Canyon Country itself. To Newberry, unlike Macomb, this was not simply Bad Land—but neither was it
Good Land, certainly not like the pleasant and cool Rocky Mountains. Previously held geographic dichotomies were breaking down. Newberry saw
the Canyon Country with a combination of intrigue and repulsion that was
approaching Burke's definition of sublimely horrific landscapes.[35] For perhaps the first time, in the written word at least, someone found value in the
Bad Land precisely because it was Bad Land. Granted, Newberry was largely
referring to the value of the Canyon Country in quantifiable scientific terms.
But it is significant that he was finding some near-mystical or transcenden-
tal "repository of truth" in such a remote land during the lifetime of Henry
David Thoreau and a decade before John Muir would find similar solace
in Yosemite Valley. With Newberry, environmental thought took a key step
toward valuing the Canyon Country not because it was simply Good Land
or Bad Land but because of its complexity and ambiguity.

Countless travelers since Newberry's time have held similar views. Motorists drive by way of pleasant summertime mountain routes, through flowers
and trees, to designated overlooks, viewing the hot, arid expanse of the Canyon Country as it stretches to the horizon. Like Newberry or Beckwith,
today's tourists assume at first that this is a flat plain, only realizing upon
closer examination that hundreds of eroded drainages cut through the table-
land. Nearly a century after Newberry, Edward Abbey looked west from a
similar viewpoint into the Canyon Country, with a similar confusion: "I hesi-
tate, even now, to call that scene beautiful" (see his full quotation in the introduction). To both Abbey and Newberry, beauty was easy to define: distant

mountains, green pastures, trees, clear flowing streams.[36] The Canyon Country was none of these, yet it still held something for these visitors.

Macomb and Newberry both agreed that this landscape had no practical utilitarian value. Here was something even more dramatic and larger than what Newberry had originally observed on a previous trip through the Llano Estacado of Texas—a flat plain that had been carved by streams into canyons and breaks, denuded of vegetation by the desert environment and all perfectly exposed for the geologist. Noting that higher, more temperate mountains surrounded the region on all sides, Newberry described a geology that increased in depth and complexity as canyon drainages traveled from the periphery of the mountains toward the main artery of the Colorado River Canyon. Utilitarian value also decreased deeper into the canyons: he observed that only the peripheries of the Canyon Country appeared to have any potential for commercial exploitation, as the sedimentary rocks of the interior canyons could hold no valuable metals.[37]

Commercial potential aside, Newberry clearly saw a more abstract value in the Canyon Country for the purposes of science—indeed, much of his writing reveled in the region's sheer lack of practical utility. As the party turned west from its northward course between the Abajo Mountains and the Great Sage Plain, it encountered the first of several huge cliff escarpments that blocked progress toward the hidden rivers. Logically, Newberry knew that the nearer they came to the confluence, the more profound and complex erosional activity would be. Aesthetically, increased erosion meant increased beauty.

> Perhaps no portion of the earth's surface is more irremeably [*sic*] sterile, none more hopelessly lost to human occupation, and yet it is but the wreck and ruin of a region rich and beautiful, changed and impoverished by the deepening channels of its drainage systems; the most striking and suggestive example of over-drainage of which we have any knowledge.[38]

As the expedition picked its way through the cliffs into the depths of either Hart's Draw or Indian Creek Canyon, Newberry recorded the first detailed description of Jurassic and Triassic sandstones (though he did not name them): the Navajo, "yellow…and very remarkably cross-stratified"; the Kayenta, "red, foliated sandstone with some bands of red shale"; and the Wingate, "two hundred and seventy feet of reddish-brown sandstone, very massive, forming perpendicular faces."[39] Most visitors to the Canyon Country today consider these particular sandstones to form the region's most striking features, and these specific geologic layers make up the bulk of four of Utah's five national parks.[40] Nearing the river canyon and descending through many more millions of years in geologic time, the party encountered the eroded pinnacles of what is today Canyonlands National Park's Needles District, where Newberry wrote that "no language is adequate to convey a just idea of the strange and impressive scenery formed by their grand and varied outlines."[41]

The party members knew that they were reaching their goal, the confluence of the Green and the Grand Rivers, but almost every step nearer this objective was more difficult than the last. Macomb must have been completely disgusted at the terrain by this point, Newberry was overwhelmed, and we can imagine that the rest of the party was hot, thirsty, and tired in the August heat. Newberry looked toward the obvious canyon of the Grand River and noted that "perhaps four miles below our position it is joined by another great chasm coming in from the northwest, said by the Indians to be the Green River. From the point where we were it was inaccessible, but we had every reason to credit their report in reference to it."[42]

This is one of Newberry's scarce references to Indians living in the Canyon Country. Like Macomb, he wrote extensively of the crumbled remains of cliff dwellings, reflecting upon the decline and fall of Ancestral Puebloans to the south and east of the Canyon Country, but he seemed to care little for the region's current inhabitants. The explorers' vision of the region, marked by adjectives such as "desolate" and "sterile," included no need to mention that human inhabitants in fact existed around them in this Bad Land. Indeed, like all American-constructed "wildernesses," for Newberry, much of the romantic intrigue of the region actually relied upon his deemphasizing of its human inhabitants.[43]

In the end, for all of the educated perspective and aesthetic appreciation that Newberry brought to this sublime region, the party ultimately fell back upon secondhand Indian reports, just as Alonso de Posada had nearly two centuries before as he conjured up mountain ranges and Edens in the interior West. Newberry never personally reached his objective, the head of the Colorado River. The country was still too broken.

As the party retreated from the area of the confluence, picking its way south toward the San Juan River, both Macomb and Newberry undoubtedly believed that they were leaving a harsh, inhospitable land. But while Macomb was leaving in simple disgust, Newberry was more reflective. The Canyon Country's rocks and rivers were very old, evidence of a deep geologic time, a dynamically changing earth, and even indirectly linked to Darwin's theories of evolution published in the same year. But for all the enthusiasm that Newberry mustered, this was not evolution or progress but devolution and decline. This region was once hospitable, its cliff dwellings "evidence that these dreadful cañons were once the homes of families…formerly spread over all this region now so utterly sterile, solitary, and desolate."[44] Not only was the human culture of the Canyon Country in decline, but the very land itself was eroding, disintegrating, crumbling toward the Colorado and ultimately the ocean. This place was beautiful, instructive, and even enlightening, but it had passed well beyond the realm of human habitation or utility.

On the large canvas of the continent-spanning United States, Macomb's expedition quickly became a minor footnote. A year and a half later the North and South were at war and the public would not see Newberry's report until 1876. By that time the American wave of Manifest Destiny, expansionism, and cultivation was poised to engulf even the Canyon Country. Mormons from the north were arriving, sharing Macomb's notion of a fallen landscape and people, but with the additional obligation to mold the land and people to their own model. Just as Manifest Destiny and "rain follows the plow" optimism had apparently disproved the notion of a "Great American Desert" on the central plains, settlers would soon attempt to show that the Canyon Country too could produce and contribute to their nation on their own terms.

Perhaps this explains the curious secondhand illustrations that accompanied Macomb and Newberry's published 1876 report. Newberry had drawn sketches of the Canyon Country, as had the artist F. W. von Egloffstein, who

4.2. An 1876 adaptation of John Newberry's drawing of the "Head of Cañon Colorado: Erosion of Triassic Series." (Courtesy of the DeGolyer Library, Southern Methodist University, Dallas, Texas, Vault Folio QE79.5 N48 1876)

4.3. Looking south from Indian Creek Canyon. Compare the horizon silhouettes of the "Sixshooter Peaks" to those of figure 4.2. (Photo courtesy of Daniel Brayack, www.brayackmedia.com)

tended to emphasize the more horrific aspects of the canyons when he worked for other expeditions. But both of these men's illustrations were lost. In their place the artist J. J. Young—no doubt unfamiliar with the Canyon

Country—contributed a set of well-intentioned watercolors to the official report. While these illustrations accurately retained many specifics of the landscape that Macomb and Newberry traversed (for example, the distinctive profiles of the North and South Sixshooter Peaks along Indian Creek, as figs. 4.2 and 4.3 show), they nonetheless kept the unique landscape very much in the background, focusing more upon grassy valleys and tree-lined streams in the foreground. These secondhand illustrations failed to capture the grit and the heat of Canyonlands' Needles district in August. Indeed, the benign, pasture-like scenes amid a backdrop of unobtrusive red rock may very well have reflected the new optimism that stood ready to reject Macomb's skepticism and force the Canyon Country to bloom.

The 1850s wave of United States exploration into and around the Canyon Country—Gunnison, Frémont, Macomb—met the region at best with light scientific enthusiasm and at worst with disgust. None of them saw the place as having anything more than minor potential for exploitation; it was still very much a place to avoid. Frémont and Gunnison only brushed the northern fringes of the Canyon Country, and even Macomb and Newberry merely managed to strike toward the confluence and then quickly retreat. Even as settlers began to infiltrate the region, United States explorers had yet to traverse even as much of the Canyon Country as Escalante and Domínguez had almost a century earlier, let alone confirm the layout of its canyons, major rivers, and their crossing points. This would change in May 1869, as ten men pushed four boats into the Green River.

5

River Bottoms to Mountaintops

THE CANYON COUNTRY SURVEYS OF JOHN WESLEY POWELL

The decade following John Newberry's encounter with the Canyon Country was the United States' most tumultuous. As the Macomb expedition's report sat unpublished in government archives, hundreds of thousands of Americans died over the ideas of federal power, slavery, and the cohesiveness of a nation that had not yet even made sense of its own claimed interior. Far to the west, Mormons, whose settlements were gradually approaching the Canyon Country, viewed the war between the North and the South as a prophecy fulfilled, in which the worldly, wicked United States would destroy themselves, opening the way for Brigham Young's continent-spanning theocracy.[1] After the war ended, these same Mormons now worried about the new power of the Republican party, which as early as 1856, when John C. Frémont had run as its presidential candidate, had sworn to "prohibit in the Territories those twin relics of barbarism—Polygamy, and Slavery."[2]

For the Canyon Country, the implications of the post–Civil War federal power of the Republicans were indirect at first but significant. In 1862 Congress passed the Homestead Act, granting squared sections of 160 acres to any settler who could afford a modest filing fee. By imposing this geometric grid upon much of the interior West, the government was still assuming that all land was created equal and that it could be evenly divided by orderly lines. While this may have been true for the flat, humid regions of the East, it was utterly inappropriate for the realities of aridity and topography that unevenly distributed agricultural resources in the arid West. In following decades homesteaders throughout the area would realize that their extensive plots of land were utterly useless without access to water.

Although American settlement was gradually encroaching upon increasingly worse lands by this time, any ideas of homesteading the Canyon Country were still well in the future. This most nonlinear landscape was still beyond even the most optimistic visions of development, improvement, or transformation. While some Manifest Destiny–obsessed promoters such as William Gilpin were still arguing into the 1860s that the "benevolence of nature" called for homesteaders to reclaim the Bad Lands of the arid West, most Americans still thought of the Canyon Country as something to avoid, if they thought about it at all. For the time being even Mormons were content to remain around the peripheries of the region.[3]

The tales of the few non-Indian travelers who did pass through the center of the Canyon Country along the Colorado River corridor described an unknowable and deadly landscape that blurred the line between myth and reality, as the strange story of prospector James White confirmed. In 1867, after surviving an Indian ambush near the San Juan River that killed two companions, White allegedly floated down the Colorado, enduring its hundreds of rapids on a crudely constructed raft. By the time Mormons pulled him out of the river at Callville, Nevada, below the Grand Canyon, he was nearly dead, sunburned, starving, and completely disoriented. White's description of his river journey was so vague, and subsequently distorted by both promoters and detractors, that we have no idea where he actually was. Estimates range from him floating along nearly 500 miles of Cataract, Glen, and Grand Canyons to merely washing about in the eddies of a thirty-mile section of river below the Grand Canyon.[4] Few people took White's claim of having successfully descended the Colorado seriously, least of all Maj. John Wesley Powell, a Civil War hero who had lost his right arm at Shiloh, amateur scientist, and explorer who began trying to understand the Canyon Country, as well as the rest of the arid Southwest, just after the Civil War.

More scholarship and literature on Powell is available than for about all other Canyon Country explorers combined—and for good reason. On the broad scale of national politics, he was a model for strong federal power in the West as part of what Elliot West has termed "The Greater Reconstruction," in reference to events far to the north. Powell also was a forerunner for Progressive-era conservationists of later decades who argued for federal power to keep natural resources away from the more predatory elements of capitalism. The published account of his 1869 descent of the Green and Colorado Rivers remains adventure literature at its finest. Later, in his *Report on the Lands of the Arid Region of the United States*, he became one of the earliest proponents of the postwar Republican federal government's regulating and limiting the extent of optimistic settlement that was rapidly spreading into worse lands through the final quarter of the nineteenth century. To Powell, the optimism engrained in the 1862 Homestead Act both encouraged abuse by speculators and opened unsuitable lands to settlement that should remain closed.[5]

The legacy of Powell specifically in regard to the Canyon Country is less straightforward and without a doubt less studied. In trying to understand the Canyon Country, Powell went well beyond the dismissal and disgust of Frémont or Macomb and extended the intrigue that Newberry felt to often romantic awe at the region's beautiful canyons and buttes. Later scientists and surveyors in Powell's employ in the U.S. Geological Survey, most notably Clarence Dutton, combined their geological analyses with poetic celebrations of the region's beauty as nobody had ever done before (or perhaps since). At the same time Powell's published diary repeatedly emphasized the deadliness of the area, implying that only the boldest of men such as himself could "conquer" the canyons and rivers. Beyond this aesthetic or heroic revelry, in his *Report* Powell used the Canyon Country as a "worst-case-scenario"—an example of how to moderate resource consumption, with the attitude that what worked in a Bad Land could work anywhere.

The Colorado's First Descent

All of this was in the future on May 24, 1869. Only two weeks earlier the Union Pacific Railroad and Central Pacific Railroad had successfully joined the east and west coasts of the United States via an engineered straight line of forged iron. No longer would Americans have to yearn for navigable water-ways across the continent or toil for months across the plains in animal-drawn wagons. Technology had finally prevailed where nature had failed. At the small town of Green River, Wyoming, Powell and nine others unloaded their heavy-hulled boats and supplies from a train and pushed them into the town's namesake river.

At this Wyoming crossing the Green River is about 150 miles from its source in the Wind River Mountains. Its transformation from a swift, cool mountain stream to a slow, wide, desert river is well underway at this point. Shortly downstream from the town, the river enters a series of gorges: the now submerged Flaming Gorge, Lodore, and Split Mountain Canyons in today's Dinosaur National Monument, the 100-mile stretch of Desolation and Gray Canyons, then Labyrinth and Stillwater Canyons. Beyond this was the Green's confluence with the Grand River (so called at the time), form-ing the Colorado, which then rushed through Cataract Canyon, Glen Can-yon, Marble Canyon, and the Grand Canyon.[6] Nobody—official explorers or otherwise—had floated or mapped the length of this drainage system and its tributaries. The greatest blank spot of all on maps was in the cen-ter of the rivers' drainage basin—the Canyon Country. In total area of blank, unmapped land, the Canyon Country dwarfed even the more famous Grand Canyon to the southwest.

Despite this lack of cartographic knowledge, Powell did have some accu-rate ideas of the country before he began his first expedition. He certainly knew that the Green River did not flow westward to California: it was vir-tually certain that it would join the Grand to form the Colorado, even if Macomb and Newberry had not visually confirmed the location of the conflu-ence. Powell also knew that the Green-Colorado system did not flow through one continuous canyon. There were breaks in the gorge walls, through which the expedition could resupply or even hike out if need be. The Uinta Basin in northeast Utah, long known to Indians and trappers, was one such easy access point.[7] Later the party floated by another natural access point at what is now the town of Green River, Utah, an open region that had long fun-neled traders and explorers—including Frémont and "the lamented Gunni-son" along the Canyon Country's northern fringes.[8] By his second trip down the river in 1871, Powell knew of even more logistical access points, such as the mouth of the Dirty Devil River, the mouth of the Paria at what would become Lee's Ferry, and even the mouth of Kanab Creek within the depths of the Grand Canyon.

Additionally, despite rumors of hundred-foot falls, narrow canyons, and even subterranean caves that swallowed the entire river, Powell made a calculated guess that the rapids and declination of the river would not be wholly impassable. Based on observation and readings of surrounding areas, he concluded that the geological layers of the Canyon Country had risen slowly enough, and were composed of sufficiently soft rock, to avoid the risk of an unknown Niagara somewhere in the Grand Canyon. The party would encounter rapids, but they would be caused more by rockfall and debris flows from adjacent canyons. At the very worst the members could portage or line their boats around them. Powell's educated guess would prove correct—barely.

Though planned as a fact-finding scientific expedition, Powell's 1869 trip from Green River, Wyoming, to the foot of the Grand Canyon at the Grand Wash Cliffs was an uncertain gamble for survival. Like Domínguez and Escalante's group nearly a century earlier, most of Powell's men were experienced guides, prospectors, and trappers who knew the Rocky Mountains and Great Basin country—if not the Green and Colorado Rivers specifically—very intimately. In addition to these men and their pragmatic knowledge, Powell brought along his brother Walter, a former prisoner of the Confederates suffering from postwar trauma, who had frequent violent outbursts on the trip that annoyed and alienated the rest of the group.[9] An eighteen-year-old cook and adventure-seeking Englishman rounded out the party. Other than John Wesley Powell himself, the expedition included no scientists, cartographers, or photographers.

The party made it as far as Lodore Canyon, portaging and sometimes lowering heavy boats by rope well past the point at which the trapper William Ashley had given up in 1825, before wrecking the first of its own boats, the *No Name*, in a rapid that Powell named "Disaster Falls."[10] Shortly thereafter Frank Goodman, who had been in the destroyed boat, left the expedition. According to some reports, at this point Powell began to treat the remaining survivors of the *No Name*, brothers O. G. and Seneca Howland, with contempt for wrecking the craft and losing valuable equipment.[11]

The expedition continued through the open country of the Uinta Basin and into Desolation Canyon, where the boats splashed through the river's many minor rapids. By mid-July they were deep into the Canyon Country, beyond Gunnison's and Frémont's crossings, floating serenely through the aptly named Labyrinth and Stillwater Canyons in the wake of Denis Julien.[12] Beyond the junction of the Grand and the Green, which "united in solemn depths, more than 1,200 feet below the general surface of the country," they endured the seemingly endless rapids of Cataract Canyon.[13] These rapids may still have been in their high-water stage and were certainly the largest and most destructive that the men had yet seen. By this point wrecks, portages, and lining of boats down rapids had destroyed much of the group's food, clothing, and equipment. Powell's treasured barometers broke, and teenaged cook Andy Hall repeatedly had to strain the wet, molding flour through mosquito netting.[14]

After quickly floating through the more mild stretch of Glen Canyon, by early August the group had reached what was to Powell and the American public the climax of their expedition: Marble Canyon and then the Grand Canyon. Rapids were larger, food rations were smaller, and the river changed course so much that Powell lost all sense of when the party would reach his set coordinates at the Mormon village of Callville. His journal summarized the atmosphere in the Grand Canyon in this oft-quoted passage:

> We have an unknown distance yet to run, an unknown river to explore. What falls there are, we know not; what walls rise over the river, we know not. Ah well! We may conjecture many things. The men talk as cheerfully as ever; jests are bandied about freely this morning; but to me the cheer is somber and the jests are ghastly.[15]

The expedition had learned by this time that harder, older rock such as the limestones of Cataract Canyon or Marble Canyon (which Powell erroneously named) caused much more violent rapids than the softer, younger sandstones of Labyrinth, Stillwater, or Glen Canyons. Past the mouth of the Little

Colorado, the party members saw that the river was veering west, into the hardest rock that they had yet seen: pre-Cambrian volcanic schists and granites of the Grand Canyon's inner gorges.

After two more weeks of rapids, hunger, and enduring portages as the August Arizona heat radiated off black cliffs, the expedition members reached what they believed was the worst rapid yet. Unlike previous rapids, such as the famous Lava Falls (which Powell did not even name or specifically mention), schist cliffs rising directly from the water made this obstacle impossible to line or portage. A dispute over how to progress led to the expedition's most controversial episode. According to Powell, the Howland brothers and their close friend William Dunn decided that they had enough and announced that they would hike out of a side canyon to the north then try to reach Mormon settlements. The rest of the crew, believing that they could successfully run the rapid, begged the Howlands and Dunn not to leave, to no avail. With three guns and a pan of biscuits, the men walked out. Powell and the remaining five members successfully ran the rapid. The next day at twelve o'clock they "emerge[d] from the Grand Canyon of the Colorado." They were half-naked, sunburned, and had run out of all supplies except coffee.[16]

The main party fared better than Dunn and the Howlands, however. After hiking north up the drainage that we now call Separation Canyon, they were killed, either by Shivwits Paiutes or by separatist Mormons suspicious of any American presence in the region. Their deaths and the ambiguity surrounding their separation from the main party continue to be the darkest part of an expedition that, while daring, gathered little practical knowledge except that a descent of the Colorado River was possible.[17]

Even in the midst of Powell's confirmation that the Canyon Country region was even bigger, more formidable, and more unknowable than previously assumed, the age-old desire for a practical water route across the interior West persisted. The attempts of "Captain" Samuel Adams were laughable and, according to Donald Worster, almost "a parody of the Powell Expedition" but were still significant in showing just how resilient geographical optimism was.[18]

The importance of Adams to the Canyon Country was his denial of the region's very existence. After unsuccessfully trying to join the Powell expedition in Wyoming, Adams mounted his own attempt to descend the Grand River from around present-day Breckenridge, Colorado. His small party portaged and wrecked boats as far downstream as present-day Grand Junction (following today's Interstate 70 and still about 100 miles from the Canyon Country), before deciding that "we had come over the worst part of our route" and that he could see Callville, Nevada, in the distance.[19] Convinced that he had beaten Powell to a true understanding of the river and its surroundings, Adams hurriedly submitted a report to the United States War Department, which ignored it. Hundreds of miles of Canyon Country simply did not exist to Adams; even amid the Manifest Destiny fervor of the nineteenth century, his bright ignorance reflected a geographical outlook that was rapidly ending.

In his own way, however, Powell was also shaping the Canyon Country and his expedition to his own needs and expectations. His popular public report, first published as a *Scribner's* magazine serial and later as a book in 1875, combined events from his more thorough second expedition of 1871–72 with the more adventurous elements, as well as the crew, of his 1869 expedition. In addition to glossing over the circumstances of the Howlands-Dunn tragedy, Powell emphasized sensational heroics in his report. He exaggerated the drop and size of rapids, for example, writing that the Big Drop Rapids in Cataract Canyon fell a total of seventy-five feet (actually closer to thirty feet).[20] Accompanying illustrations, some of which were by landscape painter Thomas Moran, were rife with exaggeration and inaccuracy, from the depictions of boats to the conspicuous omission of Powell's life preserver to the depth and width of the river canyons.[21]

The actual content of Powell's published report also hinted relatively little at the knowledge that he had accumulated about the Canyon Country through the first half of the 1870s. He mentioned dozens of place-names that his explorations had bestowed upon the landscape and named each major canyon of the Green-Colorado according to its characteristic or mood: Desolation, Labyrinth, Stillwater, Cataract, and Mound and Monument Canyons, which he would later condense into a single Glen Canyon.[22] The most descriptive name of the expedition, however, certainly came just after the party had endured the rapids of Cataract Canyon and came upon a small

tributary flowing in from the northwest. When asked if it was a cool trout
stream, William Dunn disgustingly replied that it was "a dirty devil," the name
that remains to this day.[23]

Beyond these names, however, Powell's treatment of the Canyon Country
in his report was a predictable extension of Gunnison, Frémont, or Macomb.
Like his predecessors, he marveled at the unique rock formations, hypoth-
esized about their origins, and compared them to human structures ("one
could almost imagine that the walls have been carved with a purpose, to represent giant architectural forms").[24] But his report never seriously approached
the issue of what was to be done with the Canyon Country by the United
States; it was essentially a static, passive landscape, good for adventure and
masculine bravado but little else. Powell's report devoted more storytelling
time to events in the Grand Canyon, a name and place that even in the 1870s
had much more public appeal than the expanses of Labyrinth, Stillwater, Cataract, and Glen Canyons upstream. The subtleties of the Canyon Country
would have to await more thorough examination by Powell and more specifically by some of his employees.

THE SECOND SURVEY

Though barely mentioned in his published report, Powell's second expedition, which began in May 1871, resulted in a much more comprehensive
understanding of the Colorado's canyons. This was a more all-encompassing
"survey" rather than a single "expedition." Powell funded his 1869 trip largely
out of his own pocket and with small grants from state natural history associ-
ations. His second survey received ample federal funding from the Smithsonian Institution. Rather than merely floating the Green and Colorado Rivers,
this second survey encompassed overland treks, mapmaking, boundary estab-
lishments, and systematic triangulations that took years to complete. While
the rapids of the Colorado were just as formidable, the survey avoided the
desperation and uncertainty of the first expedition. As expedition member
and chronicler Frederick Dellenbaugh recalled later, the party was not "both-
ered in the least by lack of provisions" and had ample time and resources to
"note the topography and geology as we went along, climb out frequently to
examine the surrounding country, and in every way carry forward the scientific work as planned."[25]

Perhaps most importantly, instead of employing frontiersmen, trappers, and prospectors, Powell now turned to academics, scientists, photographers, and artists, who presumably could begin observing and explaining this strange region to the rest of the United States. Many of these new "experts" had family ties to Powell. His young cousin, Walter Clement Powell (called "Clem"), came along. His brother-in-law, Almon Harris Thompson, was the survey's second-in-command. Thompson's teenaged cousin Frederick Samuel Dellenbaugh came along as an artist and would later become the expedition's and the Canyon Country's first historian. Absent, not surprisingly, was Powell's disturbed brother and 1869 expedition veteran Walter.

The actual river descent of Powell's second expedition and survey was minor compared to the mapping, reconnaissance, and surveying away from the Colorado that the party accomplished. This was not a simple river trip. Powell would occasionally come and go from the survey to secure more supplies and funds. In late November 1871 the entire party left the river and wintered in Kanab, Utah, to survey the boundary line between Utah and Arizona territories. This was to be an all-encompassing examination of the Canyon Country, not just a journey through it.

Much more so than in 1869, a dynamic and expansive period for Mormon settlement occurred in the first half of the 1870s. The towns of Pahreah, Orderville, Cannonville, and Escalante had all sprung up along the Canyon Country's western peripheries, Lee's Ferry was established on the Colorado between Glen and Marble Canyons, and a fort was built at Pipe Springs. Most important was the small town of Kanab on the southwest fringes of the Canyon Country, where Powell would base his entire survey. In 1872 Kanab had been, in the words of Herbert Gregory, a "stockaded square of log houses...by 1878, it had become a prosperous village of some 400 farmers and stockmen."[26] Powell took note of how the Mormons were extending their Zion into the howling wilderness through a combination of cooperativism and authoritarianism, and his observations on this would come to form the basis of his eventual *Report on the Lands of the Arid Region of the United States*.

For logistics, Powell enlisted the help of Mormon settlers in addition to his own employees, to cache food, guide, and serve as liaisons with Indian tribes. Jacob Hamblin was foremost of these "local" employees. Described by Dellenbaugh as a "slow moving, very quiet individual," Hamblin had been a missionary to the Ute, Navajo, Hopi, and even the reclusive Havasupai Indians in the Grand Canyon since 1857. In the year between the two expeditions Powell had even traveled with Hamblin through the Navajo and Hopi country, and the two men had worked to establish a peace between the Mormon settlers and Indian raiders who lived on opposite sides of the Canyon Country.[27]

As a missionary and Indian interpreter, Hamblin already knew the main routes that would take him through the Canyon Country as quickly as possible. But even he had relatively little knowledge of how the rivers, canyons, and Indian routes within the region connected to one another. During the summer of 1871 he and Isaac C. Haight wandered through the "grand and sublime" drainages of the Escalante and San Rafael Rivers, searching unsuccessfully for the mouth of the Dirty Devil River, where Powell had requested that they deliver supplies for the river expedition.[28] Once Hamblin actually tried to follow rivers and canyons within this region, even his relatively limited vocabulary revealed that the sheer complexity of this region overwhelmed him. A. H. Thompson, waiting for the undelivered supplies with the river party, merely felt annoyance that the Mormons could not do their assigned job.[29]

By the time Thompson had begun privately complaining in his journal about inept locals who got lost in the Canyon Country, he too was realizing the dual allure and repulsion of the region. As the Green River flows southward, its transition into the Canyon Country through Flaming Gorge, Lodore, and Desolation Canyons is quite gradual. Thompson's fascination with the country likewise increased gradually. In Desolation Canyon, where Powell had left the survey to travel to Salt Lake City, Thompson merely wrote: "Fine views. Much might be gushed on the scenery…but I cannot gush. I leave this writing to read."[30] The scenery in this same section of canyon not only failed to impress young Frederick Dellenbaugh but depressed him. Constantly lining rapids, and abandoned by his idol Powell, he complained that "throughout the high narrow cliffs are peculiar holes, looking like windows from which might be seen brighter views than we can behold in this cañon of Desolation!"[31] Only in his memoirs published decades later did Dellenbaugh finally dwell upon the river's spectacular scenery.

By late August the group had emerged from Desolation Canyon, rendez-voused with Powell at Gunnison's crossing (which Thompson glumly called "poor country"), and made a serene entrance into the heart of the Canyon Country on the flat waters of Labyrinth Canyon. At this point the party members were in much better spirits to enjoy the scenery, as the drab, flat shales gradually gave way to soaring monoliths and spires of Navajo and Wingate Sandstones.[32] The afternoon monsoonal rainstorms, which are so common in the region in late summer and early fall, cooled the men off and formed ephemeral waterfalls that cascaded off 800-foot cliffs.[33]

Thompson noted that the Indian name for this country of natural "towers, castles, churches, and capitols" was Tom-fin con la-rup: "Stone House Lands," and his use of superlatives in his descriptions gradually increased.[34] In his memoirs Dellenbaugh would retrospectively give one of the finest descriptions of the Canyon Country yet written:

[The river enters] a vast plateau…that is tilting northward and increasing in altitude towards the south, so that as the river runs on its canyon becomes deeper from this cause as well as its cutting. These great terraces sloping to the north were not before understood. They terminate on the south in vertical cliffs through which the river emerges abruptly. From such features as these the Major named this the Plateau Province. The cliffs terminating each plateau form intricate escarpments, meandering for many miles, and they might be likened to a series of irregular and complicated steps. Occasional high buttes and mountain masses break the surface, but in general the whole area forming the major part of the basin of the Colorado may be described as a plateau country—a land of mesas, cliffs, and canyons.[35]

Even the knowledge that the difficulties of Cataract Canyon lay just around the next bend did not take away the awe that the men felt at the confluence of the Green and Grand Rivers. Thompson wrote that "a prettier joining of two streams to form a third was never seen. Neither absorbs or flows into the other, but like two forces of equal strength they mingle and unite."[36]

On hikes out of the canyon or at breaks in the walls the party occasionally caught glimpses of high mountain groups punctuating the surrounding
desert horizon. Some, such as the Abajos and the La Sals, already had names
given by Spanish explorers. Others had their own names from the first expedition, such as "Mount Seneca Howland," today called Navajo Mountain.[37] One
range to the west was not yet named, simply called "Unknown" by Thompson. During one observation of these distant peaks he noted correctly that
they were "said to be volcanic."[38] It would be several years, however, before
other members of the Powell expedition could definitively confirm the intru-
sive laccolithic origins of the range and name it the "Henry Mountains," after
the Smithsonian Institution's first secretary, Joseph Henry. "Weird and wild,
barren and ghostlike" from the bottom of the river canyons, these mountains
seemed "like an unknown world" to the party.[39]

After passing through the depths of Cataract Canyon, whose "power and
majesty" seemed to Dellenbaugh to be the "acme of the stupendous," the
party quickly reached the Dirty Devil's mouth on October 1, stopping only
to cache a boat and float quickly on to the site of Escalante's ford of the Colorado, where they finally met Mormon scouts with much-needed supplies.[40]
From there it was only a few days' float to the end of Glen Canyon at its junction with the Paria River: Escalante's "Salsipuedes," a spot that within a year
would be called Lee's Ferry. The party cached the remaining boats, planning
to return to descend the Grand Canyon the following season. Before retiring
to Kanab and the winter base camp, Thompson obsessively hiked and rode
around the area of the Paria River, likely searching for any sign of an overland route back to the elusive Dirty Devil. He was unsuccessful. The problem
of this river, perhaps the largest river that he knew nothing about, continued
to perplex him.[41]

Reports of the party's winter in Kanab are disjointed and certainly lack the
drama and adventure of their river descent. This newly settled town beneath
the Vermilion Cliffs, which are the Canyon Country's southwestern terminus,
must certainly have offered a respite for all the group. Although Kanab was
very much an outpost at this time, a direct road connected it to more prosperous settlements in southwest Utah. The party enjoyed fresh vegetables, molas-
ses, and even small amounts of wine throughout the winter.[42] Kanab also

was connected to the outside world via telegraph, and Powell communicated with Washington and Salt Lake City daily.[43] Dellenbaugh and Clem Powell probably flirted with young Mormon women at the town's New Year's Eve Dance, and Powell and Thompson were certainly happy to have their wives in town.

The stay in Kanab was not just rest and relaxation, however. Powell was determined to triangulate a series of fixed coordinates across the Arizona Strip—vast flatlands that lay between the Canyon Country and the North Rim of the Grand Canyon—and establish a fixed, straight line to delineate the boundary between the territories of Utah and Arizona. This cold, tedious work naturally fell to the youngest members of the expedition: Dellenbaugh and Clem Powell. Dellenbaugh's journal kept during this "work as usual on the line" mentioned little of the cold, rainy winter weather, which must have been miserable. Instead he focused on stories of the teenagers racing against each other up lava cones, rolling rocks, and climbing cliffs.[44]

Tying Together a Bad Land: A. H. Thomson's Overland Search for the Dirty Devil

In addition to surveying and triangulation work, Thompson spent the winter thinking about the larger geological picture of the Canyon Country north and west of Kanab. Describing the strata, he assigned each major layer an era: "first the Vermilion Cliffs—Triassic…then white Cretaceous cliffs [actually the Jurassic-aged Navajo Sandstone]…back of these are the Tertiary mountains, in many places cliff-like in character, often of a pink dark color."[45] Today we call this the "Grand Staircase," a portion of a series of eroded terraces that extends from the top of the 11,000-foot Paunsaugunt Plateau to the bottom of the Grand Canyon. Thompson was observing 9,000 feet of decline and billions of years in geological history.

More practically, Thompson fixated upon the problem of the Dirty Devil River (where the party had cached a boat that fall), which Hamblin had been unable to locate. Where did it originate? Were its canyons passable for human traffic to its mouth? Sometime during the winter of 1871–72, Powell and Thompson decided upon the necessity of an overland trek from Kanab to the mouth of the Dirty Devil the following summer. Thompson, Dellenbaugh,

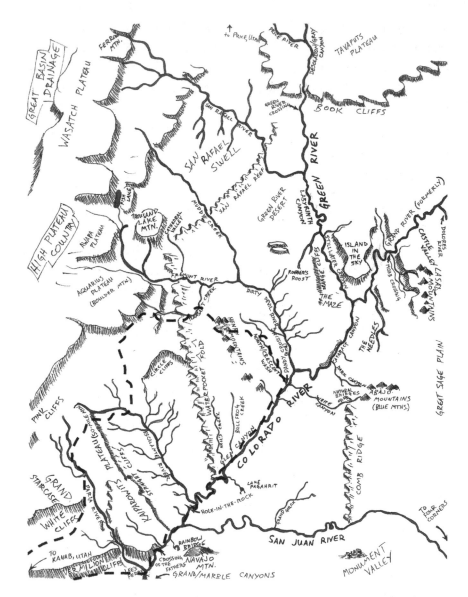

5.1. A. H. Thompson's loop through the western Canyon Country, 1872. (Map by author)

and a few others would follow a maze of canyons through the cliff layers of the Grand Staircase and across the Canyon Country west of the Colorado River (fig. 5.1).

The overt purpose of this trek was to reach the *Cañonita*, the boat that they had cached at the mouth of the Dirty Devil, and pilot it back through Glen Canyon. But it is clear that the journey through a new land that few whites and no government explorers had ever seen was perhaps even more important than the destination. Through the summer of 1872 these men found new major rivers and unknown mountains and pieced together the Canyon Country with unprecedented leaps of quantification.

Riding up the Paria, the geologist Thompson noted that the Cretaceous layers contained coal seams, hinting at possible future exploitation of this country. By June 1, however, his diary had abandoned both geology and utilitarianism, and the party's mood grew darker. In one of the Paria's upper tributaries they came across the remains of Elijah Averett, a Mormon man killed by Indians six years earlier. Wolves had apparently dug up his bones. Two days later the party's guide "Indian Tom" inexplicably left the group. They were left without a guide and the canyons were becoming deeper, making orientation increasingly difficult.[46]

Eventually the party entered an uninhabited valley that had already received a name from a Mormon militia on reconnaissance in the previous decade: Potato Valley (see chapter 8).[47] Within the year Thompson and Powell would rename the valley and its river for Fray Escalante, although the Franciscan had never seen the area. But Thompson was certainly not thinking about colonial Spanish history at this point. Though the future Escalante River ran through a "fine grassy valley" in its upper reaches, Thompson saw that it quickly turned south into the Canyon Country. If the reports of Jacob Hamblin, who had been through the region the previous August, were correct, the river's canyon would quickly become impassably narrow.[48]

More troubling was the increasingly blatant evidence that the party members had stumbled upon an entire major drainage system that they had not known existed. As Thompson and Powell had pored over maps and notes at their Kanab base camp, they had assumed that only a short divide separated the upper Paria from the Dirty Devil drainage; crossing from one basin to the other promised to be fairly simple. After four days of wandering the canyons of the Escalante through rain and flash floods, however, Thompson managed to catch a glimpse of the familiar peaks of the "Unknown" Mountains to the east. Knowing that this range lay to the west of the Dirty Devil, Thompson realized that they were descending the wrong river. Writing a description of this newly discovered river, which Thompson now assumed flowed in its canyon "40 miles east of south to the Colorado at a point thought to be a little above the mouth of the San Juan," he emphasized their mistake: "*It is not the Dirty Devil.*"[49] Thompson must have been perplexed as to how Powell had managed to float by this river's mouth unknowingly twice. This would be the last time that an explorer came across a drainage basin of this size in the contiguous United States.[50]

It was clear by this point that the Canyon Country, with still unmapped rivers and unnamed mountains, was more complex than even Powell had assumed while descending the Green and Colorado Rivers. The future Escalante River was a dead end—at least for horse or boat travel. They struggled out of its canyons, up raging creeks brimming with snowmelt, and gradually up to the high country of the Aquarius Plateau to the north. While the cool mountain air must have provided a respite from the desert below, the view was intimidating in its immensity, as the party looked "down upon the vast canyoned desert to the south as on a map."[51]

Even today, with visibility decreased by coal-fired power plants, the view of the Canyon Country from Utah State Highway 12 is astounding. The canyon of the Escalante River unwinds from the foreground toward the distant southern horizon, the uplift of Capitol Reef National Park lines the eastern periphery, and the peaks of the Henry Mountains, Navajo Mountain, the La Sals, and the Abajos punctuate the horizon. Following Thompson's route in 1880, Powell surveyor Clarence Dutton wrote that "the Aquarius should be described in blank verse and illustrated upon canvas." Comparing his climb to the top of the plateau to children's fantasy tales such as "Jack and the Beanstalk," he gushed that here an explorer "forgets he is a geologist and feels himself a poet."[52] But Dutton never did much beyond simply looking at the view of the canyons below, calling it "profound," "terrible," and "the extreme of desolation, the blankest solitude, the superlative desert." He was happy to stay in the high country.[53]

Thompson's party members knew that to reach the Dirty Devil River, however, they would have to descend into this Bad Land, from a mountain paradise into the summer inferno. After traversing the flanks of the Aquarius

Plateau for at least five days, the men reached one of the larger streams that they had encountered and began to follow it west, off the mountain and into the canyons. For all the horror that they must have felt when looking down into the red rock maze, they had actually picked one of the better routes into the Canyon Country. Had they chosen to follow other streams in the area—say, Oak Creek to the south or the Fremont River to the north—they would have encountered impassable narrows through the uplifted monocline that we today call the Waterpocket Fold. But their chosen stream gave them an easy route through the uplift, with sufficient grass and water for their livestock. Thompson's name for the waterway, Pleasant Creek, was thus quite appropriate.

Thompson's men had not found this route on their own. On June 14 the group encountered a small group of Paiutes, who told Thompson of an existing trail through Pleasant Creek Canyon and then "between two mountains," the ever-present "Unknown" peaks.[54] While Thompson only briefly mentioned this meeting, making note of the Indians' apprehension in the presence of the white men, it is clear that the group had located a well-used route on Pleasant Creek. The next day Thompson wrote of seeing "many cattle signs in the large cañon," indicators that this was perhaps a smuggling route for livestock stolen by equestrian Utes or Navajos from Mormon settlements to the west.[55] Dellenbaugh was even more uneasy about this encounter, writing that the Indians had actually been staying just ahead of the group for at least three days.[56] Later he even recalled an old Indian woman who mockstabbed one of the party with a butcher knife and speculated that this group had recently been raiding settlements on the Sevier River to the west.[57]

Regardless of these tensions, the trail that the Indians described was good. Although the usually geologically astute Thompson mentioned nothing of the Triassic and Jurassic rock layers suddenly disappearing beneath the earth as the men emerged from Pleasant Creek Canyon, he did begin noting the newer Cretaceous badlands and their numerous fossils as the party again began to climb in elevation.[58] After having found an unmapped river, the party was approaching an unnamed and unmapped mountain range.

The Henry Mountains, a series of five major peaks that cover an area of about thirty miles by fifteen miles, reaching over 11,500 feet in elevation, have long been an anomaly. Unlike the neighboring La Sals or Abajos, which rise

on the peripheries of the Canyon Country, the Henry Mountains sit nearly
in the center of the region, surrounded by at least thirty miles of desert on
all sides. Also unlike the La Sals or the Abajos, which water and shelter the
towns of Moab and Monticello, respectively, the Henry Mountains never harbored any permanent agricultural settlements. They are simply too remote.[59]

In a later detailed assessment of the range, Powell surveyor Grove Karl
Gilbert commented on the Henry Mountains' isolation and sheer uselessness: although "there is timber upon their flanks and there is coal near at
hand…both are too far removed from other economic interests to find the
market that would give them value."[60] Throughout the later 1800s prospectors
tried to find gold within the range's granite and fantasized about lost Spanish gold mines from centuries past, but Gilbert's grim assessment of the area's
utility was for the most part accurate.[61] Even grazing would be a risky proposition in the sparsely watered mountains. Gilbert cynically argued that with
"such overstocking as is often practiced in Utah" grazing would only be sustainable for "one or two years."[62]

For Gilbert, the range was most valuable for scientific observation—indeed,
"no one but the geologist" would "ever profitably seek out the Henry Mountains."[63] Observing the drastically tilted sedimentary rocks on the mountains'
flanks and the hard granite cliffs that emerged from beneath the sandstone
layers, Gilbert identified the mountains as being not a true range but rather
at least five separate "laccolytes"—blister-like uplifts from deep within the
earth.[64] Unlike the extrusive basalt of true volcanoes, which cools by direct
contact with air, the granite of the Henry Mountains cooled intrusively, while
still deep beneath the surface, only exposed later by erosion. Gilbert identified similar origins for the rest of the Canyon Country's mountains.

In late June 1872, however, Thompson noted little of the mountains' tanta-
lizing geology. Several thousand feet from the desert below, trading hot, dusty
trails for freezing rain and rough granite, and still unsure of the elusive Dirty
Devil's precise location or accessibility, the party was in no mood to make
any observations beyond obligatory elevation measurements. Moving quickly
over two days and cresting the mountains just south of their highest peak,
which Thompson named Mount Ellen in honor of his wife, the men dropped
back into the desert. Thompson noted that they had reached a creek "that is

not the one I want [the Dirty Devil River] but is one that flows into the Colorado." This route through North Wash, which finally led the party to the river, was actually more direct than any that followed the Dirty Devil and would later become the major vehicle access route to the Colorado from the north.[65]

Three days later the party members reached the Colorado near the present site of Hite and easily made their way two miles upstream to the mouth of the Dirty Devil, where they found the *Cañonita*, as "good as new."[66] Here they split: Thompson and the majority returned to Kanab the way they had come, while Dellenbaugh and three others ran the *Cañonita* through Glen Canyon. On the high-spirited float back to the mouth of the Paria, the boatmen finally noticed the mouth of the newly discovered Escalante River, which Powell had missed twice. To Dellenbaugh it appeared quite narrow and "would not be taken at its mouth for so important a tributary."[67]

Wallace Stegner later wrote that this dramatic side excursion "was Thompson's most spectacular, though probably not his most important, contribution."[68] Thompson no doubt must have realized the sheer awesomeness of the Canyon Country as he returned overland to Kanab, reflecting upon this otherworldly land of "bare rock and sand," with "very few sage brushes."[69] Surpassing Macomb's and Newberry's push toward the confluence over a decade earlier, this was the most aggressive foray across the worst of the Canyon Country that government explorers had yet accomplished. Striking overland across this Bad Land had in many ways been an even more risky proposition than descending the Colorado by boat.

POWELL'S REPORT:
"A MORE DETAILED ACCOUNT" OF THE CANYON COUNTRY?

But what was so significant about Thompson's foray through some of the Canyon Country's roughest terrain? The knowledge that he and his party members gained about how the region's rivers, ridges, mountains, and deserts fit and flowed into one another later became an integral part—along with the more detailed reports of Clarence Dutton, Grove Karl Gilbert, and others—of Powell's conclusive report on aridity, settlement, and sustenance in the American desert. Powell's *Report on the Lands of the Arid Region of the United States, with a More Detailed Account of the Lands of Utah* is one of the most important documents in the environmental history of the American West. It proposed to the American people a drastic rethinking of notions of Good Land, linear boundaries, and, above all, the distribution of water in arid and semiarid climates.

Powell biographers Donald Worster and Wallace Stegner both have given considerable attention to his *Report* and noted the debt that he owed Mormon towns of central and southern Utah for their examples of cooperative communal irrigation systems.[70] The most important arguments of the *Report* were simple yet radical. There was not enough water in the form of rain or irrigation to reclaim all of the western United States from desert. The standard 160 acre square parcels of the Homestead Act were much too small for adequate grazing in such a sparsely grassed region and much too large for farming with available water. Boundaries should abandon the traditional grid system in favor of watershed divides. Water irrigation rights should be inseparable from land rights. Above all the federal government must carefully regulate the distribution and development of the arid West, using top-down power to foster community-level, grassroots cooperation in individual irrigation districts.

As his *Report*'s subtitle states, Powell used the Mormon settlements of Utah territory as examples of sustainable water use in desert environments. Situated at the bases of mountains and high plateaus, capturing and diverting snowmelt into communally maintained canals and ditches, these agricultural communities maximized efficient water use and sometimes even thrived in a territory that is today the second most arid state in the United States.[71] Powell was careful to point out, however, that the success of these new gardens in the desert did not in any way imply that the entire desert could ever be reclaimed. Farmers, and more importantly irrigation promoters, needed to realize the profound difference between "arable" land (with suitable topography, soil, and elevation for farming), which would certainly flourish with the rainfall of the temperate East, and "irrigable" land (the amount of arable land that available water could irrigate).[72] Powell estimated that Utah Territory, for example, with thousands of square miles of arable land along its benches and valleys, had only enough water to irrigate 2.8 percent of the territory's total area.[73] In today's drought-ridden West the percentage is possibly even lower than Powell's figures.

Furthermore, as the next chapter shows, the cliché that Mormons "made the desert bloom" is inaccurate. Most of Mormondom's most successful settlements were in semiarid, not arid regions: high valleys, foothills, the mouths of mountain canyons. Powell noted that the Mormon capital of Salt Lake City was "approximate in humidity to that of Central Kansas" and that its success certainly gave "no warrant for the belief that large areas of the Arid Region can be cultivated without irrigation."[74] Under the strict authoritarian leadership of Brigham Young, the Mormons carefully selected suitable areas for settlement and passed over the worst deserts. Truly Bad Lands such as the Canyon Country were still largely devoid of attempted settlements at the time of the *Report*'s publication in 1878.

Compared to the published diary of his river trip, Powell's *Report* dwelled little on the stupendous beauty of the Canyon Country. This was not an adventure narrative telling armchair explorers about alien landscapes. Practical applications such as timber harvesting, mining, and agriculture were his main concerns. Compared to western or northern Utah, Powell saw no agricultural potential in the Canyon Country and little mineral potential beyond one "broad belt of coal land."[75] He did provide some geological information, mentioning the "volcanic" origins of mountains within the region and differentiating between Cretaceous "badlands" of loose clay and shale and the Jurassic and Triassic "alcove lands" of more massive sandstones, forming cliffs and domes (figs. 5.2, 5.3, and 5.4).[76] But the Canyon Country was still an example of where not to settle. Powell the romantic adventurer could appreciate the region, but Powell the agricultural planner had to dismiss it.

A. H. Thompson, who probably knew the interior of the Canyon Country better than any other survey member, contributed a detailed chapter on the Colorado River basin's limited agricultural potential to the *Report*. Superficially, it appeared that his assessment of irrigable lands in the region was positive—over 791 square miles of reclaimable land lay within the drainage of the Colorado River in Utah.[77] Compared to Gilbert's report that the Great Salt Lake Basin held 1,278 square miles of cultivatable land and Dutton's assessment of 109 square miles in the Sevier Valley, these were not dismal or even cautionary numbers.[78] But most of the cultivatable land within the Colorado Drainage was nowhere near the Canyon Country. It was well upstream

5.2. Powell's "Alcove Lands."

5.3. Powell's "Bad Lands." The geologists of the Powell Expeditions distinguished between the loose, largely Cretaceous shales of "Bad Lands" and the more aesthetic, Jurassic sandstones of "Alcove Lands," both of which were widespread throughout the Canyon Country. (From John Wesley Powell, *The Exploration of the Colorado River of the West and Its Tributaries*; courtesy of the Rare Books and Manuscripts Library, The Ohio State University)

of the region, such as in the Uinta Basin, or along the desert's edges, such as in the soon-to-be settled valleys of the San Rafael River's upper tributaries in Castle Valley. The entire total irrigable land in the drainages of the Escalante, Fremont, and Paria Rivers, which composed the bulk of the western Canyon Country, amounted to barely 50 square miles.[79] This land, "broken by isolated groups of rugged mountains, by plateaus…, mesas, and amphitheaters," was unredeemable.[80]

The reasons for this were many. After the abundant water from "the high table lands and the mountains" flowed from the arable mid-elevation benches into the "lower and more level country" of the desert, it was quickly "absorbed

5.4. Cañon in the Escalante Basin. (From John Wesley Powell, *The Exploration of the Colorado River of the West and Its Tributaries*; courtesy of the Rare Books and Manuscripts Library, The Ohio State University)

by the porous soil and evaporated by the higher temperature. So great is the loss from these causes that some streams fail to reach the main drainage channel during the warmer months, and all are greatly shrunken in volume."[81] In some places that were too high, such as in the upper portion of Kanab Valley, the snowmelt came earlier than the "critical period of cultivation," making irrigation haphazard.[82] In lower-elevation regions the risk of accumulated flooding was greater than the benefits of irrigation. Thompson wrote that the San Juan Basin was "much subject to overflow," predicting flood problems that Mormon settlers in Bluff would endure in the following decade.[83]

The major hindrance to settlement in the Canyon Country, however, was the age-old dilemma that even Cárdenas had noted over three hundred years earlier—the rivers within the canyons were simply inaccessible. The Green, Grand, and Colorado Rivers, by far the largest waterways in the entire territory, for the most part were so far removed from arable land that their waters were essentially useless. Only their tributaries had limited potential at best. Thompson wrote of the Escalante River, to which he must have felt a special attachment after his "discovery" of it in 1872:

Its length is nearly ninety miles, the lower three-fourths being in a narrow cañon having vertical walls ranging from 900 to 1200 feet in height. Through this gorge the river sweeps, sometimes filling the whole space from wall to wall; sometimes winding from side to side in a flood plain of sand, and always shifting its bed more or less with every freshet. Not an acre of accessible arable land is known in the whole length of the cañon, and its depth precludes the possibility of using the waters on the lands above.[84]

So settlement could not be too high or too low, too close to the mountains or too far into the canyons. Nonetheless, Mormons would successfully cultivate thousands of acres of Good Land on the middle benches of the San Rafael, Fremont, Escalante, and Paria Rivers in an expansion of settlement during the 1880s, after the publication of Powell's *Report*. These developments were largely successful. Unlike the failed towns of Caineville and Pahreah, which sprouted up deep within the Canyon Country, periphery towns such as Ferron, Torrey, Escalante, and Tropic exist to this day. But Thompson's estimates of available water for these communities far exceed today's levels. For example, in July 1876 Thompson "carefully measured" the San Rafael River's flow at 1,676 cubic feet per second, a level that it rarely reaches now.[85] Today concern and conflict among farmers about water availability in the late summer is almost an annual tradition in surviving Mormon towns around the Canyon Country.

The mixed messages contained in Thompson's *Report*—dismissal of the Canyon Country's core and promotion of its peripheries—perfectly reflect the direction that both Mormon and mainstream American attitudes toward the desert were taking in the final quarter of the nineteenth century. After the death of Brigham Young in 1877, Mormon settlement gradually became less regulated and more egalitarian and haphazard. Back in the summer of 1872, as Frederick Dellenbaugh and three others beached the *Cañonita* at the mouth of the Paria River after floating Glen Canyon for a second time, they had met a permanent settler at the riverside.[86] John D. Lee was an exile in this isolated place, which one of his wives called the "Lonely Dell," after the Mormon Church placed most of the blame for the 1857 Mountain Meadows Massacre upon him.[87] Lee's harnessing of the Paria's waters for irrigation, and more importantly his establishment of a church-owned ferry at this crucial access point on the Colorado, was a sign that the Canyon Country would not long remain a place to avoid.[88]

Although conservationists today tend to canonize Powell, he himself grad-ually grew more promotional in western water affairs. His *Report on the Lands of the Arid Region* is Powell at his most cautionary and restrained. He might not have approved of the mid-twentieth century reservoir that fills Glen Can-yon today and bears his name—it is too big, centralized, and inefficiently loses much of its volume to evaporation in the desert heat. But Powell did stress rec-lamation, incorporation, and uniformity in nature over the awe of Muir, Tho-reau, or Abbey. After the publication of the *Report*, Powell would go on to call for reclaiming Florida's swamps as cotton and sugarcane fields and look for-ward to a time "soon when all the waters of the Missouri will be spread over the great plains, and the bed of the river will be dry."[89] In 1891 the revered major even addressed the first Irrigation Congress in Salt Lake City organized by William Ellsworth Smythe, a utopian optimist who fantasized about "The Conquest of Arid America."[90] Both the romanticized prose concerning the Canyon Country in Powell's published diary of his explorations and the call for restraint and regulation in his *Report* would eventually be superseded by designs for the further incorporation and regulation of this Bad Land.[91]

In this sense Powell was certainly not the definitive proponent of rational exploration in the wake of the narrow perspectives of Gunnison, Frémont, and Macomb. He and those in his employ did exponentially expand knowl-edge of this desert and its peoples, flora, fauna, geology, and hydrology, all the while emphasizing its practical uselessness to normal American agrarian pur-suits. The Powell survey's very act of bringing more attention to the Canyon Country, however, increased the likelihood that future exploiters would take an interest in the region, perhaps following the less restrained visions of Pow-ell's later years. Later entrepreneurial explorers such as Robert Brewster Stan-ton would milk Powell's descriptions of the area for all their information, while simultaneously trying to disprove Powell's assertions of uselessness or danger, as chapter 9 shows. Above all, by the close of the 1870s the Canyon Country was no longer simply a place to avoid or dismiss as irrational or bad or as a blank spot on a map. After Powell, increasing numbers of visitors to the region began thinking seriously of how they could mold it to accommo-date rationality, democracy, commerce, and Americanness.

But in the 1870s the vanguard of settlement around and later in the Can-yon Country was arguably not rational, democratic, commercial, or even particularly American from the perspective of the rest of the United States. As Mormon agrarianism expanded into the region, its view of the nonhuman world was more a throwback to the millenarianism and geographical destiny of Posada or Salmerón than like anything in the contemporary United States. The story of Mormonism's collision with the Canyon Country begins far to the east, however, in Good Land.

6

Good Settlers and Bad Land

MORMON VIEWS OF LAND AND ENVIRONMENT

John Wesley Powell's surveys placed many names upon the Canyon Country, labeling rivers, creeks, spires, grottoes, canyons, and plateaus. Especially in contrast to the poetic names inspired by Old World mythology that he bestowed upon formations within the Grand Canyon, Powell's names in the Canyon Country were quite restrained. In addition to keeping many existing Spanish or Indian labels, such as "Abajo" and "Paria," Powell used simple, obvious descriptors in labeling Canyon Country landmarks: Stillwater Canyon, Cataract Canyon, Dirty Devil River, Echo Cliffs.[1] Not surprisingly, local prospectors, ranchers, and farmers surpassed Powell in practical description in place-names such as Icebox Canyon, Circle Cliffs, Steer Gulch, and at least half a dozen Dry Washes. Townspeople living on the fringes of the Canyon Country today still often reject official, federally imposed landform names, replacing them with their own more succinct and colloquial titles, most commonly morphing "plateaus" into simple "mountains." Dutton's beloved Aquarius Plateau is Boulder Mountain, the Abajo Mountains are the Blues, the Kaibab Plateau is Buckskin Mountain, and the Kaiparowits Plateau is Fifty-Mile Mountain.[2]

Amid all these names, descriptions, and labels from different cultures, classes, and languages lay several names as rooted in Judeo-Christian religious traditions as the old Franciscan names of the eighteenth century were. Some, such as Moab and Canaan Mountain west of Kanab, are obviously inspired by the Old Testament and conjure up familiar allegories of trial and redemption in desert lands. In particular, Moab is an area well beyond the Promised Land of Israel, quite clearly a geographical "other" to be conquered by the Hebrews. The similarities that settlers would have seen between the biblical Moab and its remote, arid counterpart in Utah, well beyond the security of the Salt Lake Valley, are obvious.

Other place-names, however, go beyond even biblical inspiration, which only those familiar with details of the Mormon religion and its scripture would recognize: Lamanite Arch, the Moroni Slopes, Kolob Canyon. In the narrative of *The Book of Mormon*, in which Israelites fleeing the Babylonian Captivity around 600 BCE sailed to the Americas, "Lamanites" are a race cursed with dark skin by God for their wickedness and are the ancestors of nineteenth-century American Indians. Moroni, a white-skinned Nephite, is the final actor of the book, dying around 400 CE after a war with Lamanites. He later appeared as an angel to the Mormon prophet Joseph Smith. Kolob does not appear in *The Book of Mormon* at all, but later Mormon scripture states that this is the name of the star "nearest unto the throne of God," a place where "one day unto the Lord" was equivalent to one thousand years on earth.[3]

While the intricacies of Mormon doctrine are not discussed here, the worldview of the religion and culture that today calls itself the Church of Jesus Christ of Latter-Day Saints is central.[4] All Euro-Christian expansion to some degree reflected the desire to shape land and peoples to preexisting models and preconceived notions (indeed, this is almost the definition of religious conversion). But Mormons of the mid-nineteenth century saw the process of exploration and settlement in the New World, especially in the arid West, in very different terms than did mainstream Protestant Americans. Perhaps it was appropriate, then, that such a unique and marginalized culture would encounter a unique and marginalized landscape such as the Canyon Country.

Mormons did not immediately set out to settle the Canyon Country or indeed any Bad Lands, however, despite the Old Testament rhetoric concerning the redemption of deserts that they so embraced. Later chapters show exactly what happened once they did attempt to incorporate the region, but the Mormon idea of how Good Lands, Bad Lands, race, conversion, and millennial destiny ultimately fit together in the interior West is as important as any actual settlement and deserves serious discussion here.

GOOD LAND, CURSED PEOPLES

Despite early Mormons' view of themselves as New World Israelites—persecuted by more powerful nations, wandering through a howling wilderness toward some sort of a Promised Land, constantly tested by their God—their faith had its origins not in Old Testament–style aridity but in the Good Land of western New York and later Ohio, Missouri, and Illinois. Founder and self-proclaimed prophet Joseph Smith claimed to have seen God and Jesus in a forest grove near Palmyra, New York, as a young teenager in 1820. Years later in the same region, under the guidance of the angel Moroni, Smith claimed to have dug up and translated "golden plates" into *The Book of Mormon.* He officially organized the church in 1830. The narrative of *The Book of Mormon* reflected a uniquely Jacksonian American perspective on humankind, race, and religion and ultimately showed a sense of entitlement for Good Land that its readers would later bring to the arid West.[5]

Later Mormon doctrines, notably polygamy, had no direct ties to *The Book of Mormon* and were the products of revelations that Smith claimed to have had later in his life. But the book's narrative contained many themes that were quite relevant to Americans of the early nineteenth century and certainly to Mormons as they later migrated to the interior West, encountering Indians, aridity, and, they hoped, redemption.[6] Perhaps most importantly, *The Book of Mormon* was the story of a journey: the prophet Lehi's family fled the corruption of the Old World for the almost utopian promise of the New World. This narrative would have been familiar to Lehi's own ancestors who followed Moses, to Gregorio López in sixteenth-century Mexico, to New England Puritans in the seventeenth century, and certainly to Mormons in the nineteenth century—a testing passage through a wilderness to reach a Promised Land. Landscape and environment were thus both a test and a reward for Mormons. Furthermore, by retelling Bible-like stories in a new American setting, the scripture served as a sort of "nationalistic text" and "patriotically honored America by giving it a biblical history," in the words of Joseph Smith's most recent biographer, Richard Bushman.[7]

The position of the Lamanites in the narrative as both "a cursed and chosen people" only augmented the sense of millenarian destiny that Mormons held even before they migrated west to Utah.[8] In *The Book of Mormon* story, the people of the Americas divided into two nations: white-skinned descendants of Lehi's righteous son, Nephi, and descendants of a wicked son, Laman, cursed for their sins with dark skin. Throughout the book's thousand-year chronology, the Lamanites are largely "a dark, and loathsome, and a filthy people, full of idleness and all abominations," especially compared to the white-skinned Nephites.[9] Like Franciscans of sixteenth-century New Spain such as Gerónimo de Mendieta, Mormons believed that converting Indians to their brand of Christianity was an essential step in bringing about Christ's second coming. Lamanites and their Indian descendants were not blissful *tabula rasa* innocents, however, or even Enlightenment-era Noble Savages. Just as most explorers of the region opined that the Canyon Country was formerly Good Land that had fallen into aridity, Mormons viewed Indians as a formerly righteous people who had then fallen into their "idleness" and "abominations," even before they specifically encountered the Indians of the Great Basin or Canyon Country.[10] Nonetheless, these cursed Lamanites could find redemption via Mormonism, brought to them by white Americans.

The parallels between converting Indians and converting land are particularly strong here and would become more so as Mormons moved westward toward increasingly worse Bad Lands. Reconverting Indians to their perceived lost faith and reclaiming fallen land into productive farms both became divine mandates to Mormons. It is no surprise that the vague prophecies of Isaiah, in which Mormons looked forward to God "comforting" their New World Zion, making the "wilderness like Eden" and the "desert like the garden," were particularly important to the faith: literal not metaphorical.[11] In fact *The Book of Mormon* even told of Jesus Christ visiting Nephites and Lamanites in the Americas and reciting chapter after chapter of Isaiah to them, emphasizing gatherings of chosen peoples and redemption in the Last Days.[12]

Racial hierarchies also played an important part for Mormons, perhaps with more divine justification than even the views that southern planters of the same era had. In one particularly controversial passage of *The Book of Mormon* Smith prophesied that Indians would actually return to being "a white and delightsome people" upon reconversion to their ancient faith.[13] While later editions of the book eventually revised this racist language to "pure and delightsome," an equating of whiteness with goodness shaped generations of Mormon thought on race and conversion while the faith was establishing itself on Indian frontiers. In 1879 future church prophet Wilford Woodruff recalled a meeting with Pueblo Indians in New Mexico and concluded that, because of "the expansion of their minds, and, above all else, their capacity to receive any principle of the gospel…I could not make myself believe I was standing in the presence of American Indians or Lamanites."[14] The Pueblo Indians were so advanced that they simply had to be white Nephites. Even well into the twentieth century another future church prophet, Spencer W. Kimball, wrote about a Navajo girl converted to Mormonism and educated in white society, who quickly became "several shades lighter than her parents."[15]

CONVERTING THE LANDSCAPE

This racial hierarchy had strong parallels and connections to land use and reclamation after the Mormons' arrival in the Salt Lake Valley in the summer of 1847. Through the Mormon gospel Indians would find conversion from degenerate to pure, red to white; and deserts would bloom, through irrigation and hard work, converted from crooked to straight, from arid brown to fertile green. As previous chapters show, the connection of Bad Indians with Bad Land was certainly nothing unique to the Canyon Country or to Mormons. But no other culture, not even the millenarian Franciscans of Mendieta's time, approached the land and people with such a self-assured sense of destiny. This would be a transformation and fulfillment worthy of Isaiah's prophecies: the New World City of God would spring up from the wasteland.

But the Mormon urge to transform the howling wilderness of Exodus to the garden of Genesis was not as unrestrained as we might initially assume. As John Wesley Powell noticed in the 1870s, the high point of Mormon leader Brigham Young's power in Utah actually coincided with an aversion to settling much of the worst land in the Canyon Country. Young carefully moderated and restrained even supposedly obvious prophecies from Isaiah or *The Book of*

Mormon about aggressively converting land. With ample stream bottoms to cultivate at the base of mountains in the Great Basin, the Canyon Country was easy for Mormons to ignore.[16]

This is not to say that Mormon settlement avoided all deserts during Young's lifetime. As the next two chapters show, Young sent an 1854–55 party to Elk Mountain, on the eastern edge of the Canyon Country. Although he did not live to see it, the 1879–80 San Juan party to the southeastern Canyon Country was very much an extension of his "mission" model of colonization. Beyond the Canyon Country Young also oversaw the settlement of deserts such as the Cotton Mission in present-day southwest Utah in the 1850s as well as the unsuccessful 1860s Muddy River Mission in Nevada.

A distinctive and less-restrained Mormon push into the interior of the Canyon Country occurred after Young's death, as church leadership was weakening in the face of federal Republican intervention, after a generation of settlers had claimed Utah's best land for themselves. These settlements, such as Caineville and Pahreah, failed completely. In the end the Mormon urge to convert both land and people to a simplified and narrow mold reflected an inability to accept either deserts or their indigenous inhabitants as anything other than tests and trials set up by their God.

Through the 1830s, as the Mormon faith expanded well beyond a book about Pre-Columbian America and began forming a distinct culture, Smith further refined exactly how notions of Good Lands and Bad Lands would fit into Mormon millenarianism. He increasingly cast Mormons, and less often the fallen Lamanites, as literal-blooded Israelites, destined to fulfill a New World version of the Old Testament gathering in Zion, their own Jerusalem— a City of God somewhere in America. In 1842 Smith composed thirteen "Articles of Faith," which summarized Mormon beliefs. The tenth mentioned this Gathering of Zion: "We believe in the literal gathering of Israel and in the restoration of the Ten Tribes; that Zion will be built upon the American continent; that Christ will reign personally upon the earth; and, that the earth will be renewed and receive its paradisiacal glory."[17]

For the earth, specifically America, to achieve "paradisiacal glory," it had to be Good Land. Smith linked this idea directly to the location of the Garden of Eden in America as perhaps nobody since Christopher Columbus had done. Yearning for the familiar geography of symmetry and polar opposites, Smith concluded that Eden, the New Jerusalem, had to be exactly opposite the globe from Old Jerusalem: in the center of the American continent. The location was Independence, in western Missouri. Much to the chagrin of non-Mormon locals already living there, in 1832 Smith dedicated a site for a future temple and also declared that outside the town was "Adam ondi Ahman," where Adam had lived after his expulsion from Eden and where Noah had built his ark.[18]

The environment at the church-owned site at Adam ondi Ahman today stands out as quintessential Good Land: well-watered, rolling green hills that obstruct nothing. Future prophet John Taylor would write a Mormon hymn about this mythical place, sung at the 1836 dedication of the Kirtland, Ohio, temple:

> *This world was once a garden place,*
> *With all its glories common,*
> *And men did live a holy race*
> *And worship Jesus face to face,*
> *In Adam-ondi-Ahman.*[19]

This would be a perfect place to build the new City of God in America. It was in Good Land situated on the western American frontier, close to contact with Lamanites supposedly yearning for conversion. Smith even drafted detailed plans for this new Zion, a city of over a square mile in area, with ten-acre blocks divided into twenty house lots and communally worked farmland outside the city limits. The planned population would be around 20,000 people, making it by far the largest city west of the Mississippi. This would be an ordered, linear city in an ordered land.[20]

Although the plotted city set important precedents for later communities in Utah, the New Jerusalem in Missouri remained unrealized, a myth. The Mormon elite, including Smith, remained comfortably in Ohio, while they sent out underclasses to Missouri not only to establish new farms but to deal with locals hostile to a separatist religion. In 1834 critic Eber Howe wrote in his exposé *Mormonism Unvailed* [sic] that "these self-made prophets and high priests are acquiring possessions of real estate in a rich and flourishing country [Ohio], while their dupes are packed off to the wilds of Missouri."[21] Similar patterns would continue in Utah as Salt Lake City leaders also ordered lower classes into the deserts of Southern Utah.

On more spiritual levels Smith's dreams of settling in already Good Land—indeed, in Eden—were geographic manifestations of a Mormon cosmology that was quite sunny in its outlook, especially when compared to the "hellfire and damnation" of contemporary evangelical Protestants. The second of Smith's "Articles of Faith" rejected the idea of Original Sin, emphasizing that "men will be punished for their own sins, and not for Adam's transgression."[22] As early as 1832 Smith began rejecting traditional notions of hell and damnation and instead described three heavens in the afterlife, each of increasing glory above the last.[23] Most radically, Smith declared that the highest level of salvation for righteous males was actually Godhood. In this era of Jacksonian democracy, in which even "the common man could hold public office...Smith out-Jacksoned the Jacksonians by proclaiming that the common man could become a god," in the words of historian Klaus Hansen.[24] This bright view of the hereafter perfectly complemented the idea of New World Edens that simply provided for righteous settlers.

This positive spiritual and geographical outlook had many qualifiers and problems, however. The entire idea of redemption rested upon some sort of fallen nature, an early state of blessedness that humanity had to reclaim. Humankind might not be punished for "Adam's transgression," but what of the Lamanites' ancestral curse of red skin or later doctrine concerning Africans and a similar curse?[25] Most relevant here, Smith eventually did teach a sort of environmental Original Sin. If earth's "paradisiacal glory" was best seen in Adam ondi Ahman's low valleys, flat rivers, and fertile fields, then mountains, cliffs, deserts, and canyons were products of Adam's transgression. At Christ's Second Coming, Smith said, mountains would "be flattened out into a gently rolling countryside" perfect for practical farming and certainly not for any sort of awe at the sublime.[26] Again, this echoed and literally interpreted familiar passages from Isaiah, such as "the crooked shall be made straight, and the rough places plain," which tied redemption to Good Land.[27] Decades later Mormon settlers in the Canyon Country, the most twisted and crooked landscape in America, would certainly think of these prophecies: making the desert green and its native inhabitants white, and perhaps even hoping for a day when the twisted canyons would straighten.

In all of his prophecies Smith never explicitly stated any sort of masochistic urge to settle in Bad Land and transform it. That would all come later. Conflicts with non-Mormons in Missouri and later in the Mormon city of Nauvoo, Illinois, eventually resulted in Smith's murder in 1844 and the emigration of most Mormons to Utah in 1847 under Brigham Young. But Smith apparently never realized that his religion would ultimately turn to arid lands for refuge. This is not to say that he did not prophesy about other bountiful lands to the west that Mormons could eventually settle. Indeed, Smith dreamed of a Mormon empire that would eventually supersede the worldly United States and even declared that "the whole of America is Zion itself from north to south."[28]

By 1844, the final year of his life, Smith was seriously thinking of empire-building well beyond the Mississippi. Aware of reports of Good Land in Oregon from boosters such as Protestant missionary Marcus Whitman, Smith ordered his twelve apostles to investigate "California and Oregon, and hunt out a good location, where we can build a city in a day, and have a government of our own, get up into the mountains, where the devil cannot dig us out, and live in a youthful climate, where we can live as old as we have a mind to."[29] He was also simultaneously considering the possibility of settlement in Texas and had entered into negotiations with Sam Houston to settle a buffer zone between the Republic of Texas and Mexico.[30]

Beyond some references to settling in the Rocky Mountains, however, Smith apparently never considered the region of Utah.[31] On those occasions when he did mention mountains he tended to emphasize visions in which the "Lord's house shall be established in the top of the mountains" much more than the nestled valleys of the Great Basin.[32] Perhaps he was still too tied to the maps and reports of boosters such as John C. Frémont and Pierre DeSmet, or perhaps the lushness of the Pacific Coast appealed more to his grandiose aspirations than the unknown wilds of Utah did. In any case nothing indicates that Smith saw his religion as embracing aridity or desert trials, notwithstanding parallels with the Israelites.[33]

A Semiarid Sanctuary

Brigham Young, the succeeding prophet of the church in the wake of Smith's murder and two years of leadership struggles and schisms, had a very different view of land and settlement. Given that friction and violence had arisen in the Mississippi Valley wherever Mormons were in competition with other settlers for Good Land, Young reasoned that only in geographic isolation could the religion thrive enough to become the empire of Smith's visions. In 1873 Apostle George Q. Cannon reasserted this idea while addressing a congregation on expansion into the Arizona desert of the Little Colorado River:

> The worst places in the land we can probably get, and we must develop them. If we were to find a good country, how long would it be before the wicked would want it, and seek to strip us of our possessions? If there be deserts in Arizona, thank God for the deserts. If there be a wilderness, there, thank God for the wilderness.[34]

After their initial arrival in the Salt Lake Valley in July 1847, most Mormons saw their call to settle arid and remote regions as a holy obligation. Those who argued for settlement in the better regions of gold rush–era California, such as soon-to-be apostate Samuel Brannan, were in the minority.[35]

Today Mormon memories emphasize the desert quality of the Wasatch Front region that their ancestors began settling in 1847. In an oft-repeated legend mountain man Jim Bridger skeptically offered Young one thousand dollars for the first bushel of corn raised in the Salt Lake Valley.[36] In the final year of his life Brigham Young looked back on this successful reclamation, saying that "we were the first to plant out orchards and to improve the desert country, making it like the Garden of Eden."[37] Of course, this narrative of fleeing, wandering, and redemption in a desert fit perfectly into the Mormons' view of themselves as New World Israelites: the United States was Egypt, the westward trek of 1847 their Exodus, Utah their Promised Land, and Brigham Young their Moses (although Young certainly did not die in Moab, Utah, before seeing the Promised Land). The geography of the region that would become the heart of Mormondom even confirmed these parallels: Utah Lake was a New World Sea of Galilee and the Great Salt Lake a counterpart to the Dead Sea. It was only appropriate that the first settlers in the region named the river connecting the two lakes "Jordan."[38]

Rhetoric emphasizing the desert qualities of the Wasatch Front was exaggerated, however, especially compared to later-settled regions of Utah that actually were deserts. The Great Salt Lake area is semiarid at worst. The earliest settlers in the Salt Lake Valley may have called it a "desert" when speaking of their perceived trials, but it is clear that they really did not see the land as particularly bad. Diaries from the first years of settlement made no mention of the region being a desert but rather praised its rainfall, grass, and soil, while adding that the dry air actually felt cleaner than in the East.[39] Nearly thirty years later John Wesley Powell compared the valley to central Kansas.[40] Even twentieth-century Mormon apologist Hugh Nibley, whose writings tended to glorify Mormon work and perseverance over the harsher elements of nature, nonetheless wrote that "Utah was a land as fair and undefiled as in the morning of creation."[41] At least before they began their incursions toward the Canyon Country Mormons saw their western sanctuary as more of a garden than a howling wilderness. The idea that the core of Mormondom had ever been a desert only emerged with later myths emphasizing the Mormons' conquest and transformation of nature.[42]

During the leadership of Brigham Young, which lasted until his death in 1877, the prophet carefully regulated Mormon expansion from the top down, quite literally as "missions." Leaders often simply "called" families to leave their homes and settle new towns, planned communities at carefully chosen locations, and preached that conforming to a uniform grid and developing irrigation projects was nothing less than a holy obligation. John Wesley Powell, and most environmental historians of the twentieth and twenty-first centuries, lauded these planned communities as efficient and sustainable—an "egalitarian, planned, unexploitive society on the American frontier," in the words of Dan Flores.[43] Although these Mormon settlements ranged widely, from what is today Idaho and Wyoming to Nevada and through a variety of ecosystems, they all avoided truly Bad Lands such as the Canyon Country, keeping near the mountains and their life-sustaining snowmelt.

The Mormon model of settlement and growth in the interior West, especially from today's perspective, was probably more sustainable and ecologically sound than settlement by groups from the mainstream Protestant United States would have been had they encountered the region first. In an era in which homesteads, townships, counties, and even some U.S. territories were bounded according to geometric grids that ignored topography, in 1849 Young planned an independent state called Deseret, 225,000 square miles bounded largely by natural features—watersheds, ridges, and deserts. It encompassed all of what would become Utah and Nevada and portions of southern Oregon, southwestern Wyoming, western Colorado and New Mexico, most of Arizona, and even much of southern California.

On the smaller community level, Mormon villages were planned on very specific topographies. The cooperative, irrigation-based towns that Powell admired so much usually sat upon rich alluvial benches at the mouths of mountain canyons, with high-country reserves for small-scale grazing, logging, and watershed protection above. Although some of these communities, such as Cache Valley in the north and Sanpete Valley in the south, were in mountain valleys surrounded by high country on all sides, most Mormon settlements were nestled between mountains and deserts. They faced either the flat expanses of the Great Basin to the west or later the maze of the Canyon Country to the south and east.[44]

In keeping with boundaries based upon watersheds, each community had its own irrigation district, limited to the stream or river upon which it rested. A grid formed the basis of town streets and irrigation ditches, following the original plans of Smith's City of Zion, with tightly packed homes, orchards, and gardens within the town limits and communal pastures on the peripheries.[45] Unlike the United States' grid system, however, which in coming decades would divide much of the West according to meridians and parallels rather than watersheds, straight lines did not form boundaries beyond the interior community level of Mormon towns. City limits, many counties, and especially the boundaries that Mormons desired for Deseret largely followed natural topography. Although this system may have risen more from "the desire to people the region with as many families as could make a living," as Leonard Arrington has noted, than from any sort of inherent environmental consciousness, it does serve as a poignant symbol of how Mormons viewed land vis-à-vis the temperate United States.[46]

Unfortunately for Young, the idea of Deseret proved only slightly less ethereal than the Spanish idea of Teguayo. Although Mormons petitioned Congress sporadically for creation of the state until as late as 1872, neighboring states and territories quickly claimed most of Deseret from the peripheries inward.[47] By 1850 the U.S.-recognized Utah Territory included only what is now Utah, Nevada, and western Colorado. Eleven years later Colorado claimed land to the 109th meridian, with some expansionist boosters even calling for a "Jefferson Territory" that would extend well into the Canyon Country from the east in gridded uniformity.[48] In 1866 the people of Nevada claimed the western section of the Great Basin, arguing that "people who discover and work mines there do not wish to be under the control" of agriculturally biased Mormon governments.[49] By the time Utah acquired statehood in 1896, its linear, boxlike boundaries (like those of Wyoming and Colorado) ignored any trace of natural topography.

Even if its size and boundaries failed, the ideas behind the state of Deseret, in which "all interests—social, political, and economic—would have been subservient to the leadership of the Mormon Church," lived on.[50] Specifically, the Mormon antimining sentiments that had been such a concern for Nevadans were only one facet of a larger escape from the evils of private enterprise that Brigham Young preached. This was nothing new. Even farther east Joseph Smith had noted the destruction that "gentile" American industry wreaked upon landscapes that God had intended for more noble agrarian purposes, writing that "before them [wicked non-Mormons] the earth was a paradise, and behind them a desolate wilderness."[51] The Mormon fixation on conversion and cultivation was organic, not mineral; sustainable, not extractive.

In Utah, Young carried this attitude even further than Smith had, tightly regulating extractive industries for common resources such as logging and grazing and forbidding Mormons to mine anything other than necessary metals. Private, for-profit ventures were contrary to the vision of Deseret. Appealing to his congregation in 1852, Young rhetorically asked:

Are you not dissatisfied, and is there not bitterness in your feelings, the moment you find a kanyon [*sic*] put in the possession of an individual, and power given unto him to control the timber, wood, rock, grass, and, in short, all its facilities? Does there not something start up in your breast, that causes you to feel very uncomfortable?[52]

Young's authoritarian regulation of resource extraction, his favoring of agriculture over mining, and his community planning represent one of the most central paradoxes of Mormon history: he was attempting to secure equality and refuge from corrupt capitalism for his Mormon flock by authoritarian means that any Jeffersonian or Jacksonian Democrat—not to mention later Lincoln Republicans—would find completely undemocratic, even un-American. Speaking of equality in Utah, Young noted that "as for the poor, there are none here, neither are there any who may be called rich, but all obtain the essential comforts of life."[53] Although class divisions certainly existed in Utah—Mormon leaders had better land, more livestock, and more wives—the model of the Mormon cooperative village gave equal resource access to all in ways that were unheard of in non-Mormon regions of the arid and semiarid West.

Furthermore, although Young was more pragmatic and less prophecy-obsessed than Smith, he also emphasized spiritual and theological reasons behind Mormon environmental consciousness. In the first two chapters of the Genesis story God orders Adam to treat the earth in two different ways. The first emphasizes human power over nature with orders such as "multiply," "subdue," and have "dominion...over every living thing." The second emphasizes a more subtle role of "stewardship," in which humans are more responsibly to "dress" and "keep" Eden.[54] Perhaps more than any part of mainstream entrepreneurial America, Young instructed Mormons to follow the "stewardship tradition" in land use.[55]

The Mormon roots of this tradition lay in the "Law of Consecration and Stewardship," first enacted by Smith in 1833, in which Mormons were to cede all their property to the church, which then reauthorized them as earthly "stewards," not owners, of the property. Although Smith's interpretation of Genesis was the basis for this law, Young continued to preach the underlying attitude: "The earth is the Lord's and man must consider his rights to land as derived and subject to church disposition."[56] While this idea of ownership was authoritarian and sometimes coercive, it could also be successful in enforcing stewardship and sustainability.

In practice, however, the Law of Consecration and Stewardship was rarely successful. Through the first three decades of Mormondom in Utah, Young periodically attempted to enforce the law in specific communities as far north as Paris, Idaho, and as far south as St. George, Utah, through what he called the "United Order of Enoch," in which all agricultural economies were communal and self-sufficient.[57] But these communities always were simply too close to outside pressures, products, and markets for their communal stewardship to be truly self-sufficient. These challenges only increased after the completion of the transcontinental railroad in 1869. It was clear that the United Order experiment required even more isolation than could be found in existing Utah communities.

Uniting and Ordering a Bad Land

In 1875 Powell's men were surveying the more remote regions of Utah for the United States government, overcrowding in planned Mormon communities gradually pushed settlers toward the Canyon Country, towns on the periphery of the Canyon Country such as Kanab gradually turned to mining and grazing in addition to traditional Mormon farming, and the health of Brigham Young waned. Mormon leadership decided upon a bold experiment at that time: an entire town would be planned and built from the ground up, based upon United Order principles. The location for "Orderville," about thirty miles north of Kanab, was consistent with other Mormon town models. Orderville sat along the upper Virgin River, just above the stream's dramatic descent into the canyons of what would become Zion National Park. It was near the security of the mountains, but surrounding terrain hinted at Canyon Country motifs. Soil was sandy, and domes of white Navajo Sandstone flecked with piñon pines and junipers abounded. Within an hour's ride to the east, west, and south were mazes of canyons and Bad Land.

Most importantly, Orderville was isolated. It had to be, in order to "prevent the development of a market-oriented economy dependent on extensive importation and exportation" and to ensure that families would voluntarily deed their property claims to the church-owned community corporation.[58] While it certainly was near Bad Land, its 150 settlers, most of whom were refugees from failed desert settlements along the Muddy River in southern Nevada, likely saw this as better terrain than their old home.[59] It is significant that the Orderville experiment was far enough into Bad Land for isolation but nonetheless not as audaciously flung out into the desert as later Canyon Country settlements such as Pahreah or Caineville would be.

Even given its isolation, however, the United Order in Orderville lasted barely a decade. Simultaneous with its establishment, mines at nearby Silver Reef to the west began producing millions of dollars' worth of its namesake metal. Validating Young's suspicions of mines, miners and their families were able and willing to purchase luxury goods from the outside secular world.[60] To the south the gaudy trappings of cowboy culture had also arrived in Kanab via the open plains of northern Arizona. The contrast between the quaint, homemade goods of Orderville and the fashionable manufactured imports of Kanab and Silver Reef was not lost on residents of any of these towns. Even other Mormons increasingly viewed residents of Orderville as backward and simple, perhaps much as modern-day residents of Hurricane or St. George see the fundamentalist polygamist residents of Colorado City in the same region.[61] An inferiority complex combined with inefficient resource management and, ultimately, antipolygamy raids by the federal government led to desertions by Orderville's residents and the official dissolution of the experiment in 1885.[62]

By the end of the Orderville experiment, however, Brigham Young was dead, the church's power throughout Utah was reaching its nadir, and, most relevant to the Canyon Country, settlements had begun to be "more spontaneous in character...and not so much under direct supervision of church headquarters," in the words of Nels Anderson.[63] The stage was set for Mormons to break free from the constraints of Consecration and Stewardship and to try their hands at moving into truly Bad Lands. As the core of Mormondom along the irrigated foothills of the Wasatch Range matured and crowded, the Canyon Country began to look more appealing. And it would be a wilderness requiring dominion and subjugation, not a garden requiring stewardship.

Although the rest of America could learn much from the Mormon model of community-building in the West, as Powell wrote, the religion's views on land were not at all clear-cut. While its communal irrigation and restraints on nonagrarian resources worked quite well in the valleys of the Wasatch Mountains in northern Utah, and even to a more limited degree in southwestern Utah's "Dixie" region, Mormon models of sustenance were utterly unprepared for the Canyon Country, as the next two chapters show.

On the broader spectrum, just as they never truly resolved whether Indians were former Lamanites yearning for conversion or simply adversarial savages, Mormons in Utah never resolved whether they were living in a bountiful garden given to them by God or in a cursed wilderness that was a product of Original Sin. While the Salt Lake Valley had seemed quite sufficient to Mormons at the time of its settlement, over the decades they developed a mythology of having made that "desert bloom," reinforcing their position as God's chosen people and justifying expansion into worse lands. The tradition of stewardship worked very well in the semiarid mountain valleys that formed the core of Mormondom. But when it met deserts and broken country, "stewardship" undoubtedly equaled "improvement." This meant viewing the Bad Land as they thought it should be, rather than as it truly was.

7

The Rim of Mormondom I

MISSIONS TO THE EASTERN CANYON COUNTRY

Less than two years after Brigham Young had led Mormons into the Salt Lake Valley, the first official exploring expedition of the church—around fifty men, under the charismatic apostle Parley P. Pratt—ventured south, away from the security of the Wasatch Front. Their intent was to find new pockets of Good Land between the Wasatch Plateau and the Great Basin suitable for Mormon villages. Their trail was well trodden, following the upper reaches of various springs, streams, and rivers before they dried up in the desert to the west. This was roughly the route that Domínguez and Escalante had taken south from Utah Lake nearly three-quarters of a century earlier and that Interstate 15 would take in the twentieth century.

It also followed an important series of Indian trails, as the Pratt party found out on December 7, 1849, along the Sevier River. That snowy, cold morning the prominent Timpanogos Ute leader Wakara rode into Pratt's camp with one companion. The meeting with "Captn. Walker," as the Mormons called him, was peaceful, offering little hint of later conflict between Utes and Mormons throughout the region. Through an interpreter Wakara spoke promisingly of good country for settlement along the Virgin River to the south, mentioning morbidly that its current residents, the Shivwits

Paiutes, were quickly dying off, probably from disease and warfare. He also impressed Pratt with his adept reading of the party's map, telling of "what country he was acquainted & what he was not, like an experienced geographer." In contrast to his rosy description of the Virgin River region that would soon nurture the towns of St. George, Santa Clara, and Hurricane, Wakara spoke vaguely and ominously of the Canyon Country to the southeast. There was "no pass over these mtns. S.E. [southeast] & no good country over there, little water, don't run far, Rocky."[1] Just as Wakara had warned William Manly a few months before (see chapter 3), the Canyon Country was a place to avoid.

Returning to Salt Lake City, Pratt expanded Wakara's description of the Canyon Country into a more poetic story. The regular terms of disgust that non-Mormon explorers such as Gunnison and Frémont would use a few years later were all there: "sandy deserts," "perpendicular rocks," "loose barren clay," and "dissolving beds of sandstone." He also gave a succinct description of the region's geological history, writing that the flat-topped mesas appeared "as if the whole country had occupied a certain level of several thousand feet or higher than its present, and had washed away, dissolved, or sunken." Beyond this accurate description of uplift and erosion (especially for a nonscientist), however, Pratt moved toward value-laden ideas of a fallen land. Before erosion had degraded the country, it had been "exalted," with a "level, smooth, and fertile surface. Poor and worthless as was the country it seemed everywhere strewed with broken pottery...it may have been the choicest portion of God's vineyard."[2] While this description was fairly brief, it hinted at Mormon ideas of Good Land and Bad Land, the Lamanite curse, and, above all, the obligation to reclaim this Bad Land's former glory.

As for Wakara's description on that cold December morning, he certainly had a motive to keep Mormons away from the Canyon Country apart from concern for their safety. For well over a decade his people had dominated slave and horse trade through the Great Basin, California, and New Mexico and would not have wanted any competition or interference with this lucrative business.[3] By the close of the 1840s Indian traders such as Wakara probably knew more of the intricacies of the Canyon Country than anyone else did.

Whether Wakara knew it or not as he met with Pratt in the winter of 1849, this era of slave and horse trading along the Old Spanish Trail was quickly coming to an end. In the following decades Mormons would begin seriously attempting to incorporate the Canyon Country into their inland theocracy. Initially these attempts were by way of carefully planned capsule-styled mission colonies sent mostly to the peripheries of the eastern Canyon Country, often with overt goals of proselytizing to Lamanites and establishing boundaries with non-Mormon Americans. Some of these colonies failed, such as the Elk Mountain Mission. Others, such as the San Juan Mission, managed to succeed—barely. Later, however, less controlled and more vulnerable waves of enthusiastic settlement (detailed in the next chapter) began to press into the very heart of the Canyon Country's western portion, armed with their predecessors' religious motivations but lacking their restraint. The results would be calamitous.

THE ELK MOUNTAIN MISSION

The first large-scale Mormon mission to the Canyon Country held few visions of overtly expanding the religion's village model to a Bad Land and changing it to a garden. Instead it was a pragmatic defense move in the face of increased hostility from non-Mormons—both Indians and white Americans. Although the 1849 California gold rush had given a much needed material boost to the Mormon economy in Salt Lake City's early years, it also threatened Brigham Young's visions of an economically isolationist society. Trails to and from the West Coast very quickly began utilizing nascent Mormon communities as essential hubs for rest and resupply and threatened to taint Mormon self-sufficiency with outside material culture. In response to heightened outside incursion, church leaders tightened restrictions on Mormons' use of goods not manufactured within Utah (which included the still-practiced taboos on alcohol, tobacco, and coffee).

Young also secured a series of forts on the fringes of Mormondom in all directions. These included Fort Limhi in the Snake River drainage to the northwest, Fort Las Vegas to the southwest, and Forts Bridger and Supply to the northeast. The region to the southeast of Mormondom remained open. Although the Canyon Country certainly served as a formidable natural barrier to encroachment, by 1854 Young had decided on the necessity of another fort to keep Colorado miners at bay, somewhere beyond Canyon Country.[4]

Gentile Americans were not the only concern, however. By this time relations between Indians and Mormons had soured considerably. As Mormons expanded south from Salt Lake City into the Sanpete Valley and beyond, Wakara's Utes began a series of violent raids upon settlements beginning in the fall of 1853. Mormons retaliated against all Indians, often killing uninvolved Paiutes. This increasing violence also may have led indirectly to John Gunnison's death. Although conflict officially ended in May 1854, and Wakara died shortly thereafter, this "Walker War" convinced Young that relations with Indians on the peripheries of Mormondom were just as important as those with white Americans.[5] With the end of the Walker War, proselytizing missionary work among Lamanites gained new importance on all Mormon frontiers, especially to the southeast. While the lofty fulfilling of Book of Mormon prophecies and redemption certainly played a part in motivating missionaries, the pacification of potentially hostile Indian tribes was the more immediate goal in Brigham Young's mind. Nonetheless, expansion into the peripheries of Mormondom through the next two decades was not just settlement but a divinely ordered mission.

To begin securing the southeastern fringes of Mormondom, in October 1854 Young sent an exploratory party of ten Mormons and one Indian guide, under William Huntington, to the Grand River.[6] Their specific goal was the present-day Moab Valley, likely the same spot that Juan María Antonio de Rivera had reached nearly ninety years earlier and long a major crossing of the Old Spanish Trail. Indian relations were at the forefront of the party's concerns as it crossed the trail of the recently killed Gunnison, passed by the canyons of the San Rafael Swell, and crossed the Green River. Although Utes and Mormons had established a peace that May, Huntington nonetheless wrote ominously of crossing this "wild, mountainous, and dreary desert…and what was still more formidable, Indian Walker, and his allies, [who] had decreed we never should pass." Later on, upon reaching the San Juan River, he added stories of Navajos who had "killed, boiled, and eaten a white man."[7]

Fortunately the group avoided confrontation, and the most dramatic event of their trip through the desert between the Green and Grand Rivers was the lowering of their wagons over a twenty-five-foot cliff. Upon reaching the river, Huntington must have been impressed at the natural location for a future mission. Even today the opening of the red rock cliffs, in an approach to Moab from the north or the south via Highway 191, signals one of the river's last natural access points and farmable valleys for hundreds of miles downstream. The nearby La Sal Mountains—which the Mormons called "Elk Mountain"—provide perennial water as well as cool solace in the summer, while the floor of the Moab Valley remains warm and mild nearly year-round, especially in comparison to the colder Salt Lake Valley to the north. It seemed a perfect location for the Mormon village model. The party cached supplies for future missionaries and even distributed melon and squash seeds to the local Indians for planting.[8]

They did not turn back at the Grand River, however. Thinking of future missionary work among larger Indian civilizations, Huntington continued south toward the San Juan River and the northern frontier of the powerful Navajos, still in a state of war with the United States. Writing of this region to a Mormon audience in the church-owned *Deseret News*, Huntington described a mythical landscape straight out of *The Book of Mormon*. Extensive ruins stretched for miles along the north bank of the San Juan, probably between the major canyons of Comb Wash and Montezuma Creek, built "in a style the present age knows nothing of." These were from a society much more "civilized" than the Utes or Navajos in their present state and also from a time when the surrounding Bad Land had been much less harsh:

> We noticed that there was no water about there, and enquired of the Indians how the former inhabitants could have managed: they told us that they had heard that a *very long time ago* there was water running there. We asked them who built those houses. They smilingly shook their heads and said that they had never heard, but surely somebody built them *a very long time back*.[9]

This was not just a general description of fallen land and fallen Lamanites, however. Huntington explicitly stated that the ruins of the San Juan area were the former stronghold of the "Gadianton Robbers," a villainous secret society from *The Book of Mormon* that had hidden out in the "mountains, and the wilderness," while attempting to subvert and destroy the righteous Nephite civilization.[10] Although Huntington believed that these ruins had been built during more temperate times when the Bad Land had been Good, the forbidding nature of the Canyon Country as it appeared to him in 1854 made it a perfect location for some of *The Book of Mormon*'s most notorious villains as they conspired in raids against the righteous. Furthermore, the Gadiantons had succeeded in weakening Nephites for their eventual defeat by the Lamanites through "secret combinations," presumably subversive hand signals and other machinations.[11] The nature of the San Juan's canyons, twisting away and out of view toward unseen hostile places, may have seemed just as covert and secretly hostile to Huntington.

With Huntington's return to Salt Lake City, and especially with his vivid *Deseret News* description written that winter, converting the Canyon Country became a significant part of the new Mormon obsession with missions to the peripheries, which itself was a product of the increasingly millenarian and separatist "Mormon Reformation" of 1855–57. The following spring, in April 1855, the major theme of the church's general conference was expansion and strengthening in the face of rising tensions with the United States. From the United States' perspective, new information from explorers such as Frémont and Gunnison, the troubling deaths of Gunnison and his party, and above all a rising apprehension over the power of Brigham Young all resulted in Congress's 1856 rejection of Utah's bid for statehood.[12]

From the Mormon perspective, rising tensions with the United States were a sign that the American Gomorrah was on the verge of collapse, that all-out warfare between the United States and Mormondom was likely, and that the continent-spanning reign of Zion that Smith had prophesied was at hand. One of Young's planned tactics in this struggle was the conversion of Indians as a means of securing them as allies against the United States. Going so far as to call the Lamanites "The Battle Axe of the Lord," Young preached that Indian aid to Mormons in war against the United States would lift their ancient *Book of Mormon* curse. All of these tensions would erupt with the Utah War and Mountain Meadows Massacre in 1857.[13]

The isolated expanses of the Canyon Country did not stand apart from this growing tension among Mormons, Americans, and Indians. The region lay between the Utes and the Navajos, both promising allies in an anticipated war with the United States. This strategic location, coupled with William Huntington's positive reports, prompted the organization of a large party to establish a fort and mission upon the Grand River. True to its name, this Elk Mountain Mission was more a "mission" than an agricultural family "settlement"—only men went to the Grand River. While they would dig irrigation ditches and plant crops, Indian conversion was their primary objective.

For a society that had not yet occupied its own capital for even a decade, it was a major undertaking to send forty-one men under Alfred N. Billings to the Elk Mountain Mission in late May 1855. Not only was the party traveling to a desert area presumably full of hostile Indians, but its men were required to fund much of the mission themselves. A young William B. Pace, recently married and settled near the southern shores of Utah Lake in Payson, bitterly wrote of having to sell his farm of "7 1/2 acres of good garden land according to fair valuation ten dollars per acre" for the price of a "19 dollar rifle and one lb of powder with a horn."[14]

But even men such as Pace saw their losses as important sacrifices for divine machinations beyond their comprehension—and prophesied ones at that. One year before Pace was "called" to the Elk Mountain Mission, he had received a special personal blessing from Mormon patriarch Isaac Morley that prophesied his role not only in "cultivating the Earth...[and being] a hunter in the mountains of Israel" but also in the "restoration and redemption" of Indians, cryptically called "that band of Dispersed people."[15] If Pace's prophetic blessing was typical of those of other missionaries, the Elk Mountain Mission must have had a deep significance that went beyond mere territorial protection.

Leaving the small town of Manti in Sanpete Valley on May 21, the Billings party crossed the Wasatch Plateau near the headwaters of today's Ferron Creek and descended into the northern San Rafael Swell. This route was not a regular spur of the Old Spanish Trail, and the party could follow no major canyons or waterways through the maze of canyons. Water for men and horses was only obtainable at times by lowering buckets into deep sandstone "potholes" that had collected months' worth of rainwater. Fortunately Indians visited the party members and showed them appropriate shortcuts across the rugged country.[16] By June 2 they had reached the more open desert of the Green River crossing. At this point, less vulnerable than he and his party had been earlier in the canyons, Billings "held a meting" with nearby Indians, telling them that his "business was to Learn them the Principle of the Gosple and to Rais Grain. They seamed to have the Spirit of the Lord uppon them and to be well pleased with wat we told them [*sic*]."[17] The missionaries looked forward to the simultaneous cultivation of souls and deserts.

The Billings party's arrival at the Grand River a week later signaled bright prospects even beyond the Indians' conversion and redemption. Indians had planted the melon and squash seeds that Huntington had left the previous year: over ten acres of river bottom land were already under cultivation. Filled with enthusiasm, the missionaries rebaptized each other in the waters of the Grand, dug ditches, and planted more crops before they even began constructing the planned defensive fort.[18] The Lord's work had started.

The missionaries realized very quickly, however, that they had settled in an area that was the intersection of very complicated relations among Navajo, Ute, and Paiute Indians—a volatile geographic bottleneck. The local Weeminuches, lacking a strong horse economy, occupied an uneasy position between the Navajos to the south and Utes to the north and east. Since the earliest days of the Old Spanish Trail they had been vulnerable to the slave raids of these more powerful horse-based tribes.[19] Just as they had in Rivera's time, the Weeminuches looked at the Grand River as a natural barrier to avoid; they remained in the Canyon Country rather than traveling through it as their more powerful neighbors did. Perhaps because of this, Billings even flippantly noted their aversion to crossing the river for fear of "snakes."[20] Like many earlier explorers, he saw them as a lesser people in a lesser land.

The Mormons quickly realized that they too were sandwiched alongside the Weeminuches between the Utes and Navajos. Barely a week into the mission, the San Pete Ute leader Arapien rode into the settlement. Efficiently multitasking, he dropped off mail to the missionaries from Salt Lake City and then continued south to deliver Paiute slave children to the Navajos.[21] Two weeks later Billings noted that the Utes were at war with the Navajos and that the Weeminuches were exhibiting signs of almost a sort of abandonment complex at any hint that the missionaries might leave and expose them to more slavers from the north and the south.[22]

Through the summer, as most of the younger, lower-ranking missionaries such as Pace dug ditches, cleared land, and traded with Indians, Billings began to reconnoiter the land surrounding the mission. On an outing that must have offered a welcome respite from the hot desert, he rode high into the La Sal Mountains, making note of the impressive view from the "San Pitch Mountains" to the north to the "St. John's" (San Juan) river to the south. From this viewpoint Billings even observed that he could "trace the Grand River where it first enters the Valley to where it and the Green River come together"—four years before Macomb and Newberry confirmed that the two streams did in fact unite.[23]

Geographic puzzles seemed unimportant, however, as temperatures rose, water levels dropped, and tensions between the missionaries and the Weeminuches grew. At the end of August Billings and four others traveled south to the San Juan to broker a peace between the Navajos and the Utes. Billings did not mention any Gadianton strongholds as Huntington had done the previous year but merely noted that the region south of the Grand River was "barron [sic] country," full of "fine red sand that a horse will sink into 5 or 6 inches."[24] Returning to the Elk Mountain Mission in mid-September, Billings mentioned that Indians had begun stealing crops from missionaries' fields during his absence. Within two weeks, as autumn began and temperatures dropped, they were stealing cattle as well, probably in preparation for the coming winter.[25]

On September 23 tragedy struck. The weather had been cold and rainy for several days by this point. That morning a large number of Indians from the Green River region crossed the Grand and angrily accused the Mormons of having herded "their cattle in a different course." Hours later Indians—including the son of the local Weeminuche chief—fatally gunned down three missionaries who had left the fort to tend livestock. In the ensuing gunfight Billings himself was shot through the finger. The next day, after Indians killed two more Mormon hunters in the mountains, the missionaries prayed and decided to abandon the mission. Although the Mormons fled under a barrage of Indian fire, by the time they reached a spring fifteen miles from the river "some Indians came along and delivered us eight cows."[26] They were clearly glad to see the Mormons leave.

Thus ended the first Mormon attempt at converting the Canyon Country and its peoples. Nobody—Billings, Young, or later historians—could ever point to one cause for the disastrous failure of the Elk Mountain Mission, although later regional chroniclers such as Faun Tanner would assert that hostilities began when Mormons refused to bed Indian women.[27] More accurately, the missionaries of Elk Mountain naïvely stepped into a very complex region with simplistic expectations of how Indians should behave. In contrast to the failures of later Canyon Country settlements such as Pahreah and Caineville, environmental factors played a negligible role in the collapse of the Elk Mountain Mission. But the expectations, optimism, and sense of entitlement in redeeming fallen peoples or land would remain the same for decades to come.

MOAB REDEEMED

Within two years of the failure of Elk Mountain Mission missionary fervor for converting Lamanites on the frontiers of Mormondom had dwindled to nearly nothing. Mormons on the Wasatch Front had more pressing concerns—first invasion by the United States army in 1857, then more Indian fighting at home, and a Civil War between the northern and southern United States through the 1860s. Although Mormons certainly looked to the Civil War as a possible fulfillment of prophecies in which the United States destroyed itself from within, the radical fervor and expansionism of the "Mormon Reformation" was over. In the face of these new problems, the incorporation and redemption of Bad Lands seemed insignificant. By 1861, when the *Deseret News* referred to one portion of the Colorado River Basin as "one vast contiguity of waste, and measurably valueless, excepting for nomadic purposes, hunting grounds for Indians, and to hold the world together," few Mormons held desires to change that howling wilderness to a garden.[28] For nearly twenty years the Elk Mountain Mission's fort stood abandoned on the open bottom of the Grand River Valley, flanked by imposing red cliffs on all sides. Indians and even white trappers and prospectors coming from the developing gold country in southwest Colorado passed by the abandoned fort, perhaps speaking smugly to one another of the failed Mormon experiment in converting Indians in the region.

But this choice location on the Grand could not remain unsettled indefinitely. Probably acting on word-of-mouth reports from members of the 1855 mission, and with no apparent prodding from church leadership, Mormon ranchers George and Silas Green began wintering 400 head of cattle on the lush river bottom range beginning in 1874. But again violence involving Indians in the region arose, this time because of displaced Colorado Utes fleeing miners from the east. Sometime in the winter of 1876–77 the Greens met violent deaths.[29] The following summer Mormons trickling into the area reported coming across a hand-written "no camping" sign along the river and meeting a French Canadian, a Texan, and an African American named Bill Granstaff who had taken possession of the Greens' remaining cattle.[30]

Through the next few years Mormons from the Great Basin, miners and loggers from Colorado, and even ranchers from Texas and New Mexico began gradually and haphazardly filling up the valley. Although Mormons had succeeded in changing the old name of Elk Mountain to the biblically inspired "Moab" by 1881, the new emerging community along the Grand River would remain culturally and religiously heterogenous, a far cry from the visions of the original Elk Mountain missionaries.[31] Today, as Moab has evolved from a uranium boom town to a recreation center for rock climbing, jeeping, mountain biking, and river-running, its diverse origins remain evident. Unique among small Utah towns, its Mormon population is a minority. Moab does not have the feeling of a typical orderly, gridded, Mormon farming village.[32]

BEYOND THE CANYON COUNTRY

Perhaps in part due to their failure to build an enduring mission along the Grand River, in the mid-1870s Mormons began once more to emphasize conversion and missionary work in and beyond the Canyon Country. In this post–Civil War era of federal raids on Mormon polygamists, increasing conflict between the church and the United States, and Brigham Young's failing health, mission work took on a new meaning. More than in the case of Elk Mountain nearly two decades earlier, this time the conversion of the landscape itself, and not just of its Lamanite inhabitants, was a divine test of Mormon righteousness. Mormons began seeing "mission" work more as a church calling to cultivate Bad Land and less as a calling to convert Indians. They would now begin testing their successes in the eastern Great Basin and Wasatch on increasingly worse lands.

The first experiment of this bold new strategy took place not in the Canyon Country but beyond it, along northeastern Arizona's Little Colorado River in the early 1870s. The scattered communities in this Arizona region south of the Navajos were arid, remote, and specifically chosen for these reasons. Indeed, Brigham Young explicitly ordered one mission group "to locate the worst place on the Little Colorado and develop its water as evidence of success to other less determined missionaries."[33] Most communities were formed around some form of the communitarian United Order, in which villagers were supposed to use all resources equally and in common. Ironically, however, they were also quite class-stratified, with elite priesthood leaders overseeing less wealthy farmers, many of whom were newly converted Mormons from the Reconstruction-era South.[34]

The Little Colorado missions such as Snowflake, Springerville, and St. Johns had much in common with contemporary and subsequent Canyon Country settlements: they encouraged cooperation, thrift, and hard work in imposing the gridded City of Zion model upon an arid land. Through the cooler, relatively rainy 1880s settlers retained a nearly Isaiah-like optimism that they were truly making the desert bloom. Furthermore, both the Little Colorado and the eastern Canyon Country (though not the western Canyon Country) were adjacent to powerful Indian tribes and encroaching non-Mormon entrepreneurs. Although this certainly meant a threat to Mormon ideas of self-sufficiency and economic isolation, it also promised access to more diverse economies, which would be essential in times of drought, flood, and crop failures.[35] The modest success of the Little Colorado settlements also resulted in steady traffic along Escalante's rediscovered trail just south of the Canyon Country. By the 1880s the route from the Little Colorado valley, across the Colorado at church-owned Lee's Ferry (formerly Escalante's Salsipuedes), and west along the Vermilion Cliffs to St. George was known informally as the "Honeymoon Trail," because of the large numbers of Little Colorado polygamists who traveled to the St. George temple to solemnize their marriages.[36]

But the differences between the deserts of the Little Colorado and the Canyon Country were significant. Although both were certainly arid, the Little Colorado was not entrenched in a canyon and was thus easily accessible for most of its length, unlike Canyon Country rivers such as the San Rafael, Dirty Devil, San Juan, Paria, and Escalante. Furthermore, the more open topography of the Little Colorado allowed for more frequent and diverse interactions with Indians and eventually, with the advent of a railroad across northern Arizona in 1881, more interactions with the rest of the United States. Because of this the Little Colorado towns eventually abandoned the exclusive agrarianism of Mormon villages to the north and became, as historian Charles Peterson has noted, a "three way cross between cattle ranch, lumber camp, and Mormon village."[37] For these reasons the Little Colorado settlements persist even to this day, while many Mormon attempted settlements in the Canyon Country, especially in its western portion, failed.

A Straight Line to the San Juan

As Mormons gradually made the desert of the Little Colorado bloom in the 1870s, church leadership began looking toward the lower San Juan River. Though this region was slightly closer to the core of Mormondom than the Little Colorado was, it was without a doubt a much more remote and hostile region in terms of Mormon ideas of settlement and community. Nonetheless, by 1879, even as more haphazard, less missionized settlements were encroaching on the western boundaries of the Canyon Country, Mormon leaders under Brigham Young's successor, John Taylor, were considering a true, top-down ordered mission of settlers along the far southeastern frontiers of Mormondom. This call for an expeditionary mission to the Canyon Country would be the church's last.

Though it is noticeably smaller than the Green or Colorado Rivers, the San Juan is the third-largest river in the Canyon Country and averages over eight times the annual flow of the Escalante, Dirty Devil, Paria, or San Rafael Rivers. From its headwaters in the eponymous mountains of southwest Colorado, the river flows through relatively open country around Shiprock, New Mexico, near the Four Corners, and into Utah. For about its last hundred miles it carves a sinuous gorge over a thousand feet deep as it flows west through southeastern Utah, roughly paralleling the Arizona border. Like the Green and Escalante, its junction with the Colorado in Glen Canyon (now beneath Lake Powell) has always been inaccessible to wheeled traffic.

More than any other Canyon Country river, the San Juan has also long been a border between peoples. Prehistoric ruins along the river and its drainages such as Grand Gulch and Mule Canyon mark the northwesternmost extensions of the eleventh- to thirteenth-century Ancestral Puebloan cultures centered at Chaco Canyon and Mesa Verde.[38] Since the arrival of the Navajos in the Southwest one or two centuries before Columbus, it has served as that people's northern frontier in their folklore and from 1884 was the officially designated northwestern boundary for the Navajo Reservation.[39] Both William Huntington and Alfred Billings had noted the significance of the San Juan as a boundary in their reconnaissance trips to the region from the Elk Mountain Mission in the 1850s. Although many rivers bring peoples and geographies together, the San Juan had long separated very different ways of life.

By 1879 white non-Mormons were also encroaching upon the San Juan country, despite at least one explorer having dismissed the entire region, writing that "this whole portion of the country is now and must ever remain utterly worthless."[40] Rumors of gold suspended in the silts of the river were circulating around Colorado mining circles (see chapter 9), and herders of Navajo sheep and even Texan cattle were gradually pushing their ranges ever northwestward. A small Mormon exploratory party sent to the region noted scattered gentile settlements and even a wedding ceremony that was "the first marriage of white people on the lower San Juan" on June 17.[41] More ominously, San Juan Mission member George Hobbs would later recall meeting prospectors Ernest Mitchell and James Merrick in the area during the winter of 1879–80, shortly before Navajos allegedly killed them in Monument Valley for finding a hidden silver smelter.[42] It was probably because of this white American encroachment onto the buffer between Navajos and Mormons that the church officially organized the San Juan Mission. The mission was to consist of around 250 men, women, and children under the leadership of Silas Smith and Platte Lyman. Leaders called for quotas of members from all towns throughout central and southwestern Utah, many with origins in the South and nearly all from the lower rungs of Mormon society.[43]

The story of the San Juan Mission's trek, also called the "Hole in the Rock" expedition, remains in Mormon memory as one of the greatest wilderness trials that pioneers ever faced. As its chief historian David Miller wrote, "there is no better example of the indomitable pioneer spirit...the story of the Hole in the Rock expedition is an excellent case study of the highest type of pioneer endeavor that broke the wilderness and brought civilization to the West."[44] Pioneer bravado aside, however, all of the hardships of the Hole in the Rock expedition resulted from its leaders' desire for a quick shortcut via straight line across the Canyon Country—a shortcut that simply did not exist.

For over a century prior to the San Juan Mission's ordeal, nearly all travel in the region—especially by wagon—skirted the Canyon Country either to the north via the Old Spanish Trail at Moab or more recently, with the opening of the Little Colorado settlements and Lee's Ferry, to the south. Both of these routes approached the region close enough to give travelers a taste of the Canyon Country's rough terrain—just enough to convince them to stay away from the intricate gorges of its central rivers. The only exception was the old Ute Ford in Glen Canyon that Escalante's party, New Mexican and Indian traders, Jacob Hamblin, and a few other horseback travelers used on rare occasions. The prevailing wisdom was that the quickest way through the Canyon Country was simply the long way around.

The San Juan Mission party ignored this. An advance exploratory expedition in the summer of 1879 had experienced dehydration and tensions with Navajos between Lee's Ferry and the San Juan; the southern route to the San Juan was thus not an option. But several scouts had reported a vague shortcut across Glen Canyon near the mouth of the Escalante River. Mission president Silas Smith wanted his congregation to reach the San Juan as quickly as possible before winter set in, to begin preparations for the planting season of 1880, so he settled upon this more direct route across the Canyon Country. The expedition was behind schedule almost from its inception, however. As winter began to descend upon the high desert in November, hundreds of settlers congregated at the tiny village of Escalante (formerly Potato Valley), itself only recently settled and barely self-sufficient. Mission leaders nonetheless anticipated a quick six-week push southeast to the Colorado and then east to the San Juan.

Stretching southeast from Escalante, an apparently open plain runs between the Straight Cliffs of the Kaiparowits Plateau and the gorge of the Escalante River, finally terminating at the rim of Glen Canyon and the Colorado River. In reality the open plain is riddled with drainages that channel sporadic flash floods and spring-fed creeks eastward into the Escalante. Most begin as minor gullies, gradually morphing into massive canyons as they near the river. Near the junction of the Escalante and the Colorado the gorges are even more sinuous and difficult to avoid.

As 250 people, 83 wagons, 200 horses, and over 1,000 cattle moved slowly toward the Colorado, they realized the first of many dilemmas in this land—most water sources to the east were tiny springs hidden in twisting canyons, while the open, more easily traveled benches to the west were completely dry. Grass feed for the huge herd was scarce as well. Platte Lyman, bringing up the rear of the expedition, complained of having no grass or water left for the stock. Through November, December, and January the party was less a single moving entity and more a scattering of people and animals seeking out every possible pocket of grass and water between Escalante and the Colorado.[45]

At the rim of Glen Canyon the vanguard of the party encountered a very narrow canyon that descended via cliffs and steep talus slopes to the river over 2,000 feet below. Because the existing slot at its head was too narrow for wagons, several Welsh immigrants with mining background used gunpowder to blast a "Hole in the Rock" to allow passage, giving the party its name and best-known landmark.[46] Below the blasted hole workers had to construct a cantilevered dugway by drilling holes into the slickrock, inserting willow stakes in the holes, and piling rocks and brush upon them to make a suspended road. Finally, on January 26, 1880, nearly three months into the expedition and weeks behind schedule, party members lowered, skidded, and sometimes let their wagons simply career down through the Hole in the Rock. Amazingly, they suffered no major accidents or injuries on the descent or on the crude ferry crossing of the icy Colorado.[47]

Although they had passed the obstacle that would give their expedition its name, the pioneers still had over 150 miles of even more difficult terrain to cross as they pushed east across the triangle plateau formed by the San Juan and Colorado River canyons. Party member Elizabeth Decker would recall that "this was the roughest country you or anybody else have ever seen; it's nothing in the world but rocks and holes, hills and hollows."[48] The only respite that the settlers found came on the day of the leap year, at the unique Lake Pagahrit, where a sand dune had dammed a small creek in a canyon, creating a "beautiful clear sheet of spring water," in the words of Lyman.[49] This welcome refuge in the desert must have evoked a sense of the sacred and mythical in the weary settlers. Decades later Lyman's son would speculate on the lake's "effectual defense for the few that have fled the many" and suggest that it had "perhaps been the security of robbers many times since the days of Gadianton."[50]

Book of Mormon connections aside, beyond the lake the party's faith began to dwindle. Amid the bitter cold of winter's last gasps in mid-March, they had to make a northern detour of nearly eighty extra miles in order to pass the head of Grand Gulch near today's Natural Bridges National Monument. Two weeks later the uplifted sandstone monocline of Comb Ridge—the eastern-most extension of the Canyon Country—forced them into a grueling uphill battle that was the steepest portion of the entire trail aside from the Hole in the Rock itself.[51]

Beyond Comb Ridge, and into the more open country of the middle San Juan, the mission simply broke up in the first days of April. Although church leadership had planned the original site of the San Juan Mission to be at Montezuma Creek, still twenty miles away, many settlers simply said "no more!" and settled at what became the town of Bluff. Perhaps their sheer exhaustion was made more unbearable because they were beginning to realize that they had contrived the hardest way possible through the Canyon Country. A trip that they had thought would take six weeks had stretched into six months and thousands of dollars in expenses.[52] Looking back on the ordeal, member Samuel Rowley bitterly commented that "before we left our homes we were told that the country had been explored, and that the road was feasible. But now we found that someone had been mistaken."[53]

Even though they had sent out preliminary scouting parties, this expedition was nonetheless crossing country that few people knew anything about. By 1880 the Powell surveys had completed their work in the Canyon Country, but those who had come nearest the Hole in the Rock party's trail, such as A. H. Thompson, had only reached the Escalante's northern fringes. The maps of the area that the Powell surveys had created gave little hint of the actual terrain, other than it being very rough. They told nothing of how to make an actual crossing of the broken country.[54]

Further complicating matters, the Hole in the Rock pioneers were not the first members of the mission to have reached the San Juan. Some families had arrived in the area the previous summer as part of an exploratory party via Lee's Ferry and the Navajo country. Though instructed to establish the time-honored, tightly gridded Mormon village, these families quickly realized that this model simply could not work along the San Juan after a flash flood washed out their communal irrigation works. Out of necessity these families spread farms and livestock out along every inhabitable bottom of the San Juan and even north to the summer ranges of Cedar Mesa and the Abajo Mountains. Just as their fellow Mormons were realizing at the same time on the Little Colorado, the vanguard of the San Juan Mission saw that mountain agrarianism was not sustainable in this desert and began relying more on dispersed herding and less on concentrated farming.[55]

Having just survived a harsh winter, these families were barely in a position to welcome the new arrivals, let alone feed them. Within days of the arrival of the Hole in the Rock group, bitter conflicts erupted over how to allot land to the new families. After arguments, "illiberal feelings," and even the unsuccessful casting of lots to determine new land ownership, acting bishop Platte Lyman finally used his priesthood authority to seize all of the original settlers' land and redistribute it to the entire mission.[56] This did not allay the problem that what little arable and irrigable land existed was of low quality and was certainly not what the settlers, familiar with land in the U.S. South or even along the semiarid plateaus of central Utah, had expected. The San Juan Mission was off to a very rough start.

Within a year travelers had completely abandoned the route through Hole in the Rock. Ferry operator Charles Hall, probably tired of the poorly accessible location, scouted a new route between the Escalante and the San Juan that connected existing canyons across the Escalante River to meet the Colorado at the foot of the Henry Mountains near the creek that bears his name. Although this route was also difficult—one canyon that it followed became known as Muley Twist because it was so circuitous that it could "twist a mule"—it avoided the sheer absurdity of lowering wagons through a blasted, forty-five degree slope of slot canyon.[57] The new "Hall's Crossing," as well as later-developed "Dandy Crossing" near the mouth of the Dirty Devil River, which A. H. Thompson had used during the Powell expeditions, soon became the major points at which to cross the Canyon Country, if it was absolutely necessary to do so.[58] Hole in the Rock quickly became a curious monument to perseverance, faith, and little else.

For the remaining two decades of the nineteenth century the Mormon settlements of far southeastern Utah along the San Juan gradually came to terms with life on a desert river. Although the layout of the village of Bluff superficially resembled the Mormon communities of the Great Basin, with its Lombardy poplars lining ordered streets, it lacked the most essential element of a Mormon village: the security of mountains behind it. For irrigation, Platte Lyman and Silas Smith immediately ordered the construction of a small dam across the San Juan in April 1880. Unlike the small mountain creeks to which Mormons were accustomed, however, the San Juan has an upstream drainage basin of thousands of square miles. The river would flood with late summer rainstorms and repeatedly take out dams and irrigation infrastructure. During one particularly bad flood in 1884 nearly every house in Montezuma, twenty miles upstream, was carried away.[59]

External pressures apart from Mormon agriculture also converged upon the San Juan country. Colorado miners and Texas cattle ranchers continued to enter the region just as they were doing in Moab, straining a range that was already under the dual pressures of Mormon cattle and Navajo sheep. Overgrazing eventually extended northward from the desert into the Abajo and La Sal Mountains, resulting not only in erosion and more severe flash floods but in the depletion of deer herds on which Paiutes relied. At least one Indian bitterly stated that the destruction of Indians' game resources by ranchers "justified them [Indians] every once in a while in killing a cow."[60] Although most resulting violence of the 1880s, including at least two fatal attacks, was between non-Mormons and Indians, it was clear that the San Juan Mission had inserted itself into an even more rapidly crowded and fragile ecosystem than the Elk Mountain Mission had done twenty-five years earlier.

The descendants of the San Juan Mission gradually adapted to a less traditional mixed economy of trade, ranching, and farming and even moved their county seat from Bluff to the new town of Monticello, which was closer to the refuge of the Abajo Mountains and less vulnerable to large floods. The Mormons in the San Juan region did in fact find a way to live in this Bad Land. Perhaps their most obvious success was the communal pooling of all Mormon ranchers' herds under President Smith's successor, Francis Hammond. Using restrained and self-regulated grazing styles that certainly would have made Brigham Young proud, while stockpiling reserves of raised alfalfa on their farms, this "Bluff Pool" of ranchers actually managed to outlast larger herds owned by absentee Texan ranchers in the region through a period of droughts and bad winters and eventually secured the entire range of southeast Utah for exclusively Mormon use.[61]

The San Juan Mormons, not surprisingly, continued to tout the familiar rhetoric of faith, trials, and above all restoring gardens in the desert. Second-generation settler Albert Lyman would write in one of the region's first histories that the San Juan Mission had established "a little Zion in spite of (or because of) the difficulty and limitations to which it had to accommodate," taking pride in some of the desert's environmental determinism.[62] Most of the settlers' successes came as a result of grassroots community-level improvisation, however, and actually abandoning the rigid, hierarchical guidelines established by Salt Lake City leadership.

In his study, *The Mormon Landscape*, historical geographer Richard Francaviglia lists a dozen or so quantifiable elements that make farming communities uniquely "Mormon" in style, such as wide, gridded streets, Lombardy poplars, pastures on the peripheries, close proximity to mountains, and cows and sheep grazed in common fields. Some of these practices were specifically ordered by church leadership, others were more implied cultural mores. Francaviglia also maps and quantifies twenty-nine Mormon farming communities through Utah, listing the amounts of "Mormon-ness" that each has. Not surprisingly, communities near the core of Mormondom, such as those in Cache and Sanpete Valleys, have the highest number of these "Mormon" elements and are labeled as part of the "nucleus" of classic "Mormon Country." The three towns that Francaviglia examines near the Canyon Country—Loa,

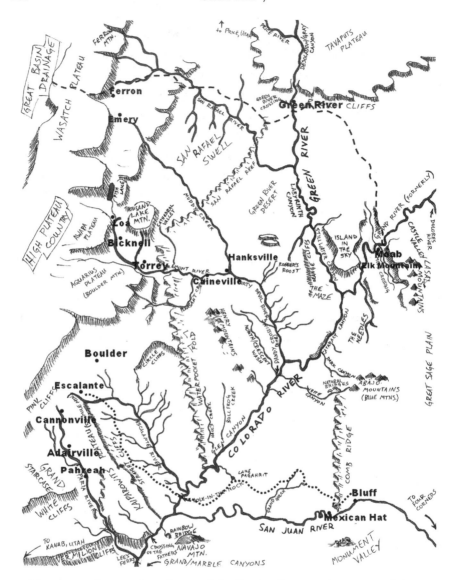

7.1. Mormon settlements in and around the Canyon Country, 1855–1909, and the route of the Elk Mountain Mission (1855: dashed line), and route of the San Juan Mission through Hole in the Rock (1879–80: dotted line). (Map by author)

Escalante, and Monticello—lack many classically Mormon elements and are designated as "fringe" communities. In other words, in order to survive, Canyon Country towns could not be completely "Mormon" in layout, economy, or culture.[63]

Most obviously, the San Juan settlement quickly ceased to be a "mission" in all but name. Early on, Mormons had stressed the "civilized," semiagrarian nature of the adjacent Navajo nation as evidence that these Indians were prepared to convert to Mormonism and abandon the Lamanite curse. Mormons also emphasized, perhaps a little too much, the similarities between the two peoples' religions, perceiving some sort of link to the *Book of Mormon* narrative. In the Mormon view Navajos also considered themselves an "elect" people, just as the Mormons did, granted a sort of Promised Land with very specific boundaries and surrounded by less agricultural "inferior" tribes.[64] At least one missionary even spoke secondhand about a converted Navajo's revelatory vision, in which he saw his desert homeland promised to be "a Garden of Eden, a level plain; all things looked beautiful," if only the rest of his people converted to the Mormon faith.[65] Certainly this Indian nation would be the one to fulfill Smith's original prophecies.

But despite these optimistic expectations, the conversion of the Navajos by the San Juan Mission never took place. Conversion of land had been a compromise of semiarid values in order for the settlers to eke out some sort of minimal existence; conversion of Indians was even less successful. In part this was because the Mormons were barely self-sufficient on their own and in part it was because they were competing with the Navajos, as well as Utes and Paiutes, for scarce resources in the region. Although minor mission work persisted on the Navajo reservation well into the twentieth century, success was so limited that eventually it lost all its millenarian rhetoric of Lamanite redemption.[66]

The San Juan Mission was the last gasp of mission-style settlement by the Mormon church in the West. By the end of the 1870s Brigham Young was dead and federal prosecution of polygamists and church leaders had become so aggressive that Young's successor John Taylor spent most of his presidency in hiding. Even as prophets and bishops "called" members to sell all they owned and trudge across a maze of slickrock to a muddy desert river, less organized Mormon towns encroached on the headwaters of rivers such as the Fremont, Escalante, San Rafael, and Paria on the western fringes of the Canyon Country, as the next chapter details (see fig. 7.1). The reasons for these new communities' settlement were less self-assured and less faith-based than those for settlements along the San Juan or Little Colorado—people simply overflowed into new valleys and onto new ranges because their existing homes were getting crowded.

Even closer to the San Juan, Moab had already established itself as one of Utah territory's most diverse and secularized towns and the antithesis of the strictly organized San Juan Mission. The differences between Moab and the communities of today's San Juan counties continue to this day. Despite the economic compromises that the San Juan Mission made, the towns of Monticello, Blanding, and Bluff remain predominantly Mormon communities. As historian Charles Peterson wrote concerning the origins of these two regions, "the Moab area was settled; the San Juan area was colonized."[67]

Ironically, however, the settlements that resulted from the San Juan and Little Colorado missions managed to sustain themselves with diversified economies and careful self-regulation. Bluff, Monticello, and Blanding in Utah and Snowflake, Springerville, and St. Johns in Arizona still exist; none of them became ghost towns. Perhaps the rigid leadership established by Brigham Young, combined with improvisation necessitated by the missions' remoteness, resulted in success. This would not be the case for communities to the north and west of the San Juan, as they pushed more audaciously into land that was even worse.

8

The Rim of Mormondom II

Success and Failure in the Western Canyon Country

In the wake of the Elk Mountain Mission's failure in 1855 and the brief but tragic Utah War and Mountain Meadows Massacre of 1857, Indian attacks on Mormon towns increased. Conflict was especially bad in frontier settlements along the plateaus extending south from Salt Lake City and dividing the Great Basin from the Canyon Country. Although most of these skirmishes— grouped together as the "Black Hawk War"—were between Mormons and Utes, Paiutes and Navajos also increased raiding activities, especially in isolated southern hamlets along the Sevier and upper Paria Rivers. In early 1865 Navajo raiders attacked settlers at Pipe Springs and Long Valley in the southwest corner of the Canyon Country. In response Mormons abandoned the burgeoning community of Kanab and would not resettle it until the time of the Powell surveys seven years later.[1]

In the midst of this violence, in August 1865 a Mormon militia under Captain James Andrus set out from St. George with orders to examine the Colorado River country thoroughly from the area of Kanab to the confluence of the Green and the Grand. They were supposed to learn all they could of "facilities and resources of the country," with particular attention to river crossings. Furthermore, they were to seek out all Indians in the region, "chastising" hostile groups and "conciliating" friendly ones.[2] Although the party followed roughly the same route that both Jacob Hamblin and A. H. Thompson would take seven years later, Andrus was no geographer. The tense atmosphere of conflict and violence prevented him from gathering in-depth information on the Canyon Country's topography.

After riding up the Paria River, losing member Elijah Averett to an Indian attack, traversing the headwaters of the yet to be named Escalante River, and ascending to the heights of the Aquarius Plateau, the Andrus party decided to go no farther.[3] From the area of 11,000-foot Bown's Point, with the topography of the Canyon Country laid out in a maplike view below, Andrus and Franklin Wooley convinced themselves that they could see much more of the region than they actually could. They mistook the canyon of the Fremont River for the Green, the open country of Hall's Creek for the Colorado, and even the still unnamed Henry Mountains for the La Sal range. Given the complex jumble of canyons in what is today Capitol Reef National Park, it is not surprising that they made such errors. With these false orientation points in mind, Andrus and Wooley convinced each other that they could see the confluence of the Green and the Grand and then turned around, eager to leave this Bad Land.[4]

Like explorers who preceded and succeeded him, Andrus failed to find an easy way through the heart of the Canyon Country; he even wrote in frustration of repeatedly encountering slot canyons on the Escalante "hundreds of feet in depth and but a rod or two in width."[5] The maze of the Escalante River would certainly confound many in coming decades, including A. H. Thompson, Jacob Hamblin, and scouts of the Hole in the Rock expedition. In this sense Andrus reaffirmed that the Canyon Country was a place simply to observe from the edges and to avoid.

The Andrus party did succeed at rediscovering existing routes and possible settlement sites along the southern and western fringes of the Canyon Country, however, and opened this area to the possibilities of Mormon travel and settlement. Although the future "Honeymoon Trail" route along the base of the Vermilion Cliffs between Kanab and the Colorado had long been known to Indians and even whites such as Domínguez and Escalante, Andrus's touting of the route spurred the establishment of church-owned Lee's Ferry on the Colorado in 1872 and the settlement of missions on the Little Colorado (see chapter 7).

Equally important, Andrus made occasional mention of pockets of Good Land north of Kanab, scattered among the slot canyons and barren cliffs of the upper Paria and Escalante drainages. Writing of Potato Valley, Andrus noted enthusiastically that it was a "beautiful park [with] green grassy meadows, groves of timber on sloping hillsides, [and] streams of cold clear water."[6] Sites such as this, along mountain streams, below the high plateaus but above the desert, fit the preexisting criteria for self-sufficient Mormon town sites. In the decade following Andrus's reconnaissance, and certainly immediately after A. H. Thompson's more thorough survey in 1872, Mormon farmers and herders moved into the upper river valleys on the Canyon Country's western fringes.

Because these were not specifically organized missions but rather diffuse movements, it is difficult to pinpoint precise dates for settlements in the western Canyon Country. Kanab was the first, settled in 1864, abandoned, then resettled in 1870. The lower Paria River was settled shortly thereafter.[7] Settlers enthusiastically settled in Potato Valley and by 1875 had adopted the name "Escalante," which Powell and Thompson had given to the river, for their town.[8] By the end of the 1870s Mormons were also living in the area of the upper drainages of the San Rafael, Fremont, and Paria Rivers, in what would become towns such as Castle Dale, Ferron, Emery, Loa, Bicknell, Teasdale, Cannonville, Henrieville, and Tropic.

With the exception of Kanab and the Paria, these early Mormon settlements along the Canyon Country's western edges were not prompted by the desire to farm but in order to find more range for livestock. As older Mormon settlements in Sanpete and Sevier Counties matured, expanded, and began to thrive, their existing ranges became saturated with cattle. Without explicit orders from Salt Lake City, without mission calls, and without millenarian desires to establish Eden in Bad Land, Mormon ranching cooperatives simply moved east, over the plateaus and into the Colorado basin. In 1873 a treaty with local Paiutes gave Sevier Valley residents permission to move their herds into Rabbit Valley on the upper Fremont, about twenty miles above the river's descent into the Canyon Country of Capitol Reef.[9] Two years later and eighty miles to the north, Sanpete Valley residents such as the Bennion and Swazey families made similar moves east along tributaries of the San Rafael River in what was to become Castle Valley.[10]

In both Rabbit and Castle Valleys the Canyon Country dominates the eastern horizon with the bizarre buttes and canyons that simultaneously repulsed and intrigued explorers of the 1870s like Clarence Dutton and A. H. Thompson. Rather than gaze into the abyss and wax poetic, however, Mormon ranchers quickly moved into it. Within a year of crossing the high plateaus to the San Rafael River's upper tributaries, cattlemen such as Joe Swazey were riding deep into the canyons of the San Rafael Swell in search of stray cattle and occasionally carving their names into remote alcoves far from civilization.[11] The lower elevations and slightly warmer temperatures of the desert provided sufficient range for the winter months when the upper valleys and plateau tops were freezing. While grass and water were obviously scarce, the small numbers of cattle that these early ranchers moved into the canyons spread across sparsely vegetated benches, congregated at sporadic springs and along rivers, and for a time managed to eke out a precarious sustainability in this Bad Land.

Unfortunately, as cattle numbers increased and Mormons began settling permanently in the upper valleys, livestock put an increasing strain on the desert. Despite its rugged appearance, the Canyon Country was turning out to be surprisingly fragile. Livestock's depletion of grass and trampling of the soil increased erosion and runoff, creating a vicious cycle in which new grass could not grow and streams entrenched themselves in less accessible gullies. Even as early as 1880 Powell survey employee Grove Karl Gilbert was making note of Mormons' destructive grazing practices in the area of the Henry Mountains.[12] Glynn Bennion, a second-generation San Rafael rancher, later lamented this range destruction and placed the blame squarely on the importation of ranching practices developed in more temperate and fertile valleys to the north and west. His 1966 recollections are worth quoting in full:

> Those early Utah herdsmen had all recently come from more humid climates where grass grew green all summer. They had no idea what the carrying capacity of desert ranges might be, nor gave any thought to the

harm that might be done to such dry ranges when repeated cropping was permitted during the short season of green growth in the spring. Grazing livestock take the most flavorable [*sic*] forage first, and when these forms are killed out they adjust their taste to the kinds of lesser nutrition. This process under a regime of unlimited grazing goes on until in a tragically short time the vegetation left alive on ranges of six to twelve inches of annual rainfall bears little resemblance to the original forms. So when I remember how my father and uncles and their fellow herdsmen used to rave about how wonderful the ranges were in the early days, and how fat the horses and cattle and sheep got on them, I feel only a bitter sense of irony in it all. Why did they have to wreck those ranges at a time when they gained pitifully little from doing it?[13]

After three years of failure on the San Rafael and the loss of nearly 300 head of cattle, the Bennions eventually simply moved their ranching back to better land in the West.[14] But other ranchers remained in the desert. Some even moved farther into the interior of the Canyon Country, such as Joe Biddlecome, who established the Robber's Roost Ranch between the Green and Dirty Devil Rivers in the early 1900s. With varying degrees of success and failure, cattle continued to stress the Canyon Country on both sides of the Colorado as well as the mountains surrounding it well into the twentieth century.[15]

But how uniquely Mormon was this overgrazing? Range depletion, damage, and its resultant erosion and increased flash floods were widespread throughout the entire arid West, especially prior to the passage of the Taylor Grazing Act in 1934. It is arguable that Mormon overgrazing in the western Canyon Country coincided with the death of Brigham Young in 1877 and the decline of the Mormon tradition of moderated stewardship over natural resources. Indeed, an implicit part of Young's environmental stewardship was simply avoiding the Canyon Country altogether, as he never sent a mission to the region after the failure of Elk Mountain. Furthermore, the one true top-down delegated "mission" venture in the Canyon Country, the San Juan Mission, actually managed to sustain large cattle herds in the desert more successfully than settlements in the western canyons. Initially competing for scarce range with Texas and even British-owned ranches, San Juan ranchers such as Al Scorup lived full-time with their herds on the range and used home-grown grain and grass stores to survive droughts that actually destroyed larger non-Mormon herds in the 1890s.[16]

In this sense the story of grazing in the Canyon Country reinforces the established idea among Mormon and Utah historians that communal, cooperative efforts were the key to environmental sustainability in this Bad Land and that only with the influx of outside market forces did Mormons begin to overtax their resources.[17] As Wallace Stegner wrote, "Mormons discovered what the cliff-dwellers had discovered centuries before: that the only way to be a farmer in the Great Basin and on the desert plateaus of the Colorado watershed was to be a group farmer." The same rules applied to ranchers.[18]

While cooperative herding may have managed to achieve a sort of coexistence with the desert, this does not imply that the Great Basin Mormon village model of communal water development and ordered grids could simply impose itself successfully upon the Canyon Country. Much of Young's original environmental ethic had encouraged restraint and moderation in the selection of locations for town sites. When Mormon visions of converting the desert to a garden began to follow the winter cattle herds into the interior of the western Canyon Country, armed with the assurance that they were doing God's work, their village model collapsed.

Pahreah

Through the 1870s, even as Mormons in central Utah pushed their cattle onto the desert during winters, most of their nascent towns remained with the security of mountains and spring runoff behind them, just as Mormon villages had done for a generation. Despite the benefits of predictable snowmelt, better soil, and cooler temperatures that the base of the plateaus offered, however, portions of the Canyon Country enticed settlement with the promise of longer growing seasons and larger rivers. The first Mormon settlement to establish itself completely within the western Canyon Country, rather than on its peripheries, was on the middle portion of the Paria River, about forty miles east of Kanab.

The Paria, occasionally spelled "Pahreah" (Ute for "muddy water"), is the smallest waterway in the Canyon Country to receive the title "river."[19] Originating in the Pink Cliffs of Bryce Canyon National Park, the small stream flows south through multiple layers of uplifted Jurassic sandstones, which we today call the "Grand Staircase." Although it drains a huge area northeast of Kanab, perennial streams are rare, and by the time it passes beneath Highway 89 near the Arizona border the bed of the Paria is often completely dry, especially during the summer months. For the final forty miles above its mouth at Lee's Ferry the stream experiences a sort of rebirth—it descends into one of the Southwest's most impressively narrow canyons, where springs literally gush from the sandstone walls. Unfortunately for potential settlers, at this point the Paria's canyon is so narrow that it has no space for grazing, let alone settlement.

For this reason the central portion of the river's course, just as it emerges from the Grand Staircase into a series of more open clay hills but before its waters sink into the hot sand, was the ideal point for settlement. In 1868 six families from southwestern Utah, led by Thomas Smith, attempted to establish a Mormon village at this point. Initially this settlement, called Rock House, was a modest trading hub for Indians. It was located at a crucial point between the Colorado River and the thriving towns of southwestern Utah, where trails from both the old Ute Ford in Glen Canyon and soon to be established Lee's Ferry intersected.

Despite this prime location, agriculture was not successful at Rock House. Within three years Smith complained of "water sinking in sand and gravel at the creek bottom," and the settler families abandoned their original site to spread out along about ten miles of the river bottom. Throughout the 1870s the twin settlements of Pahreah and Adairville grew, and each "developed into a very prosperous cattle and farming community," in Smith's own words.[20] By 1877 at least eighteen families were farming and herding along the river, and the Mormon church organized the two communities into an official ward, called simply Pahreah.[21]

According to a letter that Bishop Allen Smithson sent to the Salt Lake City's *Deseret News*, the spring of 1878 promised to be an excellent year:

> Weather is fine, although the last month we have had occasional wind squalls and now and then we are visited with nice showers of rain, which is very good for fall and spring wheat, of which we have in about 3 or 4 times as much as in any years previous. Fall wheat does very well

on our clay lands. Prospects were never better for a good crop than the coming season. Our people appear to have regained in a great measure their usual cheeriness. All are busily preparing for a good crop, grass upon the ranges are [*sic*] fine, our country is second to none in this part of the territory. As far as good feed is concerned stock is doing splendid...This is good country for grazing and farming. Anyone wishing a new home, here is the place: a liberal invitation is extended.[22]

But these hopeful words marked the zenith of Pahreah's success. Beginning in 1883, increasingly violent flash floods began sweeping down the river canyon, destroying homes, drowning livestock, and, perhaps most serious, completely washing away the fertile alluvial soils that were the foundation of agriculture along the river. Thomas Smith could only watch in horror as he saw the formerly tiny stream swell to such a muddy, raging torrent that the waters extended across the entire canyon, "from rock wall to rock wall."[23]

These were not predictable spring snowmelt floods but the results of late summer cloudbursts nearly one hundred miles away, in the high country of the Paunsaugunt Plateau. Increased ranching in the mountains in the late 1870s (the same type of overgrazing that Grove Karl Gilbert had noted in the Henry range in chapter 5) had destroyed the grasses and brush that staved off erosion and eased violent flooding along mountain streams. While the upstream villages of Cannonville and Tropic only suffered flooding of smaller streams, the lower Pahreah Ward bore the brunt of dozens of combined waterways, all funneled into a single channel. The advantages of staying near mountains were becoming clear.

On September 7, 1884, after over half of its families had given up and left, church leaders in Kanab officially dissolved Pahreah Ward. About fifty settlers, many of whom were children under the age of eight, remained scattered along the river.[24] The poverty and desperation of those who lacked the means or desire to leave the Paria must have been profound. Five years later the minutes of an 1889 Kanab church meeting reported that an undetermined but shrinking number of families still remained on the Paria, in "bad condition both spiritually and temporally."[25] In 1892 Kanab church elder Andrew Jensen rode through the ruins of Pahreah, still occupied by a few impoverished families, and reported a dreary sight:

The village of Pahreah...lies in a narrow valley in which the soil is sandy. Nearly the whole Valley is subject to heavy floods, and there is always danger of the land being washed away, when the Pahreah Creek or River is high. On this account the people have suffered great loss, and some of them have become discouraged and moved away. It may be said that the country surrounding the little Pahreah settlement is one of the most broken and haggard looking regions in Southern Utah.[26]

In fourteen years "good country for grazing and farming" somehow had become "most broken and haggard." The Paria River was clearly a lesson in failure for close-knit Mormon villages, although squatters would remain at the site of Pahreah until 1930 and ranchers from Kanab continue to use the Paria's limited winter range to the present day. Strikingly absent from any documents of the short-lived Pahreah Ward is any hint of a religious duty to make the desert bloom, even in Smithson's optimistic call for more settlers in 1878. During the ordeal of Hole in the Rock around the same time, diaries and reminiscing accounts are rife with language of trials, tests of faith, and perseverance in doing the Lord's work; settlers of Pahreah never mentioned this. Perhaps this is because Pahreah was not a mission. A prophet ordained by God never explicitly ordered followers to settle the Paria River, so the failure of the settlement did not hint at any weaknesses in Mormon theology or prophecy in the minds of believers. A different variation of this theme of failure, however, would unfold twenty-five years later, two river basins and 150 miles to the north of Pahreah.

CAINEVILLE

The Fremont River, named for the explorer who crossed its frozen headwaters in his desperate winter expedition of 1853–54, gradually transitions from mountain stream to desert river. From its source in the cold waters of Fish Lake, at 8,800 feet, it slowly descends through the open meadows of upper Wayne County or Rabbit Valley, as settlers in the mid-1870s called it. Rabbit Valley's towns of Loa, Fremont, Lyman, and Bicknell have always had notoriously short growing seasons. Frosts and snows commonly persist into May and June, and the only practical large-scale crop is alfalfa, used to feed cattle—mostly beef, but some dairy. Just below Bicknell the Fremont veers east, passes between the flanks of Thousand Lake and Boulder Mountains, and encounters the first hint of Canyon Country terrain in the "Mummy Cliffs," formed by maroon layers of Moenkopi shale. Ten miles farther along, after flowing by the towns of Teasdale and Torrey, the Fremont plunges into the sandstone canyons of Capitol Reef National Park that A. H. Thompson passed by in 1872. By the time it emerges from these canyons into the more open badlands and clays north of the Henry Mountains, the Fremont has metamorphosed into a desert river: muddy, slow, warm, and, above all, prone to flash floods.

Mormons who followed the winter cattle herds into the canyons and deserts of the Fremont River had additional motivation that was neither purely religious nor secular: asylum. By the early 1880s the federal power of the Republican Party was aggressively pursuing and prosecuting Mormon polygamists in Utah, forcing many high-ranking church leaders to go into hiding. The isolated but well-watered canyons in what would become Capitol Reef were a perfect sanctuary. In 1882, the same year Congress passed the Edmunds Act proclaiming polygamy a felony, Ephraim Hanks and at least one wife moved into the Pleasant Creek area and established a small ranch. They may have begun operating a sort of underground railroad to move other polygamists to even more isolated sanctuaries farther down the Fremont to the east.[27] Primary documents detailing the specifics of polygamists along the Fremont are very rare, given the taboo nature of the subject among their descendants today.[28] But the folklore did leave one mark upon Capitol Reef: a small canyon where "cohabitationists" allegedly hid from federal marshals, called "Cohab Canyon."

Early 1880s polygamist refugees were acting more out of desperation than out of optimism in settling the desert, but Hanks's ranch on Pleasant Creek and the adjacent community of Fruita that formed on the Fremont ten miles to the north were fairly successful. The first settlers of Fruita noted remains of prehistoric irrigation ditches along the river, indicating sustained use by Indians that survived flooding.[29] The town site was apparently high enough in the Fremont's basin to withstand flooding, even with increased upstream grazing. With its namesake orchards (and during prohibition even illegal vineyards), Fruita survived even after its surrounding country became a national monument in 1937.[30]

8.1. The Fremont River at Caineville, Utah. The trickle of this diminutive stream little hints at the floods that destroyed Caineville in 1909. (Photo by author)

Settlers moved quickly downstream from Fruita, however, to less hospitable locations. While the hard sandstone buttes and canyons around Fruita provided some semblance of security to settlers—channeling flash floods and harboring springs—the more open clays and shale valleys of the lower Fremont did not (see fig. 8.1). As Powell had identified in his *Report on the Lands of the Arid Region*, these were quite simply "badlands."[31] Nonetheless, the promise of refuge from federal marshals, longer growing seasons, and new unclaimed land convinced settlers to move into the lower Fremont. By 1887 communities were scattered over twenty miles below Fruita: Caineville, Giles, Clifton, and Hanksville (settled by and named for Eph Hanks's brother Ebenezer).[32] Of these towns, only Hanksville still survives.

Caineville was one of the earliest of these communities and for several decades was the most successful. Like the San Juan Mission (though not in such a dramatic or expeditionary fashion), and unlike Pahreah, its original settlers were "called" by the church from their homes in the Sevier Valley to farm the lower Fremont as missionaries. The first settlers arrived in the winter of 1882–83 under Bishop Elijah Behunin. Although they quickly organized an official ward on December 13, 1882, Caineville's settlers did little else in establishing a typical Mormon village along the river. Rather than establish a tight-knit, gridded town square, they spread into individual ranches along the river, just as settlers on the San Juan and Paria had done. Work on essential canals and ditches began almost immediately, but a combination church/ school meetinghouse was not built until 1890.[33] The ward did not even begin keeping regular minutes of its meetings until 1893, after over a decade of settlement.

Though decentralized and dispersed, Caineville quickly became an agricultural oasis. Once irrigated, the broad alluvial valleys along the Fremont produced ample vegetables, melons, fruit trees, and sorghum, which could be boiled down into a thick syrup for use in canning, cooking, and even the production of distilled liquor, much to the chagrin of the town's more devout residents.[34] Some even experimented with planting mulberry trees in order to raise silkworms. By 1900 Caineville still had only a dozen families, but the *Deseret News* touted its "long growing season, cool night, good crops, [and] room for settlers."[35]

Like their neighbors on the upper Fremont and their fellow "missionaries" on the San Juan far to the southeast, the villagers of Caineville by necessity utilized the country surrounding their settlement as range for cattle and sheep. The desert environment, however, proved unusually harsh for Caineville ranchers. Their summer range in the Henry Mountains had fewer permanent springs and streams than Boulder Mountain or the Abajo Mountains, and their desert winter range along the Fremont River had a higher elevation and harsher winters than the winter range of the San Juan region. Canyon Country guide Dave Rust, who spent his childhood and teenage years during the 1880s herding sheep in the lower Fremont River valley, recalled that the region had "long, lean" winters and a "short summer with the flaming sword of frost at each entrance," a significantly different view of the region than the *Deseret News* promises of a "long growing season."[36]

Further complicating the problems of ranching both cattle and sheep on a sparse range were nonlocal ranchers who put large numbers of cattle on the Fremont's fragile desert. Because they did not live in Caineville or rely upon the Fremont River for irrigation water, these out-of-towners had less interest in the damage that their herds caused and prompted resentment from local farmers. Indeed, in her reminiscences on growing up in Caineville, Evangeline Godby wrote that most Caineville residents believed that nonlocal ranchers were directly responsible for floods that began to increase around the turn of the century.[37]

These floods culminated in the late summer and fall of 1909. June and July of that year had been hot and dry—nearly all of the snowmelt feeding the Fremont river was gone, and the remaining water was sinking into the shale or evaporating into the hot desert air. So in mid-August, when the familiar black monsoonal clouds appeared over Boulder Mountain to the west and the Henry Mountains to the south, Evangeline Godby recalled: "The people took heart. The drought was over." With the first small rises in the river, villagers thanked their God for the water while grabbing passing driftwood for use in their stoves the coming winter.[38]

But the rain continued, day after day. Squash and melons began to rot in the fields, and the crude wagon roads through the clay of the Morrison Formation became impassable, cutting off the villagers' only access to the outside world. On August 16 the ward minutes noted that "a very large flood came down Caineville Wash" from the north, taking out diversion flumes and dividing the town into two islands cut off from one another. Now both the Fremont River and the adjoining wash were overflowing, as "the men of the ward" tried to "cut the river or pile trees and rocks in so the river will not take the town."[39] Only four days later yet another flood raged down the Fremont. The unnamed ward clerk reported that the riverbanks "are carving rapidly and fast, seems as though it will take the town in spite of all the hard work to save it. Some have lost all their crops...Everybody very discouraged."[40]

The proceedings of the church meeting that Sunday after the initial flood tell us much about how the farmers of Caineville dealt with this catastrophe. Elder Andrew Sanders hearkened back to the church's original mission call in 1882 to settle the Fremont and appealed to Mormon values of faith and perseverance. "If any other people than Mormons" had experienced these trials, "they would not stay and work these ditches and roads like we do!" Less than half of the ward's usual number were in church that day to hear these words of encouragement, however—the others were either in the process of moving or were still trying to repair damage to their farms.[41] More floods followed in subsequent weeks, including one that literally flowed down the streets and through the orchards of the town.[42] Godby recalled a roaring river "an eighth of a mile across," carrying full trees and livestock away.[43]

By the time the skies cleared on September 13, the community was broken. Ironically, in this desert where a little over a month earlier the community had feared a drought, an excess of water had destroyed decades of communal work. A river that only days before had been a trickle through a narrow valley had risen to the volume of the Colorado River itself.[44] The floodwaters had destroyed irrigation diversions and gates, rotted orchards, and covered formerly lush fields in a layer of sterile, mineral-laden clay. Even with the floods over, the community was left with few resources for future irrigation farming and with nothing for the coming winter.

Through that fall and early winter the formerly tight-knit Mormon community fell apart in a debate over whether to abandon the settlement or not. Optimists for continued reclamation pleaded that "if the church would help us we could put the water back in the ditch."[45] Older members such as George Pectol tried to console others with stories of trials from the early settlement, implying that these recent floods were not as bad as some of the past. Nellie Hanks even announced in one ward meeting that the floods were punishments by a God angry at some villagers who had produced and drunk distilled rum from their sorghum crops. By this point, however, only the devout were left in Caineville; everyone else had fled.

In October Caineville Ward sent several members to Salt Lake City to report on the town's plight and appeal for outside help at the church's semiannual general conference.[46] Church leaders expressed sympathy but little else; communities in Bad Land were no longer "missions" and were on their own. We can only imagine what the Caineville delegates must have thought of Mormon apostle David O. McKay's speech at the conference, which extolled the virtues of hard manual labor, proclaiming: "What a joy it is to guide the plow, and tie up the sheaf!"[47] The remaining residents tried to stay true to this positive outlook into November, trying to justify "the disadvantageousness of this country" with the thought that "the Lord tries whom He loveth." But in the end their perseverance failed.[48] Caineville Ward's final meeting ended with the hymn "Count Your Many Blessings."[49]

As winter fell on the desert, the families packed their wagons and began their long treks through the sticky clay away from their homes: north to Green River or Castle Valley, west to Rabbit Valley and Fruita, and some even farther east to Hanksville. Settled at about the same time as Caineville in 1882, where the confluence of the Fremont River and Muddy Creek forms the Dirty Devil River, Hanksville managed to survive the floods of 1909. Though part of the town's success was because it was in more open country and able to spread away from the rivers and floodplains onto safe benchlands, the town's true strength was its position as an essential resupply station along the road from the railroad at Green River to prospecting activity developing along the Colorado in Glen Canyon. Hanksville thus did not need to follow the typical Mormon village model. For most of its history, like Moab but on a smaller scale, it has been more of a non-Mormon-style "boom and bust" town.[50]

Aside from Hanksville—which survives today largely as a refueling point for vacationers en route to Lake Powell—all of the scattered communities along the Fremont River below Fruita simply flooded and then withered away after 1909, leaving only a few cemeteries and sandstone brick buildings that still stand today. Most families left with debt and earned little or nothing for selling their abandoned properties. Dave Rust's father, George, reportedly received one horse in exchange for his flooded property before moving to Manti to work the rest of his life as a low-paid guard at the Mormon temple.[51] Evangeline Godby's family was among the last to leave the settlement. Her father, Alfred Ostburg, had an unusually strong emotional attachment to his oasis in the desert. Less than a year after the floods he began planning engineering projects to conquer the floods: "We'll put that ditch on gravity flow, blast a tunnel through Slipping Rock Hill, build a short flume across Behunin Wash, put a siphon flume over the Caineville Wash, and we can forget the floods."[52] By this point, however, the old Mormon sense of cooperative effort to reclaim the desert was all but dead. And no private enterprise was willing to take the risk.

In the wake of Caineville's failure Godby wrote bitterly of greedy, more individualistic, often non-Mormon ranchers descending on the region, presumably feeding on rich alluvium along the newly scoured river bottom.

Today small ranching operations still survive in the area of Caineville, where the tight-knit community failed.[53] The crumbling ruins of pioneer rock houses often sit amid green, irrigated alfalfa fields. In a way the animosity that the displaced farmers of the region felt toward ranchers—both those visibly damaging nearby range and those out of sight in the mountains who were increasing erosion—was well placed. But they themselves were at least partly to blame. Historian C. Gregory Crampton writes:

> Depletion of the range up-country and the plowing of banks practically to the water's edge increased the volume of floods and the result was a severe lowering of the streambed…Mormons along the Fremont below the Reef [below Fruita] found that much of their farmland had caved away to be washed downstream and that the river itself was dropping below the level of the [irrigation] headgates. The result was a contraction of the original frontier of settlement as people began to move away.[54]

In the end the settlements of the lower Fremont and Paria Rivers simply attempted to extend Mormon agrarianism too far into the desert. While the settlers of Caineville and Pahreah did spread out along the rivers rather than cluster in the neat grids of Great Basin Mormon villages, they still relied too heavily on irrigated farming and the very vulnerable infrastructures that these institutions required. Had they been nearer one of the few existing routes through the Canyon Country, they could have survived on commerce like Hanksville. Had they been nestled in secure alcoves of Navajo Sandstone and farther upstream, they could have survived like Fruita.

Much can be said for the "golden age" of Mormon village establishment during Brigham Young's lifetime, when minimal federal interference, isolation from railroads and eastern capital, and strong theocratic authority all aided in the establishment of stable, self-sufficient, and ordered communities throughout the mountain valleys and foothills of the Wasatch Range. But by the end of the 1870s virtually all Good Land in Utah was already occupied. The lower rungs of Mormon society, seeking their own agrarian stability, had no choice but to look to Bad Lands. While the ordered "mission" style of the

San Juan Mission perhaps strengthened the settlers of Bluff, the desperation of settlers along the lower Fremont and Paria Rivers led them simply to transpose irrigation practices from mountain valleys onto desert lowlands.

Geographer Lynn Rosenvall has noted that the attempted settlement and reclamation of the Colorado River region, and in particular the Canyon Country, represented the largest number of failed settlements in Mormon history. Although some scattered Mormon villages also failed in the expanses of the western Great Basin and the Mojave Desert of southern Nevada for lack of water, the most concentrated failures were in the Canyon Country, nearly all because of floods.[55] Today, as travelers drive along Highway 24, following the Fremont River from Capitol Reef to Hanksville and occasionally passing by the ruins of cabins, it seems absurd that anyone would have even considered settling in the area of Caineville or its failed sister villages. The area not only is an obvious desert, with barely a trickle of river by late summer that seems only enough to sustain swarms of mosquitoes, but is arguably not even one of the more beautiful parts of the Canyon Country. Compared to the soaring red and white amphitheaters of Capitol Reef just up the road, the gray shales and clays of the Caineville Mesas are drab and uninspiring, reminiscent of the background of a postapocalyptic music video rather than a romantic vista that would inspire an explorer-aesthete of the Powell surveys to wax poetic.

For the hopeful families who lived in this valley from 1882 to 1909, however, it seemed that they truly had established their garden in the desert. Hard work and faith had indeed brought blessings. Writing her account of the floods for the *Deseret News* over sixty years later, Evangeline Godby nostalgically recalled shady poplar trees, trickling irrigation ditches, and orderly streets, wondering if there might be some way to reclaim Eden and bring the beauty of her childhood back to Caineville:

> I still go back to the Valley and ask "where did Paradise go?" I see the brush-choked streets, the grassburs, sandburs, cockleburs, and wild morning glory. I see the decay. Power machinery should be the answer, but a band of pioneers made that valley far greater and far better than modern technology is making it.[56]

With the exception of Hanksville and a few tourist outposts, the Canyon Country today still has no permanent towns in it, only around it. We can easily map the region's boundaries simply by drawing a line to connect still-successful towns along its periphery. Like summer thunderheads that cluster around the mountaintops, only to evaporate over the desert, Mormon communal irrigation and farming halted at the flanks of the plateaus. The Canyon Country desert was simply incompatible with the livelihoods of decent, faithful people.

9

Beyond Agriculture

Desert Gold and Tourism

Even at the height of the Mormon village's ventures into the Canyon Country, the main artery of the Colorado and Green River systems below the towns of Moab and Green River remained beyond the reach of settlement, Mormon or otherwise. With the exception of a few scattered subsistence gardens and orchards at Lee's Ferry, at Hall's Crossing, and around the Dirty Devil River's mouth, they simply had nowhere to establish even a small, ordered town. Despite the superficial allure of a bountiful river in the desert, some variable always precluded settlement: canyons were too narrow, alluvial benches too vulnerable to flooding, river bottoms too inaccessible from the cliff tops.

Above all the Green, Grand, and Colorado Rivers were simply too isolated for the productive export of agricultural goods to markets, even assuming that their bottoms could produce crops. Unlike most rivers of comparable sizes on the eastern seaboard or in the Mississippi drainage, the rapids of the Green and Colorado prevented easy water transport for goods to downstream markets. By the final decade of the nineteenth century, however, outsiders were looking toward human industry, technology, and engineering as new solutions to incorporating the Canyon Country where God and Good Land had failed. Steam-powered riverboats could move goods upstream, dams could submerge dangerous rapids, and railroads could move goods completely apart from riverways. Like all human developments, however, technology came to the Canyon Country slowly: dam building is a story largely beyond the early narrative here, and attempts by steam-powered river boats to connect even the towns of Green River and Moab via the confluence were unsuccessful.[1]

Despite these difficulties it was clear by 1890 that the outside world was taking a new interest in the Canyon Country. With the ventures of Robert Brewster Stanton first to construct a railroad through the Colorado River corridor and later to extract gold from the river's sands, it seemed that the Gilded Age integration of professional expertise and capital would finally incorporate the region. While these attempts were even less successful than Mormon agricultural efforts, they did nonetheless spur further outside interest beyond simple exploitation, and eventually avocational tourists. In a way tourism was an offshoot of some of Powell's more romantic musings on the region, but it was still something new, as visitors began visiting the area precisely because it was seen as a Bad Land. The Canyon Country's time as a place to avoid was slowly coming to an end.

STANTON'S RAILROAD

In the wake of Mormondom's failures in the western Canyon Country, railroads made the most serious attempts to incorporate this Bad Land. The idea of railroads in this region extended back at least to the expeditions of Gunnison and Frémont in 1853, when both surveyed potential train routes near the Old Spanish Trail's Green River crossing. By 1883 the Denver and Rio Grande Railroad had constructed a line from Grand Junction, Colorado, to Salt Lake City that used this historic crossing, ensuring Green River's place as a valuable hub for commerce and transport on the fringe of the Canyon Country. But the rest of the region and its surrounding settlements remained isolated, although the towns of Moab and Castle Valley in particular called for more outside economic interest: more railroads, large irrigation projects, and mines.[2]

Although individual towns such as Moab certainly lacked the resources to draw serious attention from speculators and developers (at least until the uranium boom of the 1940s), by the late 1880s the entire Canyon Country was sitting between two valuable markets: California and Colorado. Around this time Colorado prospector S. S. Harper and a wealthy Denver real estate investor named Frank Brown began to think about the lack of a railroad line connecting the coal country of western Colorado to the new cities of southern California. Given that the Colorado River through Cataract, Glen, and Grand Canyons was the shortest route between these regions, it seemed simply ludicrous that no line yet existed through the Canyon Country.

Superficially, this idea for a railroad along the Colorado made sense. Railroads followed wide river valleys in the east and even narrow mountain gorges in the west, because rivers provided natural passages through mountain ranges, connected farms, and supplied water for use by steam engines. While Powell (not to mention Gunnison and Frémont earlier) had discouraged the idea of railroads through the core of the Canyon Country, stating that the terrain was simply too rough, times were different now. Engineers were building tunnels, arched bridges, and cantilevered tracks through incredibly rugged mountain country; besides, Powell was certainly known to exaggerate in his narratives. Brown and Harper simply needed to find a smart, willing engineer for their new company, the Denver, Colorado Canyon, and Pacific Railroad (DCC&P).

Today most Colorado river runners and Canyon Country aficionados know Robert Brewster Stanton as the second man successfully to descend the Colorado and perhaps as the originator of two grandiose plans to exploit the region that thankfully never came to full fruition. More than any other character in the post-Powell, pre–New Deal Canyon Country, this Ohio mining engineer embodied the desire to make the region productive. Despite the best cooperative efforts of Mormons, farming and even ranching were still barely subsistence-level activities in 1890. Stanton believed that railroad commerce and later mining could utilize the Canyon Country most fully. Along the way he became a major critic of Powell's ideas, which he considered overly cautious, selfish, and arrogant. While Powell has come to embody pragmatic restraint in resource consumption through the arid West, Stanton exuded optimism about the possibility of ingenuity, work, and massive capital overcoming the problems of the Canyon Country.

All of this lay ahead of Stanton and Brown's party on May 24, 1889, at Green River, Utah, nearly twenty years to the day after Powell's historic launch down the river.[3] Their goal was to float to the confluence with the Grand River, where they would begin seriously surveying the riverbanks of Cataract, Glen, and Grand Canyons for railroad track construction (Stanton's fellow DCC&P employee Frank Kendrick was concurrently surveying the Grand River below Grand Junction, Colorado). Company president Brown was anxious to complete the survey as quickly as possible and even offered Stanton a bonus of $10,000 if he could quickly complete the entire survey to the foot of the Grand Canyon in one trip.[4]

Even at this early stage Stanton believed that this sort of rushed survey was a bad idea. He had read all of the Powell expedition's literature diligently, "with an almost worshipful reverence," and was prepared for the worst possible ordeal.[5] Brown had a more cavalier attitude. Even before launching, Stanton complained privately in his diary that he was "awfully disappointed" when he saw the boats that the company had supplied—"light brittle cedar hunting and pleasure boats, totally unfit for the work they will have to do down the Colorado River." Within days of launching, still on flatwater, the party was using flour and lard to patch the boats' many holes.[6]

Later in his life Stanton remembered his employer warmly, writing that Brown was "a man of great ability—an optimist par excellence. He never saw an obstacle in his way, and, with all, he had an energy and determination that knew no bounds."[7] Through the first weeks of the survey, however, Stanton was clearly frustrated with Brown's naïveté and his lack of respect toward the dangerous Colorado. Not only had Brown skimped on boat quality, but he refused to purchase life jackets and had brought along a cohort of investor friends from Denver for a planned pleasure cruise instead of employing "sturdy frontiersmen" as guides.[8]

As Stanton had expected, the party's two-week passage through the rapids of Cataract Canyon during the river's infamous spring runoff was terrifying, although nobody was hurt or killed. The party did face the loss of its food boat and a near mutiny in the face of Brown's persistent demands that they hurry with the survey. However, not all was ominous. Stanton began to notice that, contrary to Powell's description of a narrow, dark, almost subterranean chasm, Cataract Canyon's walls were often "3500 feet to a mile apart."[9] The fantastic realm of the one-armed major's report was bit by bit succumbing to more manageable realities. Furthermore, while the river was certainly treacherous, Stanton noted that the actual width of the canyon was more than enough for a railroad bed and that the party could even have "surveyed the canyon more quickly on foot, not being cumbered by the boats, which were constantly breaking, capsizing, and losing food."[10] In the end Stanton concluded that Cataract Canyon could accommodate a railroad easily.

The surveyors emerged from Cataract to enjoy the slower waters of Glen Canyon on June 24 and split up, some going slow, others rushing quickly ahead to survey other features, before regrouping at Lee's Ferry on July 2. Unfortunately the disasters that the expedition members had avoided in Cataract Canyon finally caught up with them in Marble Canyon. On July 10, barely a dozen miles and two major rapids below Lee's Ferry, Brown's boat flipped in a small riffle. Without a life jacket, the president of the DCC&P Railroad drowned. His body was never recovered. Five days later, as Stanton still pressed on to finish the survey, two more members drowned. The Grand Canyon was too much, and the survivors abandoned the river.[11]

Even with the death of his employer, Stanton regrouped investors for the railroad the following year and returned to the river to finish the survey. Despite having been proven tragically right in his fears that the initial expedition was dangerously unprepared, Stanton remained optimistic. He still believed that Powell had exaggerated the danger of the river and its canyons. Better boats and life jackets would make a future survey safer. Stanton believed that a railroad ultimately could and would be completed. In his obsessed engineer's mind the canyons of the Colorado were simply a challenging problem to be solved.

Although in his memoirs Stanton mostly focused on the Grand Canyon, it was likely what he saw in Glen Canyon that ultimately convinced him to return to the river and continue the survey. In contrast with relatively wide and open Cataract Canyon, which for most of its length is lined by talus slopes that could easily accommodate a railroad bed, the narrow cliffs of Glen Canyon, which often overhung severely and dropped directly into the river, were a dream or a nightmare for engineers, depending on their love for problem-solving.

For Stanton it was a dream. Years before seeing the region he had been intrigued by stories of the Canyon Country's challenges to modern engineering and even dreamed as a child of someday building a bridge across the Grand Canyon.[12] Upon actually seeing Cataract and Glen Canyons, he noted that existing railroad routes in the Rockies and Sierra Nevadas actually went over much more difficult terrain and through harder rock. Presumably the softer Navajo and Wingate Sandstones would be easier to tunnel through than mountain granite. On one occasion Stanton even noted a prehistoric trail that scaled a portion of cliff above the river so sheer that its Indian builders had bored holes into the sandstone to suspend a small cantilevered bridge. This, he wrote, "was true engineering, and possibly one of the oldest remains of bridge construction on the continent, showing also that even the first engineers of our country had no dreaded awe of building a road, if not a railroad, in the Canyons of the Colorado."[13]

Simply put, this Bad Land was not quite so bad. Stanton's attitude was something new in this region. He did not need God on his side as Mormons did. He certainly would not dismiss the region as a simple wasteland as pre-Powell explorers had. And he exhibited little of the cautionary restraint or aesthetic enthusiasm of Powell, Gilbert, Dutton, and Thompson. For Stanton, the Canyon Country was much more than some sort of abstract outdoor laboratory or repository of geological knowledge. It required practical, pragmatic engineering skills, not seemingly passive scientific observation.

Much had also changed in Glen Canyon since Powell had floated through during the late 1860s and early 1870s. By the time Stanton descended the Colorado, Glen Canyon was the center of a gold rush. As early as 1872, as Powell's men traversed the canyon's rims and floated the river, Salt Lake City newspapers were receiving reports of "very fine" gold flakes in the Colorado's sandbars, possibly washed down the river from the known gold mining regions of the Colorado Rockies.

It was "not yet known if it would pay for working" claims in this remote region, however, and most miners believed that the gold was so finely ground that it was irretrievable from the sand.[14] Although members of the Hole in the Rock expedition mentioned occasionally running into prospectors as they crossed the Colorado in 1880, little to no evidence of successful gold claims in the region existed. Eight years later, however, longtime Canyon Country prospector Cass Hite rekindled investors' interest in Glen Canyon gold and increasingly mechanized mining practices in order to sluice the fine dust from the sand hydraulically. Through the winter of 1888–89 thirteen wagons and thirty-six horses hauled "a fifty horsepower boiler and two vacuum pumps, each capable of furnishing 1200 gallons of water per minute" from Green River to near the mouth of the Dirty Devil, now called "Dandy Crossing."[15]

That summer Stanton and Brown floated through a place alive with human activity. Elaborate ditches diverted water from the river to at least three different sandbars, and the pumps were even taking water to sediment bars well above the river level in the adjacent White, Trachyte, and Crescent (North Wash) Canyons.[16] Hite had enticed at least fifty miners to a new settlement named for himself at Dandy Crossing and hundreds more to surrounding areas. He promised claims that were "the richest discovered since the flush times of California," amid a backdrop of "magnificent" scenery and mild year-round climates.[17] Just as Stanton was beginning to believe, this Bad Land was not so bad.

Still, the region remained isolated, certainly more so than the gold fields of California or Colorado (though not so much as the Yukon). Fifty miners certainly would not have constituted a "rush" anywhere but in the Canyon Country, and the Glen Canyon camps lacked any saloons, brothels, or gambling facilities. It is not surprising, then, that when Stanton and Brown floated by the mining camps, announcing that they planned to build a railroad through the canyon, miners were overjoyed at the prospect. Stanton described the economic potential of Glen Canyon and the symbiotic relationship that the railroad and the mining claims could have:

Everyone in this country is highly interested in the [rail]road. We have been greatly surprised at what is told us as to the resources of this country that will give the road local business. It is stated, and from what I think with truth, that there are some 25,000,000 cubic yards of pay gravel that will net 25 cents per yard between the mouth of Cataract Canyon and the San Juan River. These bars are what are on the bluffs above the river and do not include the bars in the river.[18]

The miners at Dandy Crossing went on to extol economic benefits of the Canyon Country that went beyond mining. Stanton learned that the region had as many as "one and one half million cattle tributary to this river which would use this [rail]road, especially as it would be along a river so as to have plenty of water." The area around Cedar Mesa and upper Dark Canyon about twenty miles to the east was valuable timber country and even had maple trees, which one local had used to produce "3000 pounds of sugar!"[19]

As historian C. Gregory Crampton noted, the placer mining figures that Stanton reported are "doubtful," the cattle numbers "too high," and the maple sugar story an obvious "yarn spun for one who was willing to listen."[20] But it is not surprising that people at this remote crossing in the heart of the desert Canyon Country would exaggerate in order to convince a major railway to come through, connecting them to outside markets.

Furthermore, the almost desperate pleas for outside investment by the miners, most of whom were not Mormon, were quite different from the ideals of isolated agrarian self-sufficiency that had marked Mormon missions such as the Hole in the Rock party. Miners wanted outside help in incorporating the Bad Land. This transformation would come by way of industry, not in organically reclaiming a garden from the desert. By the turn of the century even Mormon farmers would begin to join the demands for outside interest and investment.

For Stanton, it probably mattered little whether the Dandy Crossing miners' positive stories were yarns or not. They were only secondary confirmations of what he already knew—the railroad was essential. Unfortunately for Stanton, and fortunately for most of today's preservation-minded Colorado River lovers, the DCC&P Railroad never came to be. Although his second river expedition in 1890 successfully and safely ran the Colorado to the foot of the Grand Canyon and resulted in a general demystification of Powell's dramatic writings, the economic panic of 1890 and subsequent depression caused all investors to pull out of the company. Isolation and marginalization would outlast all of the prospectors at Dandy Crossing.

To the end of his life Stanton held considerable resentment toward financial powers, which he believed had interfered with his pure engineering goals. Writing later of the failed railroad venture, he almost defensively stated that "the commercial question—the value of the whole proposition in 1890, or at the present time, that is, will it pay?—is not within the scope of this work. Conditions have changed materially since 1890, as regards all transcontinental transportation problems, and the question has new aspects."[21] Stanton held to the idea that he could have built his railroad, contrary to naysayers that even included John Wesley Powell, who by this time was exhibiting almost selfish resentment that "anyone else might put foot in *his* canyon or in *his* river."[22] Capitalism and financing only had to catch up to existing technology and ingenuity. From Stanton's perspective during the depression of the 1890s, it was clear where the blame for the railroad's failure lay: in lack of financial interest, not in the Bad Land.

STANTON'S DREDGE

By the early 1890s prospectors like Cass Hite had come to realize the difficulty of separating tiny gold flakes from the Colorado's mud and sand, even with powerful engines, pumps, and vacuums. Writing to the *Beaver Utonian* newspaper in 1893, Hite noted the difference between the "course [*sic*] gold" nuggets of California and Colorado, which were very near their mountain granite sources, and the "fine gold" of Glen Canyon, which had been ground to a flour-like consistency in its journey of hundreds of miles down the river from its origins. In the mountains prospectors could simply sluice gold-containing gravel with clear stream water, allowing heavier gold flakes and nuggets to sink to the bottom. But Hite noted that the Colorado's water supply in Glen Canyon was so muddy itself that tiny gold bits, often as small as 3,000 to a cent, remained suspended in the silt. It was simply too difficult for most individuals to extract gold profitably from Glen Canyon. Hite observed: "I never found anything that a poor man could work, although I am convinced I know of much good gold property in that section that could be worked at a good profit with capital enough to put it in good working order."[23]

A call such as this for a large-scale venture was enough to bring Robert Brewster Stanton back to the Canyon Country. Even after the failure of the DCC&P, he was not finished with the region. With enough ingenuity and capital, he believed that the region would turn a profit beyond the expectations of even its most optimistic prospectors. In late 1897 Stanton returned to the Colorado once more, this time armed with new investors' money. The chief investor and company president of the new Hoskaninni Mining Company (named for a Navajo chief who had hidden from federal troops in Glen Canyon during the 1860s) was Columbus, Ohio, industrialist Julius F. Stone.

With Stanton as chief engineer and superintendent, this was the largest mining venture ever to attempt to exploit Glen Canyon. From 1898 to 1900 employees of the Hoskaninni Company improved the road from Hanksville to Hite, built dams across several of the Colorado's tributary streams to procure clear water for sluicing, planned several low dams across the Colorado itself (which never came to be), and even chipped steps in the steep trail down the old Hole in the Rock trail for easier access to the river.[24]

By the winter of 1897–98 the company had purchased nearly every claim along the Colorado River for $200,000, after which Stanton floated the Colorado again from Hite to Lee's Ferry to inspect these claims. The trip was miserable, including several days of breaking their boats out of ice jams. To this day we do not know if Stanton named one particular camp "Klondike Bar" as an optimistic comparison to that concurrent gold rush or simply because he was cold.[25] Despite the temperatures, Stanton remained his typical upbeat self. On one cold December day he wrote of visiting prospector George Gillham, an amateur inventor who had been experimenting with several small sluicing machines, with little success:

> Mr. G reports that the work of the machine (Little Water Washer) is a failure at working this gravel. There is so much Slimey [sic] mud or "Slums" in the gravel that the water gets thick and carries the gold (and even large pebbles) pass *up* the waste spout. He made various experim'ts in panning this water, the Slums tailings etc. and the results all showed heavy loss. While the panning seemed to save it all.[26]

Unlike Cass Hite, Gillham believed that the only way to extract gold from the muddy Colorado was by individual hard work—panning gravel and mud by hand, with no help from technology. Of course, from Stanton's perspective,

Gillham's problem actually resulted from not having enough machinery and Stanton had the ultimate solution for extracting the wealth of Glen Canyon.

The position of Glen Canyon just below the turbulence of Cataract Canyon's rapids and its relatively level grade made it "nature's sluice-box," according to Stanton. Sediment and gravel from the mountains of Wyoming and Colorado simply dropped heavy gold flakes in the slow water of Glen Canyon. The current of the river swept gold "into the main channel...especially in the level portions of Glen Canyon, the gravel has been washed over and over, and concentrated to a much higher grade."[27] Furthermore, Stanton argued that Glen Canyon's floor was so flat that gold had been distributed along its length completely uniformly. He estimated that all of this great canyon's sediment contained a constant 25 cents of gold per square yard and that extraction would be a "purely mechanical business operation."[28] Finally there was order, even benevolence, in this Bad Land. Perhaps the linear had finally triumphed.

Of course, the means for extracting the gold dust would be very expensive. The main channel of the Colorado, even at its lowest seasonal levels, was thus far inaccessible to individual prospectors. But Stanton had a solution: a giant dredge, powered by a gasoline engine, which could float up and down the Glen Canyon bars as its engineers pleased. From the summer of 1900 to spring of 1901 Hoskaninni employees hauled timber, metal, pipes, boilers, and engines from the railroad depot at Green River to Hanksville and then over rough roads and trails to the Colorado before floating them to the junction of Hall's Creek and assembling them into the dredge. The result was the largest floating structure ever seen in the Canyon Country: 105 feet by 36 feet, powered by five gasoline engines. Forty-six buckets fastened to a chain would dredge up alluvium and dump it into a rotating cylindrical screen, where it would be sprayed with high-pressure water. Tailings were discarded onto a belt and put back into the river, while the finer washed material was sluiced over pans then finally put into a mercury amalgam, producing pure, free gold (see fig. 9.1).[29]

At least that was Stanton's theory. River levels rose and fell erratically that spring, and the huge dredge continuously ran aground. Even worse, the gold particles were still too fine, even for the dredge's elaborate amalgamation

9.1. The Hoskaninni Company's gold dredge in Glen Canyon, 1901. (Photo by R. B. Stanton; courtesy of the Marriott Library Special Collections)

process. On May 7, 1901, Stanton recorded the Hoskaninni Company's total take: $66.95.[30] Operations by the company ceased two days later, the company dissolved, and the dredge was sold to local prospectors for several hundred dollars. For Stanton, this was another failure of capital to provide adequate support, just like the DCC&P. He would later argue that, given more money, he could build four more dredges and fully exploit the canyon. After spending around $300,000 on the venture, however, Stone and the rest of the investors had enough.[31]

In this age of rising industrial integration, monopolies, and robber barons, the Canyon Country had confounded mass production and extraction. While there certainly was gold in Glen Canyon, as well as in the San Juan River and even in the Henry Mountains, individual prospectors with shovels and pans seemed to be the only ones to turn a profit in the region. Just as the cooperative Mormon ranchers in Bluff had succeeded over larger Texas ranchers in the preceding decade, and just as many hardscrabble local prospectors of the mid-twentieth century would sell questionable uranium claims to international corporations, small-time operators prevailed.[32]

The Hoskaninni Company marked the zenith of human activity during the Glen Canyon gold rush. For decades, until its submersion in the waters of Lake Powell, Stanton's dredge served as an Ozymandian monument to river runners, warning them of human folly in a Bad Land. But this was not the last attempt to extract gold mechanically from the Colorado. From 1909 to 1911 Charles H. Spencer, whose visions were perhaps even more grandiose and less grounded than Stanton's, embarked on two unconventional attempts to mine gold from the canyons. First, he attempted to crush stone with steam-powered grinders on the San Juan, reasoning that any gold lying in the sand of the riverbeds would certainly be in the hardened, 200-million-year-old sandstone. When this was unsuccessful, Spencer constructed a hydraulic operation at Lee's Ferry to blast the Chinle shale slopes with water power. To power these hoses, he planned to haul coal from deposits several dozen miles upriver in a 92-foot boat. This also failed: the mudstones and shales of the Chinle Formation were too sticky for sluicing, and the Colorado's current was so strong that the boat had to use all the coal it could carry simply to power itself.[33]

After its gold rush Glen Canyon was a transformed place. Although this placid section of river had long nurtured Indian groups, now the signs of a white American presence were unmistakable. By 1915 travelers in Glen Canyon could see both telegraph lines and Indian footpaths; prehistoric cliff dwellings and the sunken remains of Stanton's dredge; steps chipped in slickrock slopes by Indians to ancient granaries, Spaniards at the Crossing of the Fathers, and Americans at Hole in the Rock; and carvings on rock walls by Indians, trappers, river expeditions, and dozens of prospectors. Glen Canyon and dozens of its tributaries were strewn with, though not overwhelmed by, the marks of humankind.

Furthermore, even after the gold rush the canyons maintained an intangible attraction for some that extended beyond financial gain. Unlike earlier explorers such as Macomb or Frémont, many Glen Canyon miners such as Cass Hite and his brothers Ben and John actually began to appreciate the region for its beauty and isolation and remained there long after the boom years of the rush had ended. Cass lived in the bottom of Ticaboo Canyon below Dandy Crossing until his death in 1914, planting grapes and apricots along the creek bottom. Until the canyon was drowned beneath Lake Powell in the 1960s, Hite's vineyard and orchard reportedly thrived around his neatly fenced grave.[34]

Cass's brother John stayed in Glen Canyon nearly as long and even sent Hoskaninni investor Julius Stone samples of the mineral carnotite from the Chinle Formation of Trachyte Canyon for testing in 1914. When Stone informed him that, though the samples were most definitely radioactive, there was simply no demand for the mineral yet, Hite seemed unfazed by yet another failure.[35] He wrote much later, in the autumn of his life, that he had no regrets over barely eking out a living in "God's Country." "Although I did not make a fortune on the Colorado River I do not regret the time I spent there, there is a fascination about the wild life I lived there that will always be pleasant to think about even if I did not make a fortune."[36]

John Hite, however, was still a minority in his less pragmatic approach to the Canyon Country. Beyond the gold rush of Glen Canyon, Moab and the towns of Castle Valley on the headwaters of the San Rafael were clamoring even more for outside investment to make this landscape productive. In 1897, one year after Utah gained statehood, Moab's *Grand Valley Times* laid out its plan "How to Bring Prosperity" in an editorial. Moab's poverty and isolation were not the fault of its people or even its environment. "Nature here has supplied about all the material that man needs for the production of what he wants." But Southeast Utah could only be "placed on a prosperous basis" if the outside world was let in through better roads.[37] Echoing Stanton's anger at investors, the people of Moab believed that the problem was not the Canyon Country's terrain or aridity but a lack of interest in the region by outside government and capital.

Given the religiously diverse and not exclusively agricultural origins of Moab, such boosterism is not surprising. Moab had long looked to the outside world in ways that more homogeneous Mormon communities did not. By the end of the nineteenth century, however, the Mormon farming towns of Castle Valley—Ferron, Castle Dale, Emery—were perhaps even bolder in their demands for outside capital. Older traditions of self-sufficiency, economic isolation, and largely agricultural sustenance were waning; now residents clamored for outside investment in extractive industries to provide wage-paying jobs. In the early 1900s promoters, investors, and purported reclamationists traveled through Castle Valley and the rugged San Rafael Swell to its east, promising everything from "the greatest oil field in the world" to "homes...for 300 families" on a reservoir oasis in "the heart of Emery County."[38] None of these promises amounted to sustainable communities or economies, and the only successful mining in Emery County to this day is well to the north of the Canyon Country.

TOURISTS IN A BAD LAND

In the midst of these island communities wanting nothing more than to become a part of national market economies—aridity, terrain, and isolation be damned—upper-class outsiders influenced by rising outdoor recreation movements were beginning to appreciate the Canyon Country for completely different reasons.[39] After the Hoskaninni Company's failure, its chief investor Julius Stone presumably would have had enough of the Canyon Country. Robert Brewster Stanton certainly had and was content merely to pontificate about the Canyon Country and Colorado River from the comfort of his Ohio home after the failure of his dredge. Stone, however, remained intrigued by the idea of exploring the region directly. In the fall of 1909 he funded an entirely different type of venture never before seen in the Canyon Country: a privately funded and nominally recreational trip down the Colorado River.

It is unclear if Stone or the four men accompanying him realized that they were pioneering the Canyon Country's place as a tourist destination. In theory their trip had scientific and historical purposes, to "follow the course of Major J. W. Powell" from Green River, Wyoming, to the mouth of the Grand Canyon and to confirm some of Powell's geological observations.[40] The expedition's two hired men, guide Nathaniel Galloway and cook Seymour Dubendorff, were both southern Utah locals who likely saw the trip as just another way to make money in a hardscrabble and difficult region, and they interspersed the trip with trapping forays to supplement their wages.

Furthermore, as of 1909 little to no distinction was made between tourism and exploration in the Canyon Country, and the Stone party certainly had more in common with Powell's expedition than with today's commercial rafting parties. They ran short of food and resorted to pilfering a prospector's garden on the Green River.[41] In Cataract Canyon they came upon several recent camps of a mining party only one day ahead of them that suddenly disappeared, "evidently met with disaster," and drowned in the Big Drop rapids.[42] This was still a dangerous journey.

Yet in a way Stone was doing this simply for fun, not for any original scientific research as Powell had and certainly not for profit as Stanton had. The gap between recreation and vocation became embarrassingly obvious on October 21, when Stone and his custom-made boats that had cost thousands of dollars floated by the two remaining impoverished prospectors at Dandy Crossing, John Hite and Fred Gibbons.[43] By this point the Glen Canyon gold rush was almost completely dead. Gibbons told Stone that it had been over two years since even a wagon from Hanksville had visited Glen Canyon.[44] Many former employees of Stone and Stanton's Hoskaninni Company had never even received their final paychecks.[45] Yet the former company president evidently was still able to afford to fund an expedition merely to enjoy scenery.

Ultimately the intrigue at the surrounding landscape overcame any bitterness that Stone must have felt about the money that he had lost in the Hoskaninni venture. In subsequent recollections of the expedition he said little of passing by the wreckage of his dredge in 1909. Three decades later, however, when he returned to Glen Canyon for yet another expedition at the age of eighty-three, his party stopped to camp at the remains of the dredge. That morning one of the group kindled a fire from pieces of the dredge, and Stone quipped that their morning coffee likely cost him $5,000.[46]

For the rest of Stone's long life (he died in 1947 at the age of ninety-two), his major obsession was the Canyon Country: traveling in it, studying it, and writing about it. In his 1932 work *Canyon Country: The Romance of a Drop of Water and a Grain of Sand*, Stone synthesized the Powell surveys' scientific and aesthetic observations with more down-to-earth relations of the appreciation that locals such as John Hite and Nathaniel Galloway had for the region. Compared to the writings of Powell or even Stanton (and certainly compared to the more sensationalistic "daredevil" accounts of Colorado River running that were widespread by the 1920s), *Canyon Country* refrained from the hyperbole that lent itself so easily to the region, gaining a sort of respect from locals who were suspicious of outsiders coming into their homes.[47] Longtime river guide and ferryman Frank Dodge would write to Stone that *Canyon Country* held a "total lack of exaggeration: the total absence of building up thrills so that the reader really gets a true picture of a river trip."[48]

Stone's 1909 voyage down the Colorado ushered in the age of what we would today call "adventure tourism" in the Canyon Country. Nonprofessional interest in the region was increasing. In 1908 Powell survey veteran Frederick Dellenbaugh published his version of the expedition in *A Canyon Voyage*. The following year—indeed, only months before Stone's river trip, on August 14, 1909—University of Utah antiquities professor Byron Cummings, guided by local John Wetherill and Navajo Nasja Begay, made the much publicized "discovery" of Rainbow Bridge in a remote tributary of Glen Canyon just below the San Juan confluence. While Navajos and Paiutes had certainly known of this awesome natural bridge for centuries, and it is likely that even white prospectors had come upon it in the 1890s, it was the publicity of this dramatic natural feature in the depths of America's last remaining frontier that truly mattered to the American nation.[49]

Within months of the discovery Cummings authored an article in *National Geographic* on "The Great Natural Bridges of Utah." The article, complete with photographs, detailed Rainbow Bridge and three neighboring bridges to the north that had been designated as Natural Bridges National Monument since 1908 (Rainbow Bridge gained a similar designation in 1910).[50] Basing visitation and publicity upon singular natural features such as natural bridges gave a sense of tangibility to the Canyon Country that earlier explorers had been unable to capture. It was impossible to experience the vastness of this country in a lifetime, let alone in a single trip, but it was quite possible to make an expedition through a portion of the country to see a specific feature like Rainbow Bridge. For most of the first half of the twentieth century legislation to protect the Canyon Country's scenic resources was concerned with specific easy-to-define natural features.

Beyond this, however, it became clear to other wealthy adventurers that they could still explore a wild landscape at their leisure and find an adventure in the United States on a par with an African safari or a polar expedition. In 1912 the archetypal tourist-adventurer-conservationist Theodore Roosevelt made the arduous journey over Navajo Mountain and into the canyons, guided by John Wetherill, to see Rainbow Bridge for himself.[51] In response to this new interest in the Canyon Country, some locals who knew the area well from decades of attempted mining, ranching, and trapping discovered a new way of making a living in this Bad Land: guiding. Early guides like John Wetherill of Kayenta, Arizona; Zeke Johnson of Blanding, Utah; Nathaniel and Parley Galloway of Vernal, Utah; and Dave Rust of Kanab, Utah, were at the vanguard, taking customers by horseback over old Indian and rancher trails and by boat down major rivers.

Like Julius Stone, most of the paying clients still thought of themselves as explorers, carrying on the work of Robert Peary or Ernest Shackleton, albeit on a much smaller scale. Also like Stone, some would later publish accounts of their travels that were logical continuations of the Powell narrative. Even with the benefit of a guide, "pleasure" expeditions in the Canyon Country from the 1910s to the 1930s could contain much more isolation and adventure than a sightseeing trip to one of America's more publicized national parks. By this time parks such as Yellowstone, Yosemite, and even the south rim of the Grand Canyon were well established as scenic wonderlands where rangers and concessionaires catered to visitors with railroad spurs, paved roads, and grand lodges.[52] The Canyon Country had none of these. Its few federally protected areas—Natural Bridges and Rainbow Bridge—were national monuments, a designation that received much less publicity, funding, and management than national parks.[53] The explorer-tourists of the Canyon Country saw it very much as a place for active adventurers, not passive sightseeing.

Charles Bernheimer, a millionaire shirt-making magnate and self-described "tenderfoot and cliff dweller from Manhattan," was one such explorer-tourist. From 1921 to 1924 he obsessed over finding an alternate route to Rainbow Bridge from the Navajo town of Kayenta via the north slope of Navajo Mountain or, as he called it, his own "Northwest Passage."[54] Bernheimer knew that these "explorations" were certainly not grand innovations in North American travel. His memoirs are rife with self-deprecating humor as this mild hypochondriac and asthmatic traveled across the Bad Land, "exploring" past inhabited Navajo hogans and sheep herds. More important to him was the illusion of exploration, the unknown, and seeming to be the first in discovering a landscape so completely removed from the comfort of his New York home.[55]

The remoteness and hostile appearance of the Canyon Country provided this illusion of authenticity arguably more than any other landscape in the contiguous United States, especially as the rest of the nation was growing increasingly connected and developed. Guides realized the importance of seeming to be "first" as their clients played explorer and refined the illusion almost to an art form. John Wetherill would frequently point out allegedly "unnamed" buttes, mesas, and spires to clients such as Bernheimer and invite them to name the landforms for themselves or for family members.[56] Zeke Johnson even carried the illusion of discovery to a point that would be illegal today, stashing a Navajo mummy in a cave for clients to dig up repeatedly.[57]

Not surprisingly, many locals in and around the Canyon Country were perplexed as to why rich easterners would spend hundreds or even thousands of dollars to see this Bad Land. For most townspeople living in and around the Canyon Country, the region had long been an obstacle to agrarian progress or more recently a container of minerals or fossil fuels simply needing extraction. Not all locals saw the harsh desert as sentimentally as John Hite at his Glen Canyon hermitage. Perhaps for this reason, when Wall Street attorney George Fraser stopped in Monticello, Utah, with his guide Dave Rust for supplies after a grueling trek from Rainbow Bridge in July 1916, he felt reluctant even to mention being a sightseer to locals. "To say we were looking at the country seemed to be regarded as equivalent to 'none of your business,'" Fraser noted. Instead he told townspeople that he was "just prospecting around" the canyons, a more utilitarian and understandable pastime.[58]

This gap between local and out-of-state tourists' views of the Canyon Country is perhaps illustrated even more profoundly by Bernheimer's account of a July 1920 town gathering in Bluff, on the San Juan River. Between expeditions Bernheimer received an invitation from the town's bishop to give a speech at the local congregation's church. The speech was to be "'arbitration,' a theme particularly appropriate as all government [in Bluff], judicial and otherwise, was on the patriarchal basis of the forefathers, the bishop being arbiter, judge, and father of all his flock."[59] Though Bernheimer wrote nothing of the specifics of his speech, we can certainly imagine this wealthy, worldly New Yorker speaking knowledgeably on broad subjects like Woodrow Wilson's growing unpopularity, the recent world war, Prohibition, women's suffrage, and the upcoming presidential election of 1920 to a group of first and second generation Hole in the Rockers, mostly women.[60]

After Bernheimer's elaborate lecture he received only one question, from an older woman whom he called "Aunt Mary." Probably trusting his financial insights, Mary simply wanted to know if the price of sugar would drop that fall, as the town was unable to can any fruits for the winter with current prices. This simple question struck Bernheimer, who would reflect that "arbitration and other world questions were…secondary to her world of vision…Aunt Mary was right to shift the discussion to the actual needs of the town."[61] The divide between local concerns about living in an isolated, harsh country and wealthy tourists who sought out that very isolation and harshness was immense.

This vanguard of upper-class adventurer-tourists in the Canyon Country in many ways reveled in how completely separate the region was from the nation and commerce that had given them their wealth. Julius Stone, who owed a significant part of his fortune to Appalachian coal country, only made note of the Canyon Country's Cretaceous coal country in abstract geologic terms; he neither explicitly nor implicitly called for mineral exploitation in the region as Stanton had done.[62] Stone had made his wealth elsewhere and could afford to see the Canyon Country as an avocation.

Furthermore, though a mere "tourist," Stone also adopted the mantle of the older nineteenth-century explorer-aristocrat and portrayed the Canyon Country as a repository of solid objective truth. Earlier Spaniards or Mormons could see this New World desert in Old Testament terms as a place for trial and redemption by their God. Stone, however, saw the complex region as a place more for engaged, educated visitors to discover secrets; all others "who never look below or beyond the surface of things are shut out from the greatest enchantments Nature can bestow. There is a far finer joy in knowing a thing is *true* than in saying it is *wonderful*." He even went on to criticize religion in the obstruction of the Canyon Country's revealed truth: "Nature cannot reveal all the glad surprises held in store if our eyes are dazzled by the presence of imaginary gods that exist only for the purpose of dancing attendance on the childish credulity of our prayers, and which have the effect of making the universe so pleasantly incomprehensible to the timid."[63]

We do not know how much forceful statements such as this were shaped by the dozens of nightly campfire discussions that Stone had with his Mormon guides along the Colorado River. It is clear that to him, however, the Canyon Country was no longer a haven for God's people: it required the careful, rational observations of the scientist-explorer.

Religious test-piece or rational font of knowledge, the Canyon Country remained a landscape completely separate from the rest of the United States. As the first recreational tourists were riding to Rainbow Bridge or floating down the Colorado, the region still rejected nearly all attempts to incorporate it agriculturally. Its mineral wealth remained inaccessible and untapped. No railroad managed to penetrate its interior. Throughout the 1920s its people remained impoverished, barely noticing the financial crises of 1929 and beyond. As one traveler to Moab, Dr. J. E. Broaddus, noted in 1930, its people were still "more or less isolated and live without any of the ordinary conveniences of life. If they were not imbued with the pioneer spirit they would have moved years ago."[64]

Despite whatever curiosity, apprehension, or suspicion locals may have felt about the first tourists in the Canyon Country, however, it became increasingly clear that the very elements that had so confounded previous attempts to incorporate it might actually be resources. With the right development and help from outside, the scenery itself could pay. The type of adventure tourism that Dave Rust and John Wetherill were promoting clearly would provide no profit beyond salaries for a few guides. But what if the Canyon Country were to garner the same type of public attention as the Grand Canyon, Yellowstone, or Yosemite? Even southwestern Utah was starting to reap the economic rewards of Bryce and Zion, both recently promoted from their lowly national monument status to full national parks.[65]

The ever-present problem of access to this remote region still remained, however. Bryce and especially Zion lay near major routes from Utah to southern California; the Canyon Country was en route to nowhere. In a passionate plea Dr. Broaddus called for state and national attention to be given to the Canyon Country in the form of roads for automobiles:

The commonwealth of Utah cannot afford to let one fifth of its land which contains incomparable scenery lie idle and useless for want of a road...We owe something to the people...Hope keeps them here, hope of better conditions for the country they have learned to love, hope that they may find employment for their children so they may remain at home. It is a worthy ambition and one that should be aided.[66]

Industrial incorporation had failed. Farming and mining were only possible on subsistence levels. Ranching had only been profitable for a few. But perhaps visitation, paved roads, national park designation, and tourist dollars could finally bring Eden to this Bad Land.

Coda

For sixteen days in September 1922 a small party of Utahns took a scenic detour: Salt Lake City to Flagstaff, Arizona, via the Canyon Country. From Richfield they drove new automobiles over rough roads to the headwaters of the Fremont River and descended into the jumble of slickrock canyons around Fruita, Utah, that would later become Capitol Reef National Park.[1] The going was rough, especially through the deep sands of Capitol Gorge, and when the party members reached the tiny outpost settlement of Notom, they switched to horse-drawn wagons. From there they turned south, making their way through the rough desert between the uplifted Waterpocket Fold and the Henry Mountains, eventually descending into the huge canyon of Grand Gulch, which the diminutive Hall's Creek had carved on its trickle toward the Colorado River.[2] At one point the gorge became so narrow that it forced the wagons into a detour high over a ridge to the east. Still, several members of the party opted to walk and wade through the magnificent overhanging alcoves, pools, and winding slots that allowed only foot travel, simply to see what there was to see. After reaching the Colorado for a rendezvous with boats, the men drifted downstream for several days before emerging from Glen Canyon at Lee's Ferry, where they resumed their automobile trip to Flagstaff and finally boarded a train east to Santa Fe, New Mexico.

Among this group was John Widtsoe: agricultural scientist, former university president, and recently ordained Mormon apostle.[3] For decades he had also been an enthusiastic proponent of dry-farming, the practice of relying solely upon rainfall for water. In his 1911 book *Dry-Farming: A System of Agriculture for Countries under a Low Rainfall* Widtsoe had laid out plans for farming in Bad Lands that even irrigation could not reclaim, prophesying a time when the "desert is seen covered with blossoming fields, with churches and homes and schools, and, in the distance, with the vision is heard the laughter of happy children."[4]

Through the 1910s hundreds of Mormon farmers, spurred on by Widtsoe's optimistic analyses of the West's higher than average precipitation (the same rains that had recently destroyed Caineville), moved away from existing irrigation infrastructures into arid regions such as the high desert of Park Valley in northwestern Utah and portions of Kane County in the western Canyon Country. One of Widtsoe's most fervent followers, Canyon Country guide Dave Rust, even established small dry-farms near his tourist camps in the depths of the Grand Canyon.[5] All of these ventures were short-lived, especially Rust's.

It is easy to assume that Widtsoe, as both a Mormon and a "scientific" reclamationist, would have thought of nothing but turning this Bad Land green as he traveled through it. His 1922 scenic detour, however, somehow changed his attitude from the relatively simplistic rhetoric of *Dry-Farming*. His brief account of the journey is a rich combination of scientific analysis and aesthetic reverence on a par with the writings of John Newberry or Clarence Dutton. While Widtsoe did occasionally mention the trials of his Mormon forefathers in the Hole in the Rock party and never failed to note scattered pockets of potential farmland in the desert, he also revered the harsh country for the way in which it had forged and tempered earlier Mormons much more than he disdained it.[6] There was more to this country than simply the agricultural.

Widtsoe was also quick to point out the limitations of industrial society in this region. Passing by the remains of Charles Spencer's ill-fated coal operation in Glen Canyon on September 16, he wrote: "In the river a few rods from the Ferry lies a steamboat, half submerged in the sand with a steam boiler, two smokestacks, etc., exposed. Another steam engine plant, partly dismantled, lies further on. Wrecks of human ambition lie scattered all about. It is an interesting commentary on how the world is conquered."[7] While not dismissing the potential of modern technology and enterprise that was so rapidly evolving by the 1920s, Widtsoe still carried some of the older, Brigham Young–era Mormon distrust for commercialism and unchecked mineral greed. He could look down knowingly, almost smugly, at the failures of the Glen Canyon gold rush.

But above all Widtsoe was simply taken aback by the beauty of the region. Traveling through what would become Capitol Reef National Park, he and his fellow delegates marveled at the slot canyons and the exposed geology and rushed about to gather arrowheads and other archaeological artifacts that the desert had preserved. He could not see why this area did not receive the federal protection and promotion that full-fledged national parks such as the Grand Canyon received: "To go down this way, then up the river and back by way of Hanksville would be one of the great trips of the world. Publicity should be given to this region." Joining his faith with this aesthetic appreciation, he later waxed religious on the mastery of a God who had created the majestic Rainbow Bridge.[8] Although Widtsoe never explicitly said it, perhaps he believed that his God meant for people to thrive upon tourism in this land where agriculture and mining never succeeded beyond subsistence levels.

For all the awe that he expressed at the untouched creation of his God, however, Widtsoe was not above promoting Progressive doctrines that human ingenuity, especially with government support, could vastly improve this region. In addition to calling for promotion and more national park designation, he saw no conflict between the enjoyment of nature and further development and reclamation of precious water resources. In the drainage of Grand Gulch he noted high water marks showing the awesome levels to which the trickle of Hall's Creek could swell during floods. Why not create small dams along the drainage to store these huge—if ephemeral—surpluses of water? They would not only prevent the types of disasters that had befallen Caineville and Pahreah but would open even more pockets of irrigable land.[9]

In the end Widtsoe admitted that dams such as these were simply too remote and floods too erratic; no irrigated villages would ever sprout along

Hall's Creek. During his detour through the Canyon Country, Widtsoe had not only observed the past failures of the Canyon Country. He also had hinted at what was to come for the region: conservation, reclamation, and recreation. But Widtsoe's foray through the western Canyon Country had not been a mere pleasure trip of the sort that Stone, Bernheimer, or Fraser enjoyed. He was part of a Utah delegation en route to a Santa Fe conference set to draft the Colorado River Compact, which would allot the waters of the Canyon Country's main hydraulic artery among its seven states.

By the 1920s it was clear that the Canyon Country would somehow have to contribute to and be incorporated by the nation's escalating economy and ever-increasing optimism, despite the repeated failures of the past decades and centuries. This complicated, perhaps unknowable land and its rivers simply had to fit into the American consciousness, if not through traditional agriculture or mineral exploitation then perhaps through the tourism that some towns had been promoting, at which Widtsoe had hinted. The most thorough and transformative exploitation of the region would not come through its land, however, but from the very rivers that flowed through the canyons on their journeys from the Rockies to the Gulf of California.

Robert Brewster Stanton had failed in his objective to conquer the Bad Land through engineering ingenuity, but his ideological heirs persisted as they increasingly looked upon the Colorado and its tributaries as sources of potential hydroelectricity, if not mineral wealth or railroad routes. While Stanton had planned a few small dams across Glen Canyon tributaries and even the Colorado itself as power sources for mining machinery, it was not until 1916 that Eugene Clyde LaRue seriously called for a large dam across the river in the Canyon Country. In addition to controlling floods, storing water, and generating power, a dam around the Utah-Arizona state line, just above Lee's Ferry, could effectively regulate water use across political boundaries of the upper basin states of Utah, Wyoming, Colorado, and New Mexico and the lower states of Arizona, California, and Nevada.[10]

Glen Canyon was not the only site where hydrologists considered building dams. Indeed, beginning in 1921, crews with funding from both the U.S. Geological Survey and private power companies, under the direction of secretary of commerce Herbert Hoover, had surveyed all of the major river canyons of the San Juan, Green, and Colorado Rivers, noting dozens of suitable future dam sites. The first of these large dams was, of course, Hoover's namesake below the Grand Canyon, in 1930. While almost none of the reclaimed water would ever turn the Bad Land of the Canyon Country itself green, the eventual creation of Lake Powell in the mid-1900s flooded nearly all of Glen Canyon while creating a recreational motorboater's Mecca, forever changing the heart of the Canyon Country.

Despite the views of his Mormon predecessors, and despite his own previously published goals of establishing dry farms in deserts, John Widtsoe realized that the incorporation and exploitation of the Canyon Country would not come through simple individual or collective farming. The time had come to let the rest of the industrialized United States into the Bad Land, both as tourists and as large-scale, federally funded dam builders. In many ways Widtsoe's visions embodied the Progressivist impulses for conservation, efficiency, and the triumph of educated professionals over nature that had crested through the rest of the nation during the previous decade. Change came more slowly to the Canyon Country than to the rest of the nation, after all.[11]

Another notion arrived rather late in the Canyon Country, however: the aesthetic, reverential view of the wilderness preservationist. Nearly ten years before the Colorado River Compact authorized dams and the allotment of the Colorado, mainstream conservationists such as Gifford Pinchot had battled preservationists such as John Muir over the damming of the Tuolomne River in Yosemite National Park's Hetch Hetchy Valley.[12] This well-known episode came to serve as a rallying cry for future advocates of protected wilderness areas within national parks and beyond.

Given the Canyon Country's isolation from any population centers, and the fact that very few people knew it well (even John Muir himself visited only the popular Grand Canyon), debates such as the Hetch Hetchy controversy would not occur there until much later. Whenever early observers marveled at the Canyon Country's scenic wonders, their awe was nearly always, like Widtsoe's or Dr. Broaddus's, accompanied by the lament that few people could ever see the region's beauty in its present state and a call to state and federal governments to build more roads to the area. Until the end of the

1920s few if any people wanted the Canyon Country simply to be left as it was, wilderness or not.

The subsequent bitter debates between preservationists and advocates for further development, a uranium boom, and the damming of Glen Canyon are all topics for the industrialized, modernized twentieth century and beyond this story's largely premodern scope. Indeed, stories of farmers, explorers, and mapmakers simply trying to make the Bad Land Good seem quaint when compared with the much better documented twentieth-century Canyon Country. The common thread running through all of these narratives, however, is that nearly all people who feel strongly about the Canyon Country—water developers, mining speculators, tourist promoters, and even self-identified environmentalist nature lovers—continue to impose lofty expectations upon its rivers, soils, and minerals and are often unable to accept it on its own complex terms.

In the twentieth and early twenty-first centuries we have seen this in the debates concerning wilderness designation and restrictions on extractive industries and commercial development in the region. After the completion of Glen Canyon Dam and the passage of the Wilderness Act, both in 1964, more people than ever saw the Canyon Country as not only a uniquely beautiful place but a refuge from a corrupt modern world that needed protection. It was still a landscape completely unlike the rest of the nation, but now with beneficial purposes. In 1968 Edward Abbey's *Desert Solitaire: A Season in the Wilderness* was published. This narrative of Abbey's time as a seasonal ranger in Arches National Park would forever link him to the Canyon Country and draw thousands of new, often counterculture-associated wilderness enthusiasts to the region, ironically crowding its canyons in their search for Abbey's romanticized solitude.

In *Desert Solitaire* Abbey simultaneously condemned not only the encroachment of mining, logging, and water interests into the Canyon Country but also increased development of roads, manicured trails, and other elements of "industrial tourism" that the National Park Service was pushing on its lands.[13] This indictment struck at the heart of what many locals had been demanding for years—infrastructure to bring more people and more revenue to the region. As hostility to the apparently nonlucrative "wilderness" designation increased, southern Utah residents began to decry federal intrusions on land use while simultaneously demanding federal money for road projects, an attitude described by Bernard DeVoto much earlier as "Get out and give us more money."[14]

The vision of prosperity that most residents of the communities surrounding the Canyon Country held had been consistent for generations: they desired small national parks and monuments centered around specific landmarks, not vast ecosystems, which were neither remote nor untouched wildernesses. They hoped that ample paved roads to attract money-spending motorists would link these tourist attractions, while the rest of the non–national park lands remained open to extractive industries such as mining and grazing. This completely opposed the anticonsumerist ideas of Abbey and later wilderness advocates for the region. They argued not only that essentially the entire southeastern corner of Utah had sufficient aesthetic value to be one large national park but that it should be an unpaved, undeveloped outback for hikers who presumably would spend very little money in local motels, restaurants, or gas stations.

The anticonsumerist fixation on wilderness has perhaps begun to seem trite after September 11, 2001, especially with the more recent economic downturn and calls for domestic energy independence. Following the 2010 elections in which the far-right and antipreservationist "Tea Party" dominated, Utah governor and former realtor Gary Herbert has aggressively pushed for more state ownership of federal lands that make up much of the Canyon Country and fewer roadless wilderness areas.

Even wilderness advocates such as the Southern Utah Wilderness Alliance have in some ways turned away from their anticonsumerist roots and argued the case for wilderness in the Canyon Country in economic terms. According to this new argument, an "amenities" economy in southern Utah towns, catering to adventure tourism and wilderness enthusiasts, could replace old extractive industries and bring prosperity to Canyon Country communities. Even this view of the Canyon Country has profound problems, however, as voiced by regional writer Jim Stiles in his recent essay "The Greening of Wilderne$$ in Utah." He argues that the Canyon Country should not be reduced to any sort of commodity, wilderness or otherwise, and that the region is in equal danger of being "loved to death" or being destroyed by dams, overgrazing, mining, and highway construction. The current condition of Moab supports Stiles's point, as well-meaning backpackers clog popular canyons and environmentally sympathetic Canyon Country lovers build vacation homes in new housing developments.[15]

The roots of locals' apprehension over large amounts of federally protected wilderness in the Canyon Country extend far back to the New Deal era. In 1936, in the wake of the Colorado River Compact, increased automobile visits to national parks through the nation, and a gradually stronger federal presence in the area, Franklin Roosevelt's Interior secretary Harold Ickes proposed a huge new "Escalante National Monument" over the areas of both Glen Canyon and the confluence of the Green and Colorado Rivers. We will never know exactly how this park would have affected future mining or grazing interests in the area and it probably would not have prevented the future Glen Canyon Dam from being built, because powerful water interests had already staked their claim in the Canyon Country.[16] The monument still encountered bitter opposition from state and county-level politicians, however, as well as from most residents of the Canyon Country's nearby communities.

The reasons for this opposition were complex but would resonate with anyone familiar with the Canyon Country wilderness designation controversies of the later twentieth or twenty-first centuries. They included the regular rural western, proto-libertarian distrust of New Deal federal intervention, which had recently imposed restrictions on the livestock use of federal land with the Taylor Grazing Act of 1934.[17] Opposition was also based on the attitude that national monument designation would hinder potentially lucrative mining in the area, although the prosperity of the uranium boom was still over a decade into the future. Most of all, however, the proposed monument was simply too big. At almost 7,000 square miles, it would have occupied nearly all of the present boundaries of Capitol Reef and Canyonlands National Parks, Grand Staircase–Escalante National Monument, and Glen Canyon National Recreation Area.

While Utah's governor Henry Blood conceded "frankly that scenery and recreation were the most important economic assets of the state," he and most other Utahns preferred small monuments such as Arches, Rainbow Bridge, or Natural Bridges.[18] Furthermore, the idea of creating a national monument with the stroke of a president's pen rather than through representative legislation angered residents of an area that had long been marginalized as a territory by the rest of the nation. Governor Blood worried that "some morning we may wake up and find that…the Escalante National Monument has been created by Presidential proclamation, and then it will be too late to forestall what we in Utah think would be a calamity."[19]

Blood's fears of federal forces making decisions contrary to local interests would be realized almost prophetically in 1996, when Bill Clinton designated much of the original area of the proposed Escalante National Monument in the new "Grand Staircase–Escalante National Monument." Though it may have been mainly a political move (Clinton had no votes to lose in conservative Utah, but the action may have won him Arizona in the November election), this was a victory for wilderness advocates nationwide. Many locals still remember it with hate.

Two Views of a New "Wilderness" in the Canyon Country

As the Canyon Country was becoming slightly less unknown and heading toward the controversies of the proposed national monument, two young men visited the region who would embody the intrigue and reverence that later, post-Abbey hikers and campers would bring to the canyons. Both Clyde Kluckhohn and Everett Ruess, who visited the Escalante area in 1927 and 1934, respectively, sought out the Canyon Country as a place to come of age and develop their manhood free from the constraints of modern society in true *Bildungsroman* fashion. The two men valued it as an undeveloped, wild, and even dangerous place.

Though both from upper-middle class backgrounds, Kluckhohn and Ruess were not wealthy expeditioners in the mold of Julius Stone or Charles Bernheimer. Their trips were do-it-yourself, budget affairs, with no professional guides, muleskinners, or camp cooks. In this sense they were forerunners of the anticonsumerist backpackers that today's Canyon Country locals sometimes resent for not contributing to local economies: Utah representative James Hansen complained that they "come in with a twenty dollar bill and the same underwear, and…do not change either one of them while they are here for twenty days or so."[20] At the same time these vanguards of modernity were among the last of the horseback-based "explorers" before the popularity of the automobile.

Each of the men's visits culminated in the drainage of the Escalante River. The Escalante, named for the friar who never saw it, is today a popular back-packing and canyoneering destination, known for its verdant stream bottoms, arches, and soaring, cathedral-like canyon walls. Geologically and emotion-ally, many feel that it is reminiscent of what was lost in Glen Canyon under the waters of Lake Powell. Despite its growing popularity, solitude is still easy to come by in dozens of tributary canyons. The Escalante also has long been a very isolated part of the isolated Canyon Country. A. H. Thompson and Jacob Hamblin had traversed its upper reaches with the Powell surveys of the 1870s, the San Juan Mission party had skirted its canyon's rims en route to Hole in the Rock in 1880, and the basin's maze of streams and canyons was still a sort of no-man's-land frontier between Mormondom and the Navajo reservation even in the 1920s.

Kluckhohn's experiences with the Canyon Country began to the south, in the country of the Navajo Indians, to whom he would later devote his career as an anthropologist. Beginning in 1925, when he was still an undergradu-ate at Princeton, Kluckhohn embarked on a series of horse and mule trips across the Navajo Reservation, first to Shiprock, then to Canyon de Chelly, and finally to Rainbow Bridge. Just these travels entailed more area than most Canyon Country visitors see in a lifetime. Kluckhohn's account *To the Foot of the Rainbow* (1927) likened the journey to a pilgrimage that culminated at the sacred Rainbow Bridge. This was not enough for Kluckhohn, however, as he looked from Rainbow Bridge toward the Escalante region, across the Colo-rado and beyond even the guiding routes of John Wetherill. Kluckhohn had to go deeper into the Bad Land, *Beyond the Rainbow*, as his 1933 account of the expeditions was titled.

Kluckhohn's specific destination across the Colorado was not the Escalante River or its canyons but the high country just southwest of the river. Explorers had named it the Kaiparowits Plateau; locals still call it Fifty Mile Mountain. Kluckhohn, steeped in romanticism, called it Wild Horse Mesa. This was never a common name for the plateau and seems to have been limited mainly to clients of John Wetherill's guiding business out of Kayenta, Arizona. Indeed, concurrently with Kluckhohn's explorations, Western novelist and frequent Wetherill client Zane Grey authored a book called *Wild Horse Mesa* (1928), based upon the little-known region. Whatever the origins of the name, it represented the romantic and unknown to Kluckhohn. One of Wetherill's employees, no doubt accustomed to whetting potential clients' interests with tall tales, told Kluckhohn what he had heard about the plateau:

> When you get to the top of that little rise where you'll find your last Navajo hogan, look off to the north and west and you'll see a big high mesa stretchin' back a hundred miles into Utah. It's way over across the San Juan and Colorado, way beyond Rainbow Bridge, and they say no white man's ever been on it. Zane Grey tried to get there this last year, but the river was too high, and he didn't make it. Some people say there's Mormon villages of "sealed wives" on top of it, but I can tell you there ain't nothing to that. Nobody could ever get on top of that mesa.[21]

This mythical place immediately intrigued Kluckhohn. For him, it repre-sented "the longing for wide, open spaces implicit in every human being" and "the lust for danger and adventure in exploration and discovery." As a college student eager to tie this remote corner of the nation to ideas such as Fred-erick Jackson Turner's frontier exceptionalism, Kluckhohn would go on to write that for "Americans this memory [of exploration and discovery] is fresh and strong" and that even in New Mexico and Arizona he felt "crowded even by Mexicans and Indians, with the Machine Age too close." This was Kluck-hohn's personal frontier. It was time to close it.[22]

Kluckhohn actually attempted to reach the top of the mesa twice, in 1926 and 1927, before finally succeeding in 1928. His final successful expedition, with several college companions, was almost farcical in his account, though it could easily have proven tragic. Kluckhohn himself, despite his past trips, was still inexperienced with handling pack mules over slickrock trails, and his friends were even more inept. Their "expedition" lost trails, killed several pack mules in falls, and nearly drowned while crossing the Colorado. But they finally did succeed in reaching Kluckhohn's three-year objective: the mythical lofty heights of Wild Horse Mesa.

The cool plateau top, with ample grass feed, evergreen trees, and springs, proved welcome to Kluckhohn's party after over a week in the hot desert: "we had expected inferno, but we found paradise."[23] It appeared that his romantic expectations were fulfilled, and he had stumbled upon an untouched Eden in the wilderness. But this was not to be. Upon closer inspection of the mesa-top, Kluckhohn found campfire remains, littered tin cans, and inscriptions on rocks by cowboys from the town of Escalante.[24] Ironically, he had traveled the most difficult route to the Mesa, avoiding the trails of ranchers and prospectors coming from the north, and contriving his own wilderness quest. He had forgotten, perhaps as Turner had, that one person's frontier is another's backyard.

But to Kluckhohn it mattered little that his Virgin Land was not what he had expected:

> Had our introduction to this region been from the Utah side, we should doubtless have heard of the cow outfits. The Mesa must be better known in Utah...But, though the trading posts of the northern Navajo Reservation are as close in miles to the Utah ranches as they are to Flagstaff, the Colorado severs Utah and Arizona so completely that there is no exchange of news between north and south. We had been so long steeped in the Arizona beliefs about the Mesa that the finding of dates, initials, and cattle altered our fundamental attitudes but little. Psychologically, Wild Horse Mesa was still the one virgin outpost of the vanishing frontier. Psychologically we claimed the Mesa as our domain by right of discovery, and we had all the thrill of getting to know it that a Spanish Grandee or an English Cavalier must have had in exploring the unknown slice of New Spain or Virginia granted him by his King.[25]

Similar to generations of backpackers after him, somehow the Canyon Country was still Kluckhohn's personal frontier; that was what was truly important. However many cattle ranchers, prospectors, or fellow hikers have come before today's Canyon Country visitors, the vast otherworldly nature of the land still provides the illusion of discovery and exploration.

Beyond the personal and introspective, however, Kluckhohn wondered to himself how the authenticity of his experience, however illusory it might be, could best be preserved for future visitors. Initially he thought, like many, that the beauty of the region unequivocally deserved full national park status. Kluckhohn backed away from this thought quickly, however, and settled on a more subtle conclusion:

> this is not a cheap scenery; it must be bought with time and sweat. At Grand Canyon one does get cheap scenery in this sense. One can look down into Grand Canyon without having abandoned a single comfort or luxury, while the view from the rims of Wild Horse Mesa is purchased at high price, and perhaps is therefore understood and appreciated more.[26]

National park status for this region seemed "a little too near commercialized wilderness" for Kluckhohn. Somehow the Kaiparowits, Escalante canyons, and even the whole Glen Canyon region needed protection without the promotion and development of modern national parks, with their paved roads, visitors' centers, and grand lodges. Kluckhohn believed that the region needed some other sort of designation as "a national preserve denied to settlement."[27] Though he did not elaborate further, he was proposing a type of protection quite ahead of its time that would not see realization until the passage of the 1964 Wilderness Act, which legally defined a "wilderness" as a place "untrammeled by man."[28] Ironically, Kluckhohn's own Wild Horse Mesa wilderness was anything but untrammeled (see fig. 10.1).

Everett Ruess was nine years younger than Kluckhohn, his father a Harvard-educated Unitarian minister and his mother a patron of the San Francisco arts scene. Even in the depths of the Great Depression Ruess was a child of relative affluence. From his high school graduation in 1930 to 1934 he wandered the desert Southwest accompanied only by a dog or perhaps a burro, living off of artwork sales, the generosity of locals, or, when all else failed, funds sent by his parents. Though he initially stayed away from the Canyon Country, he did follow the paths of Kluckhohn around the Navajo Country to Rainbow Bridge, Mesa Verde, and Canyon de Chelly. Like Kluckhohn, he met veteran guide John Wetherill, who apparently did not hold Ruess in high regard and considered him a bit of a "pest."[29]

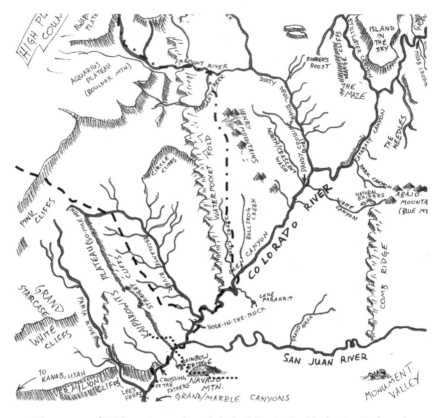

10.1. The routes of Widstoe (1922: dotted-dashed line), Kluckhohn (1928: dotted line), and Ruess (1934: dashed line) through the Canyon Country. (Map by author)

Ruess's substantial collection of letters, poetry, and woodcuts shows a young man on a mystical quest for the ultimate aesthetic experience. While he shared Kluckhohn's apprehensions about modern industrial society, his writings lacked Kluckhohn's concerns about the externalized social and cultural values of wilderness areas. Ruess wished simply to lose himself in natural beauty, cut himself off from the superficiality of urban American culture, and build a direct personal relationship with sublime landscapes. In the late fall of 1934 this quest brought him to the town of Escalante.

Rather than ascend the heights of the Kaiparowits as Kluckhohn had done, Ruess left Escalante via the old Hole in the Rock trail with vague plans to explore the maze of sandstone canyons that drained into the Escalante River. In a November 11 letter to his brother he wrote:

As to when I shall return to civilization, it will not be soon. I think I have not tired of the wilderness; rather I enjoy its beauty and the vagrant life I lead more keenly all the time. I prefer the saddle to the streetcar and star-sprinkled sky to a roof, the obscure and difficult trail leading into the unknown, to any paved highway, and the deep peace of the wild to the discontent bred by cities. Do you blame me then for staying here, where I feel that I belong and am one with the world around me?[30]

After this the details of Ruess's adventure are hazy. He followed the trail about fifty miles southeast of Escalante, plateau on his right, canyons on his left. He was not completely alone—a week into his journey he shared a camp with two local herders and declined their offer of a mutton side.[31] Shortly thereafter he veered east, taking a rough route to the floor of Davis Gulch, a tributary of the Escalante River. He left his two burros in a crude brush corral, with easy access to grass and water, and probably then began exploring the scenic little canyon. He may have wandered upstream, to the canyon's impassable dry waterfall, or downstream, past an angular arch and to the river. He also searched out the canyon's abundant archaeological sites, marveling at a pictograph panel, carving his pseudonym "NEMO, 1934" nearby, and arranging four prehistoric pots at the base of the panel into a sort of altar.[32]

After entering Davis Gulch around the third week of November, Ruess simply disappeared. Through the winter his parents worried about his lack of letters but were not surprised at first; he had gone for long periods without writing during his wilderness sojourns before. Eventually, however, it became clear that Ruess was missing. On March 1 a search party from Escalante followed his tracks into Davis Gulch. Although he had written earlier that "when I go, I leave no trace," abundant signs indicated that he had spent some time in the canyon bottom: his rock carvings, boot prints, bridles, rope, and plenty of garbage scattered around.[33] The two burros even remained in the corral, starving but alive. His art supplies, cook set, and journal were missing.

In the years since his disappearance, and especially since Edward Abbey boosted interest in the Canyon Country in the late 1960s, Ruess has become a sort of cult figure among many enthusiasts of the region, who see him in almost martyr-like terms, as someone who gave himself completely to this

beautiful but unforgiving land. There is an annual "Everett Ruess Days" festi-
val in Escalante, the Southern Utah Wilderness Alliance uses one of his woodcuts in its logo, and bookstores in and around Canyon Country national
parks are always amply stocked with various biographies and collections of
his journals and sketches.

Not surprisingly, there are also many theories regarding his disappearance
or death. He could have fallen off a cliff into an inaccessible slot, and his body
washed away in a flash flood toward the Colorado. He may have taken his
"Nemo" identity seriously, crossed the Colorado to the Navajo Reservation,
romantically married into the tribe, and remained hidden for the rest of his
life. Or he may have been murdered.[34] Of the many variations on this murder
theme, one particular version is more common among southern Utah cattle
ranchers than among modern-day Ruess enthusiasts. It follows this rough
scenario: two Escalante cowboys come across the young man on the benches
above Davis Gulch. He has just killed one of their cows and is in the process
of butchering it. They shoot him and bury his body.

While this story is no more or less reliable than other theories concerning
Ruess's disappearance, its symbolism, if not its accuracy, is important. Ruess
clearly saw the desert as a refuge away from all people where he could live by
and for himself, finding individual abundance in a region that mass society
had rejected for its sparse resources. It may not have occurred to him from
this romanticized perspective that less affluent users of the region saw it not
as a sanctuary for voluntary withdrawal but as a place where it was very hard
to make any sort of living in the best of scenarios, let alone in the hard times
of the Great Depression.

At the same time many of those living around the Canyon Country were
becoming concerned with the ways in which outsiders were viewing the
region. Against the backdrop of federal restrictions on grazing and the threat
of national monument designation, here was a vagabond artist with the time
and resources simply to wander about in the desert before killing local livestock. This was not the type of increased visitation that local towns wished to
attract. To this day similar resentment sometimes still arises between locals
and wilderness enthusiasts in Escalante, albeit with none of the fatal conse-
quences of the supposed Ruess story.[35]

In the end the experiences of both Ruess and Kluckhohn dramatically changed their perspectives on the Canyon Country. Each young man expected an untouched wilderness or a refuge from the modern world, but their idea of exactly what "wilderness" was proved to be highly relativistic. Kluckhohn's journey confirmed, rather humorously, that his expected frontier on Wild Horse Mesa was actually the cattle range of Fifty Mile Mountain. Ruess's assumption that the Bad Land was more a refuge than a harsh desert likely proved fatal, and his sad story has become one of several in which a not-so-nurturing wilderness repays love with death.[36]

BAD LANDS AND WILDERNESS: A LANDSCAPE OF EXTREMES

This new, more personal appreciation of idealized wilderness that so intrigued Ruess and Kluckhohn was yet another chapter in a long series of false assumptions and expectations about the Canyon Country. Though still one of the most isolated regions in the United States, the Canyon Country of the 1930s was no more an untouched wilderness than Teguayo had been a lush grassy plain to Fray Jerónimo Zárate y Salmerón in 1626, the Río de Tizón a haven of monsters to Juan María Antonio de Rivera in 1765, the Grand-Green confluence a worthless wasteland to John Macomb in 1858, or the Paria River a redeemed oasis to Bishop Allen Smithson in 1878. In speculating about and observing the region of the Canyon Country throughout the centuries, all of these men, including Kluckhohn and Ruess, were imposing preconceived assumptions upon an unfamiliar, "other" landscape.

This is the common thread that runs through nearly all perceptions of the region and connects mapmakers of the sixteenth century to tourists of the twenty-first. The Canyon Country has always been a profoundly misunderstood region and continues to be one to this day. It is no surprise that modern proponents of extractive industries and increased development in the area ignore the Canyon Country's repeated confounding of past efforts. Perhaps more subtly today's wilderness advocates continue to assume that it is simply "virgin land" to be completely protected from all outside forces, ignoring the ways in which longtime locals have continued to live in the Bad Land—sometimes struggling, rarely thriving, but always knowing and loving the harsh landscape in ways incomprehensible to mere visitors.

In his essay "The Trouble with Wilderness," William Cronon argues that the idea of wilderness as officially established in 1964 (and as envisioned by Kluckhohn in 1928) actually negatively establishes a "set of bipolar moral scales in which the human and the non-human, the unnatural and the natural, the fallen and the unfallen, serve as our conceptual map for understanding and valuing the world."[37] By labeling certain areas as "untouched" or "virgin," we both denigrate other landscapes and establish expectations for "wildernesses" that they may never be able to fulfill, as Kluckhohn realized so humorously on his Wild Horse Mesa. Whether in dismissing it as simply Bad Land, as I have emphasized in these pages, or seeking it out as wilderness, we have always viewed the Canyon Country through a particularly polarized, dichotomized lens. This land that used to repulse visitors now attracts those who seek some sort of authenticity in its still overwhelming remoteness and otherness.

In the decades since the 1930s our civilization has without a doubt permanently altered and damaged the Canyon Country. Though New Deal legislation had imposed grazing restrictions and proposed national parks in the region, it also signaled new attempts to integrate and exploit the Canyon Country's resources. Indeed, the story of the region from the 1930s is a variation of Sarah Phillips's observation on the entire American West: "The New Deal never asked residents of the Far West to lower their expectations...but rather whetted their appetites for 'expanded horizons' by means of massive hydroelectric and irrigation facilities serving both industrial farms and industrial factories."[38]

Though the Canyon Country is still not an agricultural or industrial center, we have dammed rivers, crowded national parks, turned trails into paved highways, and even obscured views with smoke from coal-fired power plants. Even as long ago as 1968, when Abbey's *Desert Solitaire* captured the essence of the region better than any writer since Powell, he mourned the loss of the desert's wildness and called his book "not a travel guide, but an elegy."[39] Since then lovers of the region have made it the focus of some of the wilderness preservation movement's bitterest battles, striving to prevent future damage to a harsh but vulnerable landscape.[40]

The ideal of the Canyon Country as a region completely contrary to all other American landscapes still persists. Abbey's "elegy" to the wilderness was not original in emphasizing the authenticity of his experience over all future visitors and in implying that he had seen Virgin Land but for all after him it was Fallen Land. From the time of Powell, countless visitors and residents who have seen themselves as "explorers" of the region have viewed it as forbidding wilderness for themselves but as both sanitized and deflowered for all those coming later. The region fosters a sense of proprietorship (but not ownership) in many. Perhaps this is the true essence of wilderness in the Canyon Country—it is a place where we can all "play explorer" just as Charles Bernheimer did, with the illusion that we are the final ones to see it in its untouched Edenic state.

The remoteness, vastness, and ever present desolation of the Canyon Country continue to intrigue and perhaps frighten visitors, in true Burke fashion. Since the highpoint of Mormon settlement in the 1880s, few new permanent towns have sprung up (the notable exception is Page, Arizona), and agriculture has certainly not opened any dramatic new frontiers. Some population growth has occurred, particularly in the tourist town of Moab, but the whole of southeast Utah remains one of the most sparsely populated parts of the contiguous United States. For the time being, entire counties lack big-box retailers, suburbs, and even traffic lights. And unlike similarly sparsely populated expanses of the rural Midwest or southeastern United States, there it is still possible to walk for days in a continuous direction without crossing a paved road or private property lines or even seeing another person. For all its problems, whatever our cultural definition of wilderness is, much of the Canyon Country still fits it.

Compared to most other landscapes in the United States, the Canyon Country has only been lightly touched. It is still quite easy to find the illusion of complete seclusion and solitude there. But the aridity and remoteness that have for so long kept the numbers of human actors in the region minimal have also paradoxically preserved the marks of those who have traveled the region before us, belying its apparent emptiness. Cliff dwellings and granaries, rock carvings and paintings by Indians and cowboys, uranium mine shafts, decrepit cabins, rusted tin cans, jeep tracks, and even primitive aircraft landing strips appear in the most unlikely places. In one particular canyon in the San Rafael Swell, after walking for miles and feeling refreshingly far from all signs of human civilization, a traveler rounds a corner to find the rusting shell of a 1940s-era Ford truck.

The secluded desert canyons hide much more than mere uninhabited "wilderness." In a sense this makes the region even more engaging than any polarized labels can. The Canyon Country has intrigued and repulsed visitors, attracted settlement and destroyed it. Although the decades after this book's story ends have been overwhelmingly a tale of our modern society incorporating the region, imposing our linear ideas upon a crooked landscape, future exploitation and utilization of the Canyon Country will undoubtedly continue to be shaky and fraught with misunderstanding.

This is not to imply, however, that the Canyon Country will completely thwart all future exploitation. It is a fragile place. Many characteristics of isolation and beauty that lovers of the region value (myself included) are at constant risk of destruction or have already been destroyed. This risk will certainly rise in coming decades as our desperate search for dwindling fossil fuel sources leads us to previously passed-over resources such as the oil shales of the Kaiparowits Plateau. When this happens, no amount of emphasizing that "wilderness" is merely a cultural construct will allay our loss of very special places. Although we continue to impose our straight lines upon this crooked landscape, I certainly hope that strip mines on the Kaiparowits will not seem as quaintly humorous to future historians as Kluckhohn's littered tin cans on Wild Horse Mesa are to us.

Time Line

1498   Christopher Columbus speculates about an Eden on the
          Orinoco.
1540–42   Coronado Expedition reaches Cibola (New Mexico) and the
          Grand Canyon; Melchior Díaz names the present-day lower
          Colorado "Tizón."
1562   Gregorio López arrives in the New World, seeking out terrible
          deserts in northern Mexico.
1604   Juan de Oñate and Fray Francisco Escobar reach the lower
          Colorado River, name it "Buena Esperanza," and compile Indian
          reports on what lies upstream.
1612   Amsterdam cartographer Claes Visscher places an unnamed lake
          at the source of the Colorado River.
1626   Fray Jerónimo Zárate y Salmerón promotes promised riches in
          the area of the Great Basin and Canyon Country.
1673   Jacques Marquette hears reports of a large lake connecting the
          Mississippi drainage to the "Vermillion Sea" (Sea of Cortez).
1686   Fray Alonso de Posada drafts a description of the future Canyon
          Country and Great Basin and first coins the term "Teguayo."
1755   Jacques Nicolas Bellin's 1755 "Carte de L'Amérique Septentrionale"
          designates Teguayo simply as an unknown blank spot.

1765	Two Rivera expeditions journey toward the upper Colorado (Tizón) in July and October.
1767	The Jesuit Order is expelled from New Spain.
1774	Juan Bautista de Anza and Fray Francisco Garcés find a southern route from Sonora to Alta California.
1776	The Domínguez-Escalante expedition travels from New Mexico to Lake Timpanogos; Miera first draws a map of the region.
1805	Manuel Mestas traverses Canyon Country while traveling from New Mexico to Lake Timpanogos.
1808	Alexander von Humboldt draws his map of New Spain, based heavily upon Miera's descriptions.
1816	The Arze-García expedition crosses the Canyon Country, probably by way of the Ute Ford in Glen Canyon, en route to Lake Timpanogos along the "Old Spanish Trail."
1821	Canyon Country becomes part of Mexico.
1825	William Ashley attempts to descend the Green River around Dinosaur National Monument.
1826	James Ohio Pattie allegedly travels the rim of the Colorado Canyon in the winter.
1829	Antonio Armijo crosses the Ute Ford both to and from California.
1830	Joseph Smith Jr. organizes the Mormon church in New York.
1836	French trapper Denis Julien descends the Colorado as far as Cataract Canyon.
1843	Warren Ferris publishes a description of the Colorado Canyon in *Western Literary Messenger* magazine.
1847	Mormon settlers enter the Great Salt Lake Valley.
1848	Canyon Country becomes part of the United States.
1849	Mormons propose the state of Deseret; the Parley P. Pratt expedition south of Salt Lake City gathers reports of the Canyon Country from Ute chief Wakara.
1850	Utah is established as a U.S. territory.
1853	The Gunnison party surveys a railroad route through the northern Canyon Country/San Rafael Swell; the "Black Hawk War" breaks out among Mormons and Indians.

1853–54   The Frémont party also surveys a railroad route, trending slightly farther south than Gunnison; a Mormon exploratory party reaches the future site of Moab and the San Juan River in October.

1855   The short-lived Elk Mountain Mission is established on Grand River (future Moab).

1857   The Ives party surveys the lower Colorado to the foot of the Grand Canyon; the "Utah War" and Mountain Meadows Massacre take place.

1859   The Macomb-Newberry expedition nears the confluence of the Green and Grand Rivers.

1862   The Homestead Act passes.

1864   The Mormon village of Kanab is established on the southwestern fringe of the Canyon Country.

1865   The Mormon Andrus expedition traverses western Canyon Country from Kanab to Boulder Mountain.

1867   James White allegedly descends the Colorado River on a raft.

1868   Mormons first attempt to settle the middle Paria River.

1869   John Wesley Powell descends the Green and Colorado Rivers to the foot of the Grand Canyon.

1871   Powell floats the rivers for a second time to the junction of the Colorado and Paria Rivers and winters in Kanab; in the summer Jacob Hamblin and Isaac Haight explore the Escalante and San Rafael Rivers in an unsuccessful attempt to locate the mouth of the Dirty Devil.

1872   The A. H. Thompson party locates the mouth of the Dirty Devil via an overland trek from Kanab and identifies and names the Escalante River and Henry Mountains; John D. Lee establishes a Mormon-owned ferry at the mouth of the Paria; gold is first reported in Glen Canyon.

1873   Mormons begin crossing at Lee's Ferry in settlement of Arizona's Little Colorado River; Mormon ranchers of Sevier Valley begin moving into Rabbit Valley on the upper Fremont River.

1877   Mormons resettle the site of Elk Mountain Mission; Powell publishes a heavily embellished report of his first expedition;

Orderville is established on the southwestern fringes of Canyon Country as an experiment in Mormon communalism; Potato Valley is settled and renamed Escalante; Mormon ranchers from Sanpete Valley begin grazing the upper tributaries of the San Rafael River in Castle Valley; Brigham Young dies.

1878 Powell submits his *Report on the Lands of the Arid Region* to the U.S. Congress.

1879–80 Members of the San Juan Mission traverse the Canyon Country from Escalante to Bluff via Hole in the Rock.

1880 Grove Karl Gilbert and Clarence Dutton of the Powell Survey publish reports on the Henry Mountains and High Plateaus, respectively.

1881 Elk Mountain is officially renamed Moab.

1882 Ephraim Hanks establishes a ranch/polygamist sanctuary on Pleasant Creek in future Capitol Reef National Park.

1883 Flash floods begin depopulating Paria River settlements; the lower Fremont River settled by Bishop Elijah Behunin; the railroad reaches Green River, Utah.

1885 The Orderville experiment is dissolved.

1888 Steam engines and pumps are hauled to Dandy Crossing in Glen Canyon for gold sluicing.

1889 First expedition of the DCC&P Railroad surveys a railroad through the Colorado Canyons; company president Frank Brown and two others drown.

1890 DCC&P chief engineer Robert B. Stanton returns to run and survey the Colorado, but his railroad venture fails.

1896 The state of Utah is established.

1898 The Hoskaninni Company heavily invests in dredging and sluicing equipment, again under the management of Robert B. Stanton; it fails by 1901.

1908 Natural Bridges National Monument is designated.

1909 Flash floods depopulate Caineville and other lower Fremont River settlements; former Hoskaninni financier Julius Stone takes the first pleasure trip down the Colorado; Rainbow Bridge is "discovered" by white travelers.

1910 Rainbow Bridge National Monument is designated.

1911 Charles Spencer's attempt to haul coal on a steamer through Glen Canyon to Lee's Ferry fails.

1914 Cass Hite, longtime Glen Canyon prospector and resident, dies at Ticaboo.

1921 The name of the Grand River is changed to Colorado.

1922 John Widtsoe travels through the Canyon Country; the Colorado River Compact is signed.

1926–28 Clyde Kluckhohn explores Navajo Mountain and the Kaiparowits Plateau region.

1929 Arches National Monument is designated.

1934 Taylor Grazing Act passes; Everett Ruess disappears in Davis Gulch.

1936 The proposed Escalante National Monument fails.

Notes

INTRODUCTION

1. For more on this broad theme, see Frederick Turner, *Beyond Geography*. For the detailed intellectual links between Columbus's expectations and later Jeffersonian ideals, see James P. Ronda's *Finding the West*, particularly the second chapter, "Lewis and Clark in the Age(s) of Exploration," 17–28. For the details of how the United States established its linear, ordered boundaries across the interior of the continent, see Andro Linklater, *Measuring America*.
2. Roderick Nash, *Wilderness and the American Mind*, 8.
3. The phrase "Geography of Hope" was coined by Wallace Stegner, albeit in a different context, in his "Wilderness Letter" of 1960. See the anthology *Marking the Sparrow's Fall*, 111–20.
4. Stephen J. Pyne, *How the Canyon Became Grand*, 4.
5. John S. Newberry, *Report of the Exploring Expedition from Santa Fé, New Mexico*, 6–7.
6. See Hal Rothman, *Devil's Bargains*; Nash, *Wilderness and the American Mind*; and Richard West Sellers, *Preserving Nature in the National Parks*.
7. In January 2009 relaxed Bureau of Land Management regulations opened thousands of acres of land adjacent to Canyonlands and Arches National Park to possible oil and gas drilling, though the claims were later closed. The ever-present possibility of oil shale in the Cretaceous layers of the Kaiparowits Plateau will certainly receive more attention in energy crises of coming decades.
8. See, for example, Shepard Krech III, *The Ecological Indian*.
9. A large body of archaeological literature pertaining to the Ancestral Puebloans, Anasazi, or Fremont peoples who populated the Canyon Country in cliff dwellings from about 900–1200 CE is available. Most works suggest that these peoples ultimately failed because of environmental factors, overtaxing the desert's scarce resources. See, for example, Steve Simms, *Ancient Peoples of the Great Basin and Colorado Plateau*, 226–28; or, for a more general story, chapter 4 of Jared Diamond's *Collapse*, 136–56.
10. My use of the term "island communities" comes from Robert Wiebe's seminal synthesis of the Gilded Age–Progressive Era United States: *The Search for Order*.

Wiebe's analysis of exactly how isolated communities were incorporated economically, culturally, and socially into the post–Civil War United States identifies many patterns that reached the Canyon Country much later than the rest of
the nation.

11. The total area of the lower forty-eight states is about 3.1 million square miles;
the Colorado drains a basin of about 243,000 square miles.

12. The Green-Colorado system is about 1,450 miles in length, from the source of
the Colorado to its mouth at the Sea of Cortez. In terms of the longest rivers in
the contiguous United States, this puts it behind the Missouri, Mississippi, Rio
Grande, St. Lawrence, and Arkansas Rivers, in that order. The volumes of many
rivers of lesser length dwarf the Colorado, however, such as the Ohio, Kanawha,
Columbia, Snake, and Tennessee Rivers.

13. John Wesley Powell, *The Exploration of the Colorado River and Its Canyons*, 29–30.

14. Edmund Burke, *A Philosophical Enquiry into the Origins of Our Ideas of the Sublime and Beautiful* (1757), 158. See also Carolyn Merchant, *Reinventing Eden*,
87–88.

15. Burke, *A Philosophical Enquiry*, 253.

16. Edward Abbey, "The Way It Was," from Edward Abbey and Philip Hyde, *Slickrock*, 20.

17. Although there are many exceptions, for the most part state boundaries in
the eastern United States run along imaginary east-to-west latitudes but are
bounded by natural rivers, ridges, and lakes on their north-to-south, longitu-
dinal axes. As we move farther west on a map of the nation (and incidentally
into more arid regions), the state boundaries become more gridded and "boxy":
the boundaries of Utah, Wyoming, New Mexico, and Colorado are completely
devoid of any natural borders whatsoever. See Linklater, *Measuring America*, 225.

18. See James B. Allen, "The Evolution of County Boundaries in Utah."

19. Edward Geary's *The Proper Edge of the Sky* offers an excellent examination of the
Mormon communities that flank the high plateaus of this region.

20. The geographical boundaries for the Canyon Country here are essentially the
same as those described in C. Gregory Crampton, *Standing Up Country*, 15–32;
and in Abbey and Hyde, *Slickrock*.

21. Jared Farmer, *Glen Canyon Dammed*, 222.

Chapter 1. Inventing Teguayo

1. We must not confuse Escalante's Río Grande with today's Rio Grande along the
Texas-Mexican border, which in the late eighteenth century was called either
"Río Bravo" or "Río Grande del Norte."

2. Vélez de Escalante, *The Domínguez-Escalante Journal*, 112–23; and Herbert E.
Bolton (ed. and trans.), *Pageant in the Wilderness*, 216–26.

3. "Miera's Report to the King of Spain, October 26, 1777," from Bolton, *Pageant in
the Wilderness*, 244.

4. Ibid., 246.

5. See Merchant, *Reinventing Eden*, specifically chapters 2 and 3. The Edenic, virginal imagery of westward expansion in American history is also central to the theme of Henry Nash Smith's *Virgin Land*; George H. Williams, *Wilderness and Paradise in Christian Thought*; and more recent works such as Nash, *Wilderness and the American Mind*; and Max Oelschlaeger, *The Idea of Wilderness*. With the possible exception of Williams, however, none of these works seriously examine the perceptions of Spanish Catholicism in the New World.

6. These words, from Aquinas's mid- to late-thirteenth-century *Summa Theologica*, are quoted in Clarence Glacken, *Traces on the Rhodian Shore*, 235.

7. I have borrowed this phrase from the second chapter of John Phelan's *The Millennial Kingdom of the Franciscans in the New World* (particularly 24).

8. Merchant, *Reinventing Eden*, 48–49. See also the illustration of this geography in F. J. C. Hearnshaw, *Medieval Contributions to Modern Civilization* (New York: Holt, 1922). Interestingly, recent astrophysics theories have shown that the earth actually does have a very slight pear shape due to lunar gravitational forces.

9. Bartolomé de Las Casas, *Las Casas on Columbus*, 28, 55.

10. Ibid., 56. See also Genesis 2:10–14 (King James version).

11. Ibid., 55. It is also significant to both Dante's and Columbus's visions of this earthly paradise that their raised elevations presumably would have made them exempt from the Flood of Genesis 6–8, certainly because of their virgin, innocent condition. Also, Williams writes of the this polarity between Jerusalem and the Earthly Paradise that "much of the Old Testament polarity and interrelatedness of garden and desert persisted in the medieval belief that the terrestrial paradise was to be found in a warm climate at the antipodes of the Wilderness of Zion [Jerusalem]." Williams, *Wilderness and Paradise in Christian Thought*, 48.

12. The etymology of the terms "wilderness" and "desert" is diverse for such closely associated words. "Wilderness" is based upon the Germanic "wold," originally referring to a wooded area and later defining broad notions of wildness and animals within these woods. "Desert," in contrast, is much more tied to human use in its origins, with its Latin roots meaning "deserted" or "forsaken" by humanity or an elected group of humans. Interestingly, most versions of the Bible have used the two terms interchangeably. The view that wildernesses and deserts were different would only gain momentum with the more puritanical view of "errands into the wilderness," in which aridity took a backseat to the unkempt woods and dark forests of New England as the exemplar of environmental evil. See Williams, *Wilderness and Paradise in Christian Thought*, 66; and Nash, *Wilderness and the American Mind*, 3. Furthermore, the idea that land was "uninhabited" if it lacked European cultivation is a very basic part of the American image of frontier wildernesses. Puritan Massachusetts governor John Winthrop wrote that it was morally permissible to seize untilled land from Indians in his 1629 "Reasons to Be Considered for Justifying the Undertakers of the Intended Plantation in New England."

13. Alexander VI, *Papal Bull Inter Cetera II*, Rome, May 4, 1493, 34–37.

14. Las Casas, *Las Casas on Columbus*, 31.

15. Phelan, *The Millennial Kingdom of the Franciscans in the New World*, 60. Even this early, however, other views competed with this "Indians as innocents" idea. These views undoubtedly gained momentum as relations between Indians and Europeans matured and became more complicated through the following centuries. For an extreme opposite example, see chapter 1, "The Devil and the Amerindian," in Fernando Cervantes, *The Devil in the New World*, 5–39, which traces the development of the European view of Indians as devil worshipers.

16. Mendieta's view of Mexico's Indians was also fairly simple and was only one facet of a very spirited debate in the mid-sixteenth century concerning exactly how Indians could fit into a biblical worldview. See Anthony Pagden, *The Fall of Natural Man*, particularly the first two chapters.

17. Williams, *Wilderness and Paradise in Christian Thought*, 62.

18. Phelan's prologue in *The Millennial Kingdom of the Franciscans in the New World*, 1.

19. For more on this nascent scientific revolution that supplanted Mendieta's mysticism in understanding the New World, see Antonio Barrera-Osario, *Experiencing Nature*, particularly the first chapter, which details the Spanish compulsion to transform the New World into a place more friendly not just for Christianity but for European crops and livestock.

20. Williams, *Wilderness and Paradise in Christian Thought*, 18.

21. Francisco de Losa, *The Holy Life of Gregorio López*, 6.

22. Ibid., 7–8.

23. Ibid., 11. See also Jodi Bilinkoff, "Francisco Losa and Gregorio López," 115–28.

24. Williams, *Wilderness and Paradise in Christian Thought*, 28. Isaiah 35:1 also comes to mind: "The wilderness and the dry land shall be glad, the desert shall rejoice and blossom."

25. See Dennis Reinhartz, "Legado: The Information of the Entradas Portrayed through the Early Nineteenth Century," in *The Mapping of the Entradas into the Greater Southwest*, ed. Dennis Reinhartz and Gerald D. Saxon, 135.

26. For basic information on Teguayo and Copala, see Lyman S. Tyler, "The Myth of the Lake of Copala and the Land of Teguayo."

27. In 1678 Diego de Peñalosa proposed an exploration of "Tatago." Eight years later Alonso de Posada undoubtedly gave the region the name "Teguayo." See Joseph P. Sánchez, *Explorers, Traders, and Slavers*, 6–7.

28. C. Gregory Crampton, "The Discovery of the Green River," 301.

29. John Logan Allen, "Pyramidal Height-of-Land." Baja California, despite being originally and correctly identified as a peninsula like Florida in the mid-1530s, later became an island in the Spanish mind. See David J. Weber, *The Spanish Frontier in North America*, 40, 56.

30. For details on the composition of Coronado's army, see Richard Flint, "What's Missing from This Picture? The *Alarde*, or Muster Roll, of the Coronado Expedition," in Richard Flint and Shirley Cushing Flint (eds.), *The Coronado Expedition from the Distance of 460 Years*, 59.

31. The best survey of this expedition is still Herbert E. Bolton, *Coronado*, although Richard and Shirley Cushing Flint are currently at the forefront of Coronado scholarship with several excellent collections of essays and manuscripts on the expedition.

32. Pedro de Castañeda de Nájera, "Relación de la Jornada de Cíbola," in Richard Flint and Shirley Cushing Flint (eds.), *Documents of the Coronado Expedition*, 397.

33. Ibid., 397, 451. The Spanish word *barranca* is difficult to translate. It does not necessarily mean "canyon," as the Flints translated it in their 2005 collection of Coronado documents, but it also certainly means more than George Parker Winship's bland "banks" in his 1904 translation of Castañeda's narrative, *The Journey of Coronado*. Roughly, a *barranca* is a great cliff, which may or may not fall into what we would call a "canyon." Perhaps the most appropriate direct translation would be the noun "breaks," as used in the name of Cedar Breaks National Monument, where the plateau top "breaks" into lower geological strata.

34. Bolton, *Coronado*, 138. See also Pyne, *How the Canyon Became Grand*, 4–12.

35. Flint and Flint, *The Coronado Expedition*, 397–98.

36. Ibid., 394. Díaz's estimation of the Colorado's width was quite erroneous.

37. Today's average high and low temperatures at Yuma, Arizona are 100 and 70 degrees Fahrenheit, respectively. For a more general European/world history on colder temperatures of this time, see Brian Fagan, *The Little Ice Age*.

38. See Weber, *The Spanish Frontier*, 80–87. For a more complete story of Oñate, see Marc Simmons, *The Last Conquistador*.

39. Francisco Escobar, "Father Escobar's Relación of the Oñate Expedition to California," 19–41.

40. Ibid., 13.

41. Ibid., 20–21.

42. Ibid., 21.

43. Reinhartz, "Legado," 140.

44. Jerónimo Zárate Salmerón, *Relaciones by Zárate Salmerón*: see preface by Donald Cutter.

45. Ibid., chapter 6, 32.

46. Escobar, "Father Escobar's Relación," introduction, 1.

47. Zárate Salmerón, *Relaciones*, chapter 47, 66.

48. Ibid., chapter 49, 67.

49. John Chávez, *The Lost Land*.

50. Salmerón, *Relaciones*, chapter 102, 90.

51. Ibid.

52. Ibid., chapter 49, 68.

53. Salmerón's *Relaciones* actually contains one of the earliest descriptions of the Navajos.

54. Zárate Salmerón, *Relaciones*, chapter 113, 94.

55. Lyman S. Tyler and H. Daniel Taylor, "The Report of Fray Alonso de Posada in Relation to Quivira and Teguayo," 285.

56. Jacques Marquette, "Of the First Voyage Made by Father Marquette toward New

Mexico, and How the Idea Thereof Was Conceived," in Edna Kenton (trans. and ed.), *The Jesuit Relations and Allied Documents*, 333, 358.

57. Alonso de Posada, *A Description of the Area of the Present Southern United States in the Seventeenth Century*, 34.

58. Ibid., 44.

59. Tyler and Taylor, "The Report of Fray Alonso de Posada," 302–4. The Canyon Country was a frontier between these two Indian peoples for centuries.

Chapter 2. Encountering Teguayo

1. For more on Jefferson's hopes for Good Land across the continent, see John Logan Allen, *Passage through the Garden*; and Roger G. Kennedy, *Mr. Jefferson's Lost Cause*. Aside from these coincident optimisms of geographical benevolence and a positive Indian reception of Christianity, missionaries such as Domínguez and Escalante had little in common with secularized Enlightenment thinkers. For more information on differing views of Indians, for instance, see David J. Weber, *Bárbaros*, 116–20.

2. Pyne argues in *How the Canyon Became Grand* that of all European colonial powers Spain was the least prepared intellectually to deal with the sheer lack of utility of the Grand Canyon. The same holds for Spaniards' interactions with the Canyon Country and the Colorado Plateau as a whole. See Pyne, *How the Canyon Became Grand*, 8–9.

3. Austin Nelson Leiby, "Borderland Pathfinders," introduction.

4. The term *genízaro* is a derivation of the Turkish "Janissary," captive slave-soldiers of the Ottoman Empire. In colonial New Mexico, *genízaros* were a class of defeated Indians. Though often living with and serving Spaniards, they were nonetheless "permanent outsiders who had to submit to the moral and cultural superiority of their conquerors": Ramón Gutiérrez, *When Jesus Came, the Corn Mothers Went Away*, 151.

5. Leiby, "Borderlands Pathfinders," entries for July 6–8.

6. Ibid., July 13. Leiby has speculated that this village was either Hovenweep or the Lowry Ruins. Neither of these ruins are expansive enough to have been compared to Santa Fe even in the 1760s, however, and they are not situated in particularly memorable canyons; Mesa Verde seems to fit his description much more closely. If Rivera was truly describing Mesa Verde, this would be the earliest Euro-Christian mention of the ruins.

7. Ibid., July 16.

8. Ibid.

9. Bernard Cohen, "What Columbus 'Saw' in 1492." Williams also writes that horrific monsters such as satyrs, "storm devils," and even Satan himself were long associated with the biblical desert wilderness: Williams, *Wilderness and Paradise in Christian Thought*, 13.

10. Las Casas, writing of Columbus's third voyage, stated that the Indians of the

South American mainland were "rather more white than others that had been seen in the Indies, very good looking with handsome bodies": *Las Casas on Columbus*, 31. For the myth of the Portuguese bishops, see Bolton, *Coronado*, 6. For Salmerón's tale of whites, see Zárate Salmerón, *Relaciones*, 45.

11. In 1909 church president Wilford Woodruff wrote while visiting the "civilized" New Mexican Pueblos that "the expansion of their minds, and, above all else, their capacity to receive any principle of the gospel...fully equals the minds of any in the Anglo Saxon race...I could not make myself believe I was standing in the presence of American Indians or Lamanites": Armand L. Mauss, *All Abraham's Children*, 119.

12. These speculations of Austin Leiby and Myra Ellen Jenkins are found in Leiby, "Borderland Pathfinders," 229.

13. Leiby, "Rivera Diaries," in "Borderland Pathfinders," June 18.

14. G. Clell Jacobs, "The Phantom Pathfinder," 201–2.

15. The idea that prospectors would have seemed unremarkable to Utes at this time is intriguing. Although we have no documentation of prospectors other than Rivera traveling into the Canyon Country before the early 1800s, they were almost certainly there illegally and off the record. Jacobs writes: "Expeditions to trade or explore beyond the frontiers required a license or commission limited by a royal order that had existed since the early days of the New Spain era. Although that order prohibited travel to the country of the Ute nations, at least one group was known to have disregarded that decree and was known to have carried on contraband trade; it was from them that Rivera was able to obtain guides": Jacobs, "The Phantom Pathfinder," 201.

16. "Governor Cachupín's Charge," in Leiby, "Borderland Pathfinders," 170.

17. Leiby, "Rivera Diaries," in "Borderland Pathfinders," October 10. For speculation as to where they actually were, see also Jacobs, "The Phantom Pathfinder," 215.

18. Leiby, "Rivera Diaries," October 15.

19. Ibid., October 16. I have not yet concluded exactly what these "nine small rivers" that so disappointed Rivera are. Rivera's diaries make very clear that they reached the Colorado River at present-day Moab crossing; it was the only open access to the river in miles, along a well-established Indian trade route that would become the Old Spanish Trail in the nineteenth century. Problematically, however, nowhere a day's ride above Moab crossing does the river split into nine tributaries. Had Rivera ridden very quickly for the entire day, he might have reached the junction of the Colorado and the Dolores just above today's Dewey Bridge. But even this would not have fit his description of nine rivers. The closest I can come to resolving this problem is that, given that this was October and Rivera describes a very low, unimposing river, he may have reached the open valley of the Colorado above the Dolores junction, where the river tends to split into numerous meandering channels in low water. This is still very much a problem in his geography, however.

20. Ibid., 210.

21. The three or four existing Indian crossings (which Euro-Christian trails followed) between Moab and Pierce's Ferry were all difficult. In Glen Canyon,
now underneath Lake Powell, Hite and Hall's Creek would become the most
frequently used for ferry crossings by the late 1800s. The "Ute Ford," or "Crossing
of the Fathers," where Domínguez and Escalante crossed in November 1776, was
a suitable shallow ford but very difficult to access. By far the most traveled crossing was the open country at Lee's Ferry, Arizona, where the canyon walls open
between Glen and Grand Canyons. The river here was notoriously deep and
swift, however, and many travelers drowned in the crossing.

22. Leiby, "Rivera Diaries," October 15.

23. Ibid., October 17.

24. Tom Chaffin, *Pathfinder*, 237; F. V. Hayden, "Letter to Secretary of the American Philosophical Society, Oct. 10, 1867" (Philadelphia, American Philosophical
Society, American Indian Manuscripts, Coll. 2977). Continuing this tradition
of linking Bad Lands to lowly people, Mark Twain would write of the Gosiutes
as "inferior to even the despised Digger Indians of California; inferior to all
races of savages on our continent": Twain, *Roughing It* (New York: Harper and
Brothers Publishers, 1872), 131. Even historians such as William Goetzmann have
labeled Indians of the deserts "miserable Diggers—figures out of the Stone Age
who lived on rats and bugs": Goetzmann, *Exploration and Empire*, 134. In addition to the fact that these "diggers" were actually able to sustain themselves in
deserts more effectively than perhaps any other society, distinguishing them as
Paiutes from their linguistic relatives the Utes has been very much an Anglo-
imposed value judgment, in which ownership of horses is the only criterion for
designation. See Jared Farmer, *On Zion's Mount*, 31–32.

25. Leiby, "Borderlands Pathfinders," 218. I have taken "Serpanino" to mean "Serpen-
teo," an adjective used to describe a winding natural feature, such as the goosenecks of a river or canyon.

26. Rivera could very well have continued his forays into the Canyon Country as
they started, as semilegal prospecting and trading ventures. Although no documentation of any of these ventures is yet known, the possibility remains; even
Rivera's diary of his 1765 expeditions was "lost" until the 1960s.

27. In his final sentences of his report Rivera wrote accurately: "One can deduce
that the distance from the Río de el Tison, which I judge to be the Colorado
River, which empties into the Gulf of California, to the Villa de Santa Fe, is one
hundred and fifty leagues": Leiby, "Rivera Diary," November 20.

28. David J. Weber, *The Spanish Frontier in North America*, 242.

29. I have borrowed the phrase "spiritual storm troopers" from my colleague J.
Gabriel Martínez-Serna. It is important to realize that, despite the Jesuit Order's
wealth, its presence in what was to become the American Southwest was limited to future southern Arizona and always overshadowed by the Franciscan
Order in New Mexico (see Weber, *The Spanish Frontier*, 95).

30. Given the very observant writings of Jesuits experiencing their own deserts
in Baja California from the late sixteenth to early eighteenth centuries, and

especially the writings and explorations of Eusebio Francisco Kino, it is unfortunate that no Jesuits would ever attempt to understand the ultimate Bad Land of the Canyon Country. Unlike his contemporary Alonso de Posada, Kino actually explored the deserts of the lower Colorado River extensively and pieced together a geography of the region that was much more accurate than any other work dealing with the Canyon Country for centuries. Eusebio Francisco Kino, *Kino and the Cartography of Northwestern New Spain*, trans. and ed. Ernest J. Burrus, S.J. (Tucson: Arizona Pioneers' Historical Society, 1965); and Ernest J. Burrus, S.J. (ed.), *The Jesuit Relations of Baja California, 1716–1762* (Los Angeles: Dawson's Book Shop, 1984).

31. Weber, *The Spanish Frontier*, 242–43.
32. Ibid., 251–53.
33. Silvestre Vélez de Escalante, "Letter to Governor Mendinueta, October 28, 1775," in Alfred B. Thomas, *Forgotten Frontiers*, 157.
34. Ibid. Of these mythical lost whites, Escalante would write: "Because the settlement of Monterey is much more modern, it is inferred evidently that the Spaniards who have been seen on the other side of the great river of Tison cannot be from there."
35. Interestingly, the expedition has come to be associated much more with Escalante than with Domínguez, his superior, the senior leader of the expedition. Escalante left ample documentation of his visions of conversion and exploration through the arid Southwest, both before and after the 1776 expedition. He would go on to write a well-known history of New Mexico. Domínguez, however, fell out of favor in the colony. A canyon in western Colorado and a desert in western Utah along the party's route would take Escalante's name, as well as a town, river, and later National Monument in south-central Utah that were not on the party's route. Today just the name "Escalante" evokes a sense of romance and adventure in the Canyon Country, especially for wilderness enthusiasts. For some reason "Domínguez" does not. But in reality Escalante's journal minimizes the use of the first person and all final decisions were made by his superior, Domínguez. See Ted J. Warner's introduction to Silvestre Vélez de Escalante, *The Domínguez-Escalante Journal*, xiv.
36. Silvestre Vélez de Escalante, "Letter to Murillo, May 16, 1776," in Thomas, *Forgotten Frontiers*, 161.
37. Vélez de Escalante, *The Domínguez-Escalante Journal*, October 11 (88).
38. Vélez de Escalante, "Letter to Governor Mendinueta," in Thomas, *Forgotten Frontiers*, 155.
39. Vélez de Escalante, *The Domínguez-Escalante Journal*, August 27 (31). See also Warner's introduction (viii) and Frances Leon Swadesh, *Los Primeros Pobladores*, 42.
40. Vélez de Escalante, *The Domínguez-Escalante Journal*, September 1 (40).
41. For more on this complex, little-known world of the Indian slave trade to New Mexico that Colorado Mountain Utes carried on at this time, see Ned Blackhawk, *Violence over the Land*, particularly the second and third chapters, 55–118, which specifically deal with the Rivera and Domínguez-Escalante expeditions

from a Ute perspective. See also the second chapter of Swadesh, *Los Primeros Pobladores*.

42. Vélez de Escalante, *The Domínguez-Escalante Journal*, August 17 (20). A Spanish league is equal to roughly 2.63 miles. According to my boundaries of the Canyon Country as outlined in the introduction, the Dolores is not strictly part of the region. I see it as a periphery to the Canyon Country, sharing some but not all characteristics of aridity and eroded canyons. The Dolores is more of a cool mountain stream than a warm, muddy desert river, and its drainage is separated from the rest of the Canyon Country by high mountains such as the La Sals. Perhaps for this reason Escalante actually seemed to enjoy the scenery of the Dolores country in his journals.

43. Ibid.

44. Ibid. The "Sabuagana" Utes are an alternate spelling to Rivera's "Saguaganas." Perhaps because of his optimism about conversion and his brighter view of human nature, however, Escalante shared none of Rivera's disdain for the tribe.

45. Ibid., August 27 (31).

46. It is unclear whether the friars read Rivera's diary of the 1765 expedition or not. Several times in the journal Escalante mentions Rivera by name (for example, August 22, 25). On other occasions he cryptically refers to "individuals searching for silver" or "those who have come before" (August 9, 14).

47. Today this route roughly follows the courses of Highway 191, Interstate 70, and Highway 6. In the early 1800s it would form part of the "Old Spanish Trail," a route by which slaves, blankets, and horses were traded between New Mexico and California.

48. Vélez de Escalante, *The Domínguez-Escalante Journal*, August 25 (27).

49. Escalante's "Comanches" are not necessarily the powerful nation that had adopted equestrian culture, moved eastward onto the southern plains in the early 1700s, and was in conflict with both Spaniards and Apaches by the 1770s. Rather, he is speaking of what we call Shoshones, Numic-speaking linguistic relatives of the Comanches, who lived north of the Uinta Mountains in present-day Wyoming, southern Idaho, and northern Utah. His use of the word "Comanche," however, would certainly have struck any Spaniard who read his report. It is clear that Spaniards and Indians of the late eighteenth century did not make the distinction that we do between Comanches and Shoshones. See Blackhawk, *Violence over the Land*, 35–58.

50. Vélez de Escalante, *The Domínguez-Escalante Journal*, August 24 (27) and September 5 (46).

51. See, for example, Escalante's description of the Uinta Basin, ibid., September 18 (58).

52. Ibid., September 23 (64).

53. Vélez de Escalante, "Description of the Valley and the Lake of Nuestra Señora de la Merced of the Timpanogoztis, or Timpanocuitzis, or 'Come Pescado,'" in *The Domínguez-Escalante Journal*, 72. The Great Salt Lake was a sort of neutral zone between the Shoshones and the Laguna Utes, which would later lead

Mormon settlers to regard its residents as somehow "lesser" peoples and result in the birth of an inaccurate myth that this region was a "no-man's land" before it became the core of Mormondom. We see traces of this in Escalante's words. See also Farmer, *On Zion's Mount*, 50.

54. Vélez de Escalante, *The Domínguez-Escalante Journal*, October 8 (84).
55. Ibid., September 30 (77).
56. Ibid., October 2 (80).
57. Ibid., October 11 (87).
58. Ibid., October 8 (84). The Havasupai tribe still lives in a beautiful tributary of the western Grand Canyon. The stream, waterfalls, and vegetation of the red rock Havasu Canyon are a true oasis in the desert and long attracted missionaries such as Francisco Garcés, Escalante, and later the Mormon Jacob Hamblin. The prospect of reaching the Cosninas from the north held a special attraction for Escalante, who had attempted to reach them from the east, only to be turned back by the Hopis. See Vélez de Escalante, "Letter to Governor Mendinueta," 157.
59. Vélez de Escalante, *The Domínguez-Escalante Journal*, October 11 (87).
60. Ibid., October 11 (88).
61. Ibid., October 11 (90).
62. Ibid., October 15 (95).
63. Ibid., October 23 (111).
64. Ibid., October 18 (100).
65. Ibid., October 22 (108).
66. Ibid., October 26 (112).
67. Ibid., October 26 (113).
68. Ibid.
69. Particularly interesting is the term "San Benito," which referred to a "garish white cassock worn by errant brothers as a mark of punishment." Clearly the Franciscans saw this spot as a divine punishment, probably for the party's continuous trading and refusal to adhere to God's work. Vélez de Escalante, *The Domínguez-Escalante Journal*, note 364 on 113.
70. Ibid., October 28 (114).
71. Ibid., October 28 (120).
72. Ibid., November 7 (121).
73. Ibid., November 7 (120).
74. Ibid., November 7 (121).
75. Ibid., September 5 (45). Interestingly, Escalante's care in not giving the upper Colorado the same name as the lower Colorado carried over, though perhaps only coincidentally, to the later name that Anglo-Americans used for the stream. Until 1921 the true Colorado did not begin until the confluence with the Green River; above that point the river was called the Grand.
76. Ibid., September 13 (52).
77. Ibid.
78. Ibid., September 29 (77). Escalante could not bring himself even to name this river the San Buenaventura but instead called it the Santa Isabel.

79. Ibid., October 1 (78).
80. Had the Domínguez-Escalante expedition decided to head directly west from Sevier Lake, it would have encountered very dry country. Furthermore, this would have set the party up for a crossing of the Sierra Nevada Mountains in early November and in a weakened state. These are the exact conditions that caused the tragedy of the Donner Party in 1846.
81. Vélez de Escalante, *The Domínguez-Escalante Journal*, 5 (note).
82. Richard Francaviglia, *Mapping and Imagination in the Great Basin*, 40 (emphasis in the original).
83. Humboldt's *Atlas geographique et physique du Royaume de la Nouvelle Espagne* (1811) cites Miera and Escalante in numerous spots and also connects the Sevier and Green Rivers in one "San Buenaventura," which flows to the Pacific.
84. Don Bernardo Miera y Pacheco, "Miera's Report to the King of Spain, October 26, 1777," in Bolton, *Pageant in the Wilderness*, 246.
85. After dealing with a long-standing sickness that may have originated during his desperate push across the Paria Plateau, Escalante died traveling from Santa Fe to Mexico in April 1780. See Warner's introduction to Vélez de Escalante, *The Domínguez-Escalante Journal*, xvii.

Chapter 3. Old Spanish Trails and Trappers' Tales

1. Jacques Nicolas Bellin, "Carte de L'Amérique Septentrionale." The map's full description of the interior west says: "On pent [*sic*] placer isi les Provinces de Quivira et Tegouaio dont on na aucunes connoissances certaines" (translated by Francaviglia in *Mapping and Imagination*, 36).
2. Francaviglia, *Mapping and Imagination*, 38.
3. William Goetzmann, *New Lands, New Men*.
4. Aaron Sachs, *The Humboldt Current*, makes an excellent case for Humboldt's more prominent than previously assumed role in the development of our current environmental consciousness and appreciation and explicitly ties him to the western explorations of Clarence King, the polar expeditions of George Melville, and the wilderness reveries of John Muir.
5. Quoted in Francaviglia, *Mapping and Imagination*, 50.
6. Humboldt's "Carte generale du Royaume de la Nouvelle Espagne" (1809), which appears in his *Atlas geographique et physique du Royaume de la Nouvelle Espagne* (1811), labels the Canyon Country as country seen by "le Pere Antonio Velez y Escalante en 1777," getting both Escalante's full name and the year of the expedition wrong.
7. Humboldt labels these peoples as the Nabajoa, Tabequachi, Moqui, and Cosnina Indians, respectively.
8. "Miera's Report to the King of Spain, October 26, 1777," from Bolton, *Pageant in the Wilderness*, 246.
9. Ironically, the region and unknown river canyon complex on which Miera

placed his legend would come to be named for Escalante. It was not uncommon to put notes, comments, and legends over the most unknown regions of maps. In 1837 Benjamin Bonneville also placed the title of his 1837 "Map of the Territory West of the Rocky Mountains" over the most unknown section of the Canyon Country. See Francaviglia, *Mapping and Imagination*, 74–75.

10. Miera writes that in the region around Mesa Verde, between the San Juan and Colorado Rivers, were "las Ruinas de pueblos antiguos muy grandes" (ruins of very large old towns).

11. Interestingly, most archaeologists agree that environmental change to some degree caused the decline of Ancestral Puebloan culture in Chaco Canyon, at Mesa Verde, and throughout scattered sites in the Canyon Country. The Little Ice Age from about 1000 to 1400 CE may have made the Canyon Country "Good Land" to some degree.

12. See Allen's detail of the map in his book *Passage through the Garden*, 384.

13. See Robert Utley's reproduction of Finley's map in *A Life Wild and Perilous*, 86.

14. Quoted in Goetzmann, *Exploration and Empire*, 97.

15. Roy Webb, *If We Had a Boat*, 23–27.

16. Ibid., 36–39.

17. William Manly, *Death Valley in '49*, 88–89.

18. Utley, *A Life Wild and Perilous*, 92–93, 201–4. For more on the evolution from the mythical San Buenaventura to the gritty Humboldt River, see Dale L. Morgan, *The Humboldt*, especially the second chapter.

19. I have borrowed the "neither 'old' nor 'Spanish'" phrase from David Weber's introduction to Leroy R. Hafen and Ann W. Hafen's *The Old Spanish Trail*.

20. Hafen and Hafen, *The Old Spanish Trail*, 84–85; and Joseph P. Sánchez, *Explorers, Traders, and Slavers*, 101. Mestas's one-month trip from New Mexico to Utah Lake and back again borders on impossible given the distance, the terrain, and his age. According to Sánchez, Mestas tended to exaggerate some of his other frontier exploits. For more on Mestas and his family's background, see Swadesh, *Los Primeros Pobladores*, 43.

21. Sánchez, *Explorers, Traders, and Slavers*, 102.

22. Hafen and Hafen, *The Old Spanish Trail*, 85–86.

23. Sánchez, *Explorers, Traders, and Slavers*, 102.

24. The Abajo Mountains (also called the "Blues" by locals today) received their original Spanish name, which means "under" or "below," because they were "below" any easy crossing of the Colorado River.

25. See Antonio Armijo, "Armijo's Journal of 1829–30."

26. Quoted in Sánchez, *Explorers, Traders, and Slavers*, 104–5.

27. "Route Discovered from the Village of Abiquiú in the Territory of New Mexico to Upper California," in Hafen and Hafen, *The Old Spanish Trail*, 157.

28. Ibid., 157. The noun *bufas* in older Spanish seems to denote flat landforms similar to mesas.

29. Perhaps not surprisingly, discrepancies and even animosity have long existed

between traders such as Armijo who knew the geography of the Far North intimately yet left no record of it and those more educated, quantifying people of "instruction and literature" who presumably could have mapped and measured the Canyon Country had they ever visited it. Antonio Barrera-Osario points out that this uneasy "relationship between formal education and personal experience" extends well back into the early sixteenth century, when hardened sea captains were often illiterate and cartographers rarely left their drawing-rooms: Barrera-Osario, *Experiencing Nature*, 49.

30. James O. Pattie, *The Personal Narrative of James O. Pattie* (1831), 97.

31. Frank Waters, *The Colorado*, 179–80.

32. Pattie, *The Personal Narrative*, entries for March 16, April 10, and April 26, 1826.

33. Ibid., 97.

34. I refer, of course, to Frederick Jackson Turner's classic essay "The Significance of the Frontier in American History," which argues that the entire experience of American democracy is forged by contact with the broad, open land of the frontier. While Turner did not deliver this essay until 1893, its ideas have roots extending back to Pattie, Jacksonian America, and beyond. A good introduction to the Turner thesis is Richard Etulain's edited collection, *Does the Frontier Experience Make America Exceptional?* (New York: Bedford/St. Martin's, 1999).

35. Pattie, *The Personal Narrative*, 176.

36. Warren A. Ferris, *Life in the Rocky Mountains*, 397–98.

37. Ibid.

38. See the map attachment in ibid.

39. Julien's most well known and detailed inscription at Hell Roaring Canyon shows a picture of a masted boat, along with his name and the date "1836 3 Mai." Another carving near Bowknot Bend, about twenty miles upstream, is dated "16 Mai 1836," which indicates slow upstream travel. See Charles Kelly, "The Mysterious D. Julien"; and James H. Knipmeyer's two articles, "The Denis Julien Inscriptions"; and "Denis Julien: Midwestern Fur Trader."

40. See Knipmeyer, "The Denis Julien Inscriptions," for the most detailed chronological catalog of Julien's inscriptions. Although Kelly doubted the authenticity of the Julien inscription in Arches, Knipmeyer believes it to be authentic.

41. Kelly believed that Julien drowned, though this conclusion assumes that he was traveling downstream and that the 1844 Arches inscription is not genuine. Knipmeyer speculates that Julien may have followed other French trappers to California but admits that this theory is "undocumented": Knipmeyer, "Denis Julien: Midwestern Fur Trader," 263.

Chapter 4. United States Explorers

1. E. G. Beckwith, *Report of the Exploration of a Route for the Pacific Railroad*, entry for October 11 (71).

2. Ibid., October 13 (72).

3. Ibid., October 13 (65–66).

4. Ibid., October 13 (71).

5. Ibid., October 1 (67–68).

6. James Schiel, *The Land Between* (originally published in German, 1859), 90.

7. Ibid., 93.

8. Ibid., 93–94.

9. Goetzmann, *Exploration and Empire*, 283.

10. Schiel, *The Land Between*, 87.

11. Goetzmann, *Exploration and Empire*, 287; and Blackhawk, *Violence over the Land*, 231–35. Ironically, Gunnison had assumed that the Canyon Country was the most dangerous portion of his route and let his guard down upon reaching the site of his death on the Sevier River. Some have speculated that the Gunnison massacre was the work of separatist Mormons rather than Indians. For a discussion of this theory, see chapter 6 of Sally Denton, *American Massacre*. After the tragic massacre of October 26, 1853, Beckwith wintered in Salt Lake City, rebuilt the expedition, and successfully surveyed parts of the Wasatch Mountains for future railroad lines.

12. Beckwith, *Report of the Exploration of a Route for the Pacific Railroad*, October 10 (71). The expedition's route along the upper Colorado River through Grand Valley, Ruby, and Horsethief Canyons, and across open desert to the Green River just before entering the Canyon Country would eventually become a railroad route in early 1883. But this railroad swings north toward Price, Utah, rather than continuing in a direct line across the San Rafael Swell.

13. Goetzmann, *Exploration and Empire*, 25.

14. Quoted in ibid., 51.

15. At Bent's Fort in eastern Colorado Frémont dismissed hired hand James F. Milligan after finding that he had been keeping a journal. This is unfortunate, for Milligan's writings would have provided much greater insight into the Fifth Expedition's outcome. See Ava F. Kahn's introduction to Solomon Nunes Carvalho's *Incidents of Travel and Adventure in the Far West* (1858), xii; and Mark J. Stegmaier and David J. Miller, *James F. Milligan*, 86.

16. Chaffin, *Pathfinder*, 423.

17. See Martha Sandweiss, *Print the Legend*, 97. Sandweiss spends an entire chapter examining the role of photography on Frémont's Fifth Expedition, although she does erroneously place their worst winter trials in "Southern Wyoming," rather than in the Canyon Country's San Rafael Swell.

18. Ibid., 100–101.

19. Carvalho, *Incidents of Travel and Adventure*, 104. See also Ferol Egan, *Frémont*, 400.

20. Carvalho, *Incidents of Travel and Adventure*, 104.

21. Ibid., 114. The definitive work on Frémont's route through this area is Robert Shlaer, *Sights Once Seen*. Shlaer identifies one of Carvalho's daguerreotypes, which had been viewed backward for decades, as a scene from Cathedral Valley. James H. Knipmeyer, *Butch Cassidy Was Here*, 23–24, also makes a good case

for the specifics of this expedition's uncertain route. The lively debate among regional historians concerning Frémont's route through the northern Canyon Country will no doubt continue, but unfortunately few of his biographers seem concerned with it. Egan, *Frémont*, erroneously states that the route went through "today's Canyonlands National Park and Bryce Canyon National Park" (501), and the book's map of the route is equally wrong. Chaffin's more recent *Pathfinder* gives very little attention to this expedition.

22. Carvalho, *Incidents of Travel and Adventure*, 115.

23. Ibid., 118.

24. Patricia Nelson Limerick devotes the first chapter of *Desert Passages* to Frémont's view of arid lands but says nothing of his final 1853–54 expedition through the San Rafael Swell.

25. Carvalho was a Sephardic Jew of Iberian ancestry.

26. For further analysis of Egloffstein's visual depictions, see the special section "The Artist's View" in Wallace Stegner, *Beyond the Hundredth Meridian*.

27. Goetzmann, *Exploration and Empire*, 307–8.

28. Ibid., 306. Perhaps the best treatment of the Mormon War and the Mountain Meadows Massacre is Will Bagley's *Blood of the Prophets*. See also Steven Madsen, *Exploring Desert Stone* for more details on the Macomb expedition.

29. By 1859 Miera and Escalante's myth of the Green River as the San Buenaventura flowing westward to California was almost completely dead. Its postulated confluence with the Grand River (today's upper Colorado), however, was still completely unknown.

30. Captain J. M. Macomb's introduction to John S. Newberry, *Report of the Exploring Expedition from Santa Fé, New Mexico*, 6 (emphasis in the original).

31. Ibid., 6–7. Macomb was not wholly inaccurate in this observation. The high mesas of the eastern Canyon Country would have been much colder during this time of the Little Ice Age, and a well-founded theory holds that the Ancestral Puebloans actually did ensure their own demise by stripping the piñon and juniper highlands of available timber. For an overview of this subject, see chapter 4 of Diamond's *Collapse*.

32. Newberry, *Report*, 6–7.

33. Ibid., 7.

34. Ibid., 83–84.

35. Burke, *A Philosophical Enquiry into the Origins of Our Ideas of the Sublime and Beautiful*, 158.

36. Abbey, "The Way It Was," in Abbey and Hyde, *Slickrock*, 20.

37. Newberry, *Report*, 53–54. Future mining ventures, such as the gold rush in Glen Canyon during the 1890s and the uranium boom of the 1940s and 1950s, would disregard Newberry's speculation.

38. Newberry, *Report*, 54.

39. Ibid., 94. Newberry called the large canyon that the expedition traveled through simply "Cañon Colorado." His description does not make it clear

whether they were following Indian Creek or Hart's Draw, two large and adjacent drainages flowing toward what is today the Needles district of Canyonlands National Park. It makes more sense that the party followed Indian Creek, which had more water, pasturage, easier access, and is today the road route into the national park. For more information on the Macomb expedition's specific route, see F. A. Barnes, *Canyonlands National Park*.

40. Of Utah's national parks, only Bryce, which is composed of the much younger Wasatch/Claron Formation, lacks Jurassic and Triassic sandstones.

41. Newberry, *Report*, 94.

42. Ibid., 97.

43. This, of course, is one of the major themes of Nash's *Wilderness and the American Mind*.

44. Newberry, *Report*, 95.

CHAPTER 5. RIVER BOTTOMS TO MOUNTAINTOPS

1. For Mormon prophecies on the Civil War, see B. H. Roberts, *History of the Church of Jesus Christ of Latter-Day Saints*, 301–2.

2. Quoted from the official Republican Party Platform of 1856, outlined at the party's convention in Philadelphia.

3. Smith, *Virgin Land*, 40–41.

4. See Eilean Adams, *Hell or High Water*. For a more critical indictment of White's claim, see part I of Robert Brewster Stanton's hard-to-obtain *Colorado River Controversies*.

5. Two excellent biographies of Powell have been published: Stegner, *Beyond the Hundredth Meridian*; and Donald Worster, *A River Running West*. Stegner's work, while a rich example of his conservationist genre, recently has been criticized for perhaps anachronistically portraying Powell as too much of a modern-day environmentalist: see Gary Topping, *Utah Historians and the Reconstruction of Western History*, 270–71. For Powell's relation to modern western conservation, see James M. Aton, *Inventing John Wesley Powell*. For a less analytical, more mainstream account of Powell's 1869 explorations, see Edward Dolnick, *Down the Great Unknown*. The concept of a "Greater Reconstruction" in the West, mirroring federal efforts in the U.S. South, forms a significant part of Elliot West's ideas in *The Last Indian War*.

6. In 1921, at the urging of Colorado state politicians, the name of the Grand River was officially changed to Colorado and geographers began to consider the former Grand River as the true "source" of the Colorado system. The headwaters of the Green River are actually the point in the drainage farthest from its mouth, however. Thus, in addition to the Green River being easier to access by train and more navigable than the Grand River, Powell was beginning on the true source of the Colorado system.

7. Expedition member Frank Goodman left the river at this point in the Uinta

Basin. See Powell, *The Exploration of the Colorado River*, entry for July 5, 1869 (187).

8. Ibid., July 13 (199).

9. See Worster, *A River Running West*, 101, 104.

10. Powell, *Exploration of the Colorado River*, June 9 (163–64).

11. According to Robert Stanton's interview of expedition member Jack Sumner, however, "this wreck marked the beginning of many major quarrels between Major Powell and O. G. Howland": Stanton, *Colorado River Controversies*, 177.

12. Powell never mentioned the Denis Julien inscriptions along this stretch of river.

13. Powell, *Exploration of the Colorado River*, July 19, 1869 (209).

14. Ibid., July 18 (212).

15. Ibid., August 13 (249).

16. Ibid., August 28–29 (280–84). The coffee supplier for a Colorado River rafting company that I worked for several years ago printed on all its bags of fresh-roasted coffee beans "Major Powell never ran out of coffee!"

17. In addition to their part in wrecking the *No Name*, expedition members William Hawkins and Jack Sumner both later stated that Powell had demanded repayment from Dunn for a watch that was damaged in the Disaster Falls accident and even said that Dunn would be charged with food expenses if he did not leave the expedition as quickly as possible: Stanton, *Colorado River Controversies*, 147–48. Because of their subsequent deaths, Powell was never publicly critical of the Howlands or Dunn. He personally visited with the Indians who claimed to have killed the men. According to Frederick S. Dellenbaugh, Powell "never said a word in condemnation of these men…he always spoke of them affectionately": Dellenbaugh, *A Canyon Voyage*, 171. Powell never mentioned the possibility that Mormons killed the three men, although that theory has become quite widespread, especially in more popular literature. See, for example, Dolnick, *Down the Great Unknown*, 282–83; and John Krakauer, *Under the Banner of Heaven: A Story of Violent Faith* (New York: Doubleday: 2003), 240.

18. Worster, *A River Running West*, 197. Adams was not actually a captain; the title was self-given.

19. Quoted in Stegner, *Beyond the Hundredth Meridian*, 82.

20. Powell, *The Exploration of the Colorado River*, 218.

21. Dellenbaugh later wrote in his introduction to *A Canyon Voyage* that neither expedition's boats had fixed rudders as depicted in the engravings (x). Although Powell's amputation certainly necessitated use of a life preserver, he omitted any reference to using a life preserver in the 1869 expedition, when he was apparently the only member to have one: Stanton, *Colorado River Controversies*, 225. For an example of how Moran and other engravers exaggerated the very character of the canyon walls, see Stanton's *Colorado River Controversies*, 56–57, for a side-by-side comparison of the plate "The Wreck at Disaster Falls," which depicts Egloffstein-style cavernous walls, and an actual photo of Disaster Falls,

which is much more benign in appearance. See also Stegner's "The Canyon Country: The Artist's View" inset in *Beyond the Hundredth Meridian*, 92–93.

22. Worster, *A River Running West*, 181.

23. Powell, *The Exploration of the Colorado River*, 227.

24. Ibid., 230.

25. Dellenbaugh, *A Canyon Voyage*, 96–97. For the most all-encompassing view of Powell's second survey, see Herbert E. Gregory, William Culp Darrah, and Charles Kelly (eds.), *The Exploration of the Colorado River and the High Plateaus of Utah*.

26. Herbert E. Gregory's introduction to Almon Harris Thompson, "The Diary of Almon Harris Thompson, Geographer," 10.

27. Dellenbaugh, *A Canyon Voyage*, 153, 169.

28. Jacob Hamblin, "Journals and Letters of Jacob Hamblin, 1854–1877" (typescript), entry for August 20, 1871.

29. Thompson, "Diary," July 27, 1871 (30).

30. Ibid., August 21, 1871 (38).

31. Frederick S. Dellenbaugh, *Journal, 1871–1873*, entry for August 11, 1871.

32. Thompson, "Diary," August 26, 1871 (41).

33. Dellenbaugh, *A Canyon Voyage*, 106.

34. Thompson, "Diary," September 7, 1871 (44).

35. Dellenbaugh, *A Canyon Voyage*, 109.

36. Thompson, "Diary," September 14, 1871 (48).

37. Ibid., October 3, 1871 (55).

38. Ibid., September 10, 1871 (46).

39. Dellenbaugh, *A Canyon Voyage*, 109.

40. Ibid., 127.

41. Thompson, "Diary," November 3, 1871 (60).

42. Even as early as this Mormons informally called the settlements of southwestern Utah such as Santa Clara, St. George, and Hurricane "Utah's Dixie," for their mild climate and ability to produce more subtropical crops such as olives, grapes, and cotton.

43. Dellenbaugh, *A Canyon Voyage*, 166.

44. Dellenbaugh, *Journal*, January 4, 1872.

45. Thompson, "Diary," January 16, 1872 (65).

46. Ibid., June 1–3 (80–81). See also Dellenbaugh, *A Canyon Voyage*, 197.

47. C. Gregory Crampton, "Military Reconnaissance in Southern Utah, 1866," 153.

48. Thompson, "Diary," June 2, 1872 (80). Although neither Thompson nor Dellenbaugh mentioned Hamblin's prior reconnaissance, they certainly would have heard about this region from him. See Hamblin, "Journals and Letters," August 22, 1871 (54).

49. Thompson, "Diary," June 6, 1872 (81; emphasis in the original).

50. Like all medium-level Canyon Country rivers, the Escalante is quite small; in the Pacific Northwest or the eastern United States, it would barely achieve creek

status. But its drainage basin is huge—2,000 square miles (a third larger than the state of Rhode Island).

51. Dellenbaugh, *A Canyon Voyage*, 201.
52. Clarence E. Dutton, *Report on the Geology of the High Plateaus of Utah*, 284–85. Western literature icon Wallace Stegner actually wrote his Ph.D. dissertation on this aesthetic "literary naturalism" of Dutton: "Clarence Dutton: Geologist and Man of Letters" (University of Iowa, 1935).
53. Dutton, *Report*, 286–87.
54. Thompson, "Diary," June 14, 1872 (84).
55. Ibid., June 15, 1872 (84).
56. Dellenbaugh, *Journal*, June 13–15, 1872.
57. Dellenbaugh, *A Canyon Voyage*, 205.
58. Thompson, "Diary," June 15, 1872 (84). Today a section of mesa in this area is named Oyster Shell Reef for the huge amount of fossilized shells contained in its strata.
59. Hanksville, the nearest town to the Henry Mountains, obtains its water from wells or from the Fremont and Muddy Rivers.
60. Grove Karl Gilbert, *Report on the Geology of the Henry Mountains*, 2.
61. Long-time Green River, Utah, resident Bert Silliman asserted, with no real evidence, that the Henry Mountains were the site of a "cursed" mine where enslaved Indians had rebelled against their Spanish overseers. See the Bert J. Silliman Papers, 1951–1957, Utah Historical Society, Salt Lake City, folder 1, page 4, "Correspondence with LeRoy Hafen, 1952," as well as folder 9, "Legends, Traditions, and Early History of the Henry Mountains, by E. T. Wolverton."
62. Gilbert, *Report on the Geology of the Henry Mountains*, 151–52.
63. Ibid., 14.
64. Ibid., 19. Later geologists changed Gilbert's "laccolytes" to the grammatically correct Greek "laccoliths." See also Stegner, *Beyond the Hundredth Meridian*, 156.
65. Thompson, "Diary," June 20, 1872 (86). See also Dellenbaugh, *A Canyon Voyage*, 208–9. Today Highway 95 follows North Wash to Hite Marina on Lake Powell.
66. Thompson, "Diary," June 23, 1872 (86).
67. Dellenbaugh, *A Canyon Voyage*, 210.
68. Stegner, *Beyond the Hundredth Meridian*, 144.
69. Thompson, "Diary," June 21, 1872 (86).
70. Worster, *A River Running West*, 354; and Stegner, *Beyond the Hundredth Meridian*, 225–29.
71. Nevada is the most arid state in the nation.
72. John Wesley Powell, *Report on the Lands of the Arid Region of the United States* (1879), 16.
73. Ibid., 19.
74. Ibid., 94.
75. Ibid., 120.
76. Ibid., 119.
77. A. H. Thompson, "Irrigable Lands of That Portion of Utah Drained by the

Colorado River and Its Tributaries," chapter 9 of Powell, *Report on the Lands of the Arid Region*, 177.

78. For Gilbert's assessment, see "Irrigable Lands of the Salt Lake Drainage System," chapter 7 of Powell, *Report on the Lands of the Arid Region*, 139. For Dutton, see "Irrigable Lands of the Valley of the Sevier River," chapter 8 of Powell, *Report on the Lands of the Arid Region*, 157.

79. Thompson, "Irrigable Lands," 177.

80. Ibid., 163.

81. Ibid., 165.

82. Ibid., 167.

83. Ibid., 176.

84. Ibid., 169.

85. Ibid., 171. Even after we account for upstream reservoirs that decrease the flow of the San Rafael today, Thompson's flow report is very high by today's standards. For July 2008 the United States Geological Survey's real-time water data webpage recorded a level of 57 cubic feet per second (cfs) on the lower San Rafael River. Each of the river's three upper tributaries (Ferron, Cottonwood, and Huntington Creeks) averages around 100 cfs above its respective reservoir. Their net sum, even without accounting for water lost to summer evaporation, is still much less than Thompson's 1876 figures.

86. Dellenbaugh, *A Canyon Voyage*, 210–12.

87. For more information on Lee, see his biography by Juanita Brooks, *John Doyle Lee: Zealot, Pioneer-Builder, Scapegoat* (Glendale, Calif., A. H. Clark Co., 1962). For information on the Mountain Meadows Massacre, see Bagley, *Blood of the Prophets*.

88. For a comprehensive documentary history of Lee's Ferry, see P. T. Reilly, *Lee's Ferry*.

89. Quoted in Worster, *A River Running West*, 362.

90. Ibid., 526–27. See also the introduction and chapter 4, "The Blessing of Aridity," in William E. Smythe, *The Conquest of Arid America*, for a very distorted, diluted version of the Mormon communal irrigation systems that Powell lauded in his *Report*.

91. Whether Powell would be a wilderness enthusiast and preservationist today has been the subject of considerable debate, some anachronistic. In 1953 Wallace Stegner certainly portrayed Powell as a modern-day prophet-environmentalist in *Beyond the Hundredth Meridian*, while Worster has shown in *A River Running West* that this matter is much more complicated. For a more direct examination of Stegner's perspective, see Topping, *Utah Historians and the Reconstruction of Western History*, 270–71. For Powell's relation to other scientist-explorers of his time, both romantic and rational, see Sachs, *The Humboldt Current*, 255.

CHAPTER 6. GOOD SETTLERS AND BAD LAND

1. For an excellent overview of place-names in the Canyon Country, see Crampton, *Standing Up Country*, 4–7.

2. Local legend in Wayne County, Utah, also tells how the Powell surveys des-
    ignated place-names for the region's two plateaus: the descriptive "Thousand
    Lake Mountain" for the massive plateau to the south and a blander "Boulder
    Mountain" for the dryer, smaller plateau to the north. The story goes on to tell
    of a bureaucratic mix-up in Washington at the United States Geological Survey,
    in which the dry mountain to the north, which has very few lakes, erroneously
    received the name "Thousand Lake Mountain" and the lake-studded plateau to
    the south became "Boulder Mountain." I have found no record confirming this
    story, however. Powell and his employees almost always referred to the land-
    forms as plateaus, not mountains. The story's lighthearted jab at the mistakes
    of federal bureaucracy and the federal government's fundamental ignorance of
    local geography certainly carries over into more serious concerns today about
    wilderness designation and a local feeling of powerlessness in their own land
    management.
3. Joseph Smith, *The Book of Abraham: Translated from the Papyrus, by Joseph Smith*
    (1842), 34–35 (chapter 3, verses 2–4) in Smith, *The Pearl or Great Price*. See also the
    entry for "Kolob" in Bruce R. McConkie, *Mormon Doctrine*, 428.
4. Especially in recent decades the LDS Church has gradually moved away from
    referring to itself formally as the "Mormon" Church. If I applied today's stan-
    dards to my narrative, I probably would not use the term "Mormon" in as broad
    a context. But members of the religion today still often, albeit informally, refer
    to themselves as "Mormons." In the nineteenth century, when the faith was
    much more a uniquely regional culture than it is today, they saw themselves
    even more as "Mormons." Thus I retain the use of the word "Mormon" through-
    out this work.
5. The best biographical studies of Joseph Smith are Fawn Brodie's *No Man Knows
    My History*; and Richard Lyman Bushman's more recent *Joseph Smith*. Given the
    extremely controversial life and religion of Smith, the two books take very dif-
    ferent approaches to their subject: Brodie is more critical, and Bushman more
    sympathetic. For more on *The Book of Mormon* itself, see Terryl L. Givens, *By the
    Hand of Mormon*. For more on Mormonism's place in the context of Jacksonian
    America, see Klaus J. Hansen, *Mormonism and the American Experience*.
6. For more on the *Book of Mormon*'s view of polygamy, see Richard S. Van Wag-
    oner, *Mormon Polygamy: A History* (Salt Lake City: Signature Books, 1989), 3.
7. Bushman, *Joseph Smith*, 101, 104.
8. Ibid., 99.
9. Joseph Smith, Jr., *The Book of Mormon* (1830), 1 Nephi 12:23. For deeper analysis,
    see also Mauss, *All Abraham's Children*, 116.
10. Smith, *The Book of Mormon*, 2 Nephi 5:21.
11. Isaiah 51:3, King James Version.
12. Bushman, *Joseph Smith*, 99. In *The Book of Mormon* Christ preaches extensively
    from Isaiah 54. Elsewhere, notably the books of 2 and 3 Nephi and Mosiah 14,
    the prophecies of Isaiah also take a prominent role.

13. Smith, *Book of Mormon*, 2 Nephi 30:6.

14. Quoted in Charles S. Peterson, *Take Up Your Mission*, 182.

15. Spencer W. Kimball, "The Day of the Lamanite." For a detailed analysis of Mormons and racial constructions of Indians, see chapter 5, "Old Lamanites, New Lamanites, and the Negotiation of Identity," in Mauss, *All Abraham's Children*, particularly 116–20.

16. See Leonard J. Arrington, *Great Basin Kingdom*, 333–34; and Carolyn E. Grattan, "New St. Joseph, Nevada."

17. The "Thirteen Articles of Faith" were first published in the Mormon journal *Times and Seasons* in 1842 and became official church doctrine in 1882. See Joseph Smith, *The Pearl of Great Price*, 80. Interestingly, the parenthetical "New Jerusalem" did not appear in early versions of the articles.

18. John L. Brooke, *The Refiner's Fire*, 198–99; and Givens, *By the Hand of Mormon*, 67–69.

19. Hugh Nibley, "Brigham Young on the Environment," 24. The Kirtland temple dedication was transcribed in the Mormon newspaper *Latter-Day Saints' Messenger and Advocate* 2, no. 6 (April 1836).

20. Bushman, Joseph Smith, 219–21.

21. Quoted in Brodie, *No Man Knows My History*, 126.

22. Smith, *The Pearl of Great Price*, 79.

23. Brooke, *The Refiner's Fire*, 199.

24. Hansen, *Mormonism and the American Experience*, 83.

25. For Mormon views on the racial destiny and curse of Africans, see chapter 8, "The Curse of African Lineage in Mormon History," in Mauss, *All Abraham's Children*, 212–30.

26. Smith quoted in Hansen, *Mormonism and the American Experience*, 69–70.

27. Isaiah 40:4 (King James Version).

28. Quoted in Brooke, *The Refiner's Fire*, 268.

29. Quoted in Brodie, *No Man Knows My History*, 359.

30. Michael Scott Van Wagenen, *The Texas Republic and the Mormon Kingdom of God*, 39.

31. Arrington, *Great Basin Kingdom*, 39.

32. Isaiah 2:2. Micah 4:1 also contains almost this exact quotation. In 1831 Smith echoed this prophetic language when he preached that "Zion shall flourish upon the hills and rejoice upon the mountains, and shall be assembled together unto the place which I have appointed" which was later put into the *Doctrine and Covenants of the Church of the Latter Day Saints: Carefully Selected from the Revelations of God* (the Mormon canon collection first published in 1835), chapter 49, verse 25. Official church history also tells of an occasion when Smith, while drinking a tumbler of spring water, prophesied that "the saints would yet go to the Rocky Mountains; and, said he, this water tastes much like that of the crystal streams that are running from the snow-capped mountains": B. H. Roberts, *History of the Church of Jesus Christ of Latter-Day Saints*, vol. 2, 181–82.

33. Nels Anderson, *Desert Saints*, 50, 57.

34. George Q. Cannon, "Mission to Arizona," 143. See also Peterson, *Take Up Your Mission*, 9.

35. Arrington, *Great Basin Kingdom*, 64–65. For more on how nineteenth-century Mormons saw every aspect of their lives as blessed "sacred time," from cultivating land and digging irrigation ditches to simply interacting with one another, see Jan Shipps, *Mormonism*.

36. This apocryphal story is much more common in works of "pop history" and on Internet sites than in scholarly works on Utah or Mormon history. See, for example, Harold Schindler, "Pioneers Maintain Western Trek, Hear about Great Salt Lake Valley," in a *Salt Lake Tribune* series on the sesquicentennial of Mormon settlement in Utah (June 28, 1997), A2. Obviously the story reinforces Mormon themes of perseverance in a desert as well as prevailing over the skepticism of nonbelievers.

37. *Journal of Discourses* 19 (1877): 62.

38. For more on the perceived parallels and similarities between the Holy Land and the foot of the Wasatch Mountains, see Farmer, *On Zion's Mount*, 108–9.

39. Richard Jackson, "Utah's Harsh Lands," 8. The standard definition of a "desert" is a region with less than 10 inches of annual precipitation. The most recent thirty-year average for the Salt Lake Valley is 16.5 inches annually.

40. Powell, *Report on the Lands of the Arid Region*, 94.

41. Nibley, "Brigham Young on the Environment," 3.

42. For more details on the later erroneous Mormon emphasis on the desert qualities of the Salt Lake and Utah Lake Valleys, see Farmer's chapter "The Desertification of Zion," in *On Zion's Mount*, particularly 126–30.

43. Dan Flores, "Agriculture, Mountain Ecology, and the Land Ethic," 158.

44. For details on Mormon community qualities and planning, see Richard Francaviglia, *The Mormon Landscape*.

45. Arrington, *Great Basin Kingdom*, 24.

46. Ibid., 93.

47. William P. Mackinnon, "'Like Splitting a Man Up His Backbone,'" 118–19.

48. Ibid., 112.

49. Ibid., 117. For more detail on Nevada's eastward encroachment upon Mormon Utah Territory, see chapter 4 of W. Paul Reeve, *Making Space on the Western Frontier*.

50. Anderson, *Desert Saints*, xiii.

51. Nibley, "Brigham Young on the Environment," 7. Mormons of the nineteenth and early twentieth centuries frequently called nonmembers "gentiles," including, ironically enough, Jews.

52. Brigham Young, "Management of the Kanyons," 210. For more on the deep-seated Mormon aversion to rampant mining, see Reeve, *Making Space on the Western Frontier*, 91–92.

53. Quoted in Arrington, *Great Basin Kingdom*, 10.

54. Genesis 1:28 and 2:15 (King James Version), respectively.
55. Thomas G. Alexander, "Stewardship and Enterprise," 342.
56. Arrington, *Great Basin Kingdom*, 11, 25.
57. Ibid., 333.
58. Ibid., 330.
59. Ibid., 333. The settlements of the Muddy River were originally intended to serve as supply points for Mormons en route to California in the 1860s. Unfortunately they succumbed to flash floods in 1871, just as many Canyon Country towns did in coming decades.
60. Ibid., 335–36.
61. Wallace Stegner, *Mormon Country*, 126–27. Stegner opines, in his characteristic prose, that "fashion, as much as anything else" killed Orderville.
62. Ibid., 337.
63. Anderson, *Desert Saints*, 283.

CHAPTER 7. THE RIM OF MORMONDOM I

1. Robert Campbell, "Diary, Friday, December 7," in William B. Smart and Donna T. Smart (eds.), *Over the Rim*, 41–42.
2. Parley P. Pratt, "Pratt's Report to the Legislative Council, February 5, 1850," in Smart and Smart, *Over the Rim*, 181.
3. Blackhawk, *Violence over the Land*, 139–41.
4. For more on the conflict between Mormons' minimal survival and maintaining economic self-sufficiency amid gold rush settlers, see chapter 3, "The Harvest of '49," in Arrington's *Great Basin Kingdom*, 64–95.
5. For details on the Walker War, see Blackhawk, *Violence over the Land*, 237–44.
6. Throughout this study I largely retain the use of the name "Grand River" for what we now call the upper Colorado. In 1921, largely at the urging of Colorado State politicians, the name "Colorado" was adopted for the entire length of the Grand and Colorado Rivers. The bulk of my narrative occurs before this name-change, however, so I feel it most appropriate for the Grand to retain its former name.
7. William Huntington, "Interesting Account of a Trip to the Navijos."
8. Richard A. Firmage, *A History of Grand County*, 77–80. The name "La Sal" was actually much older than "Elk Mountain," dating back at least to Miera's time.
9. Huntington, "Interesting Account" (emphasis in the original).
10. Ibid. For more on the Gadianton Band, see Smith, *The Book of Mormon*, Helaman 2.
11. The precise meaning of "secret combinations" has long been debated among Mormon scholars. Fawn Brodie argued that the term was meant to be a prophecy by Smith warning of the Freemasons. Secret hand signals by the Gadiantons had brought down Nephite society, and many Americans of the early 1800s, in a wave of anti-Masonic fervor, believed that secret hand signals among

Freemasons would bring down their own nation: Brodie, *No Man Knows My History*, 63. In the 1990s Mormon folklore commonly cited inner-city gangs' hand signals as a similar harbinger of destruction. At any rate Huntington would not be the last Mormon to identify the Canyon Country as the refuge of Gadianton. In an oral history interview with Charles Peterson in 1970, longtime San Juan County resident Albert R. Lyman spoke of a group of Paiute Indians who were trapped in a pen after hostilities in 1923, saying: "This is the first time this band has been corralled since the days of Gadianton": Lyman, "Oral History Interview," 15. Farther west, on the Utah-Nevada border, Mormons were also equating the Shivwits and Kaibab Paiutes with the wilderness Gadianton Band. See Reeve, *Making Space on the Western Frontier*, 102–4.

12. For more on this "Mormon Reformation," see Farmer, *On Zion's Mount*, 92–93.

13. Bagley, *Blood of the Prophets*, argues the details of the role of prophecy and Indian relations as they culminated in the 1857 Mountain Meadows Massacre. While the strategy of whites winning over Indian allies for wars among themselves was common throughout all European nations' colonization efforts in the Americas, the separatism and millenarianism of Mormons, as well as their view of Indians' specific destiny, made Mormon conversion unusual.

14. William B. Pace, "Diary of the Elk Mountain Mission, 1855–1856" (typescript), entry for April 16, 1855.

15. William B. Pace, "Blessing Given by Patriarch Isaac Morely" (typescript).

16. Pace, "Diary," May 31, 1855.

17. Alfred N. Billings, "Personal Diary," entry for June 3, 1855.

18. Ibid., June 17–22, 1855.

19. Robert S. McPherson, *The Northern Navajo Frontier*, 13. The designation of the diverse Indians of this region as "Utes" or "Paiutes" was very much a Euro-American imposition based on the former having horses and the latter not. For more on the overall nature of the slave trade of nonequestrian Paiutes and Nuche Indians among horseback tribes of the Great Basin, the Navajos, and New Mexico, see James F. Brooks, *Captives and Cousins*; and Blackhawk, *Violence over the Land*.

20. Billings, "Personal Diary," June 23, 1855. "Snakes" may have been a reference to Shoshone Indians, although Shoshones were not significant actors in this region's economy.

21. Ibid., June 15, 1855.

22. Ibid., June 29, 1855.

23. Ibid., June 24, 1855.

24. Ibid., September 4, 1855.

25. Ibid., September 19, 1855.

26. Ibid., September 23–24, 1855.

27. Faun McConkie Tanner, *A History of Moab, Utah*, 22. The topic of missionaries who rejected the advances of Weeminuche women is probably the favorite element of this story among Moab locals today.

28. *Deseret News*, September 11, 1861. Though specifically referring to the Uinta Basin north of the Canyon Country, these words nonetheless show this low point of the Mormon compulsion to reclaim Bad Land.

29. The details of the Greens' deaths are very sparse. See Charles S. Peterson, *Look to the Mountains*, 29; and Firmage, *A History of Grand County*, 103–4.

30. Peterson, *Look to the Mountains*, 30–32. We know very little about this curious trio of ranchers, although Negro Bill Canyon, several miles up the Colorado from Moab and a popular hike for tourists, took Granstaff's name.

31. Mormons arriving from their New World Promised Land in Salt Lake City certainly showed their impressions of the Grand River by naming it Moab. In the Old Testament the people of Moab were originally descended from the incest-born son of Lot and his daughter. The Bible depicts the region as a place of ravines, flat-topped hills (similar to the mesas of the Canyon Country), and idolaters and as the death-place of Moses. In one of Moab's earliest regional histories, Faun McConkie Tanner acknowledged these biblical parallels in the naming of Moab but also pointed out that the Paiute word for "mosquito" is "Moapa": Tanner, *History of Moab, Utah*, 32. Anyone who has visited the Colorado River in the summer will attest that this is just as valid an origin for the place's name as any biblical references.

32. As of 2005 Mormons made up about 28 percent of Grand County, in which Moab is the only city of significant size. For a more modern view of the sociological and demographic anomalies in this Utah town, see Matt Canham's article in the July 25, 2005, *Salt Lake Tribune*: "LDS Future May Be Divined from Grand County Experience."

33. Quoted in Peterson, *Take Up Your Mission*, 182.

34. Ibid., 103.

35. For details on this "Oasis Agriculture" of the Little Colorado settlements, see chapter 7 in Peterson, *Take Up Your Mission*.

36. P. T. Reilly, *Lee's Ferry*, 56.

37. Peterson, *Take Up Your Mission*, 36.

38. Though Pre-Columbian ruins and rock art sites are certainly prominent farther north and west than Grand Gulch, most archaeologists see the San Juan as the northwestern boundary for various Ancestral Puebloan cultures, mostly of the Pueblo II era, which began to move into the Eastern Canyon Country around 1080 CE. Beyond the Colorado River archaeological sites are dominated by the Fremont Culture. While there is still a debate about the connections between the Fremont and Puebloan groups, the region between the Colorado and the San Juan was very much the frontier area between the two cultures. See David Madsen, *Exploring the Fremont*; Steven R. Simms, *Ancient Peoples of the Great Basin and Colorado Plateau*, 221–28; and Jeffrey S. Dean, "Delineating the Anasazi," in J. Jefferson Reid and David E. Doyel (eds.), *Emil W. Haury's Prehistory of the Southwest*, 407–13.

39. McPherson, *The Northern Navajo Frontier*, 84.

40. George Chittenden, "Report of George B. Chittenden, Topographer of the San Juan Division, 1875," in F. V. Hayden, *Ninth Annual Report of the United States Geological and Geographical Survey*, 361.

41. "San Juan Stake Camp Records," Tuesday, June 17, 1879, in David E. Miller, *Hole in the Rock*, 26.

42. "George B. Hobbs' Account of Exploration from Hole-in-the-Rock to Montezuma and Return," in Miller, *Hole in the Rock*, 91–92. Hobbs erroneously referred to Merrick as "Merrit."

43. Miller, *Hole in the Rock*, 6. George Hobbs wrote that "one of the objects" of the mission "was to select a place where the converts from the Southern States might make new homes in Utah and still be in a warmer climate." A roster of the mission indicates that the large group did not include any plural wives. In this era, at least ten years before the church began officially giving up polygamy and at a time when polygamy was mostly reserved for the upper classes, this indicates that nearly everyone selected for the mission was already at the bottom of Mormon society.

44. Miller, *Hole in the Rock*, ix.

45. Ibid., 49.

46. Ibid., 103. Today's Canyon Country aficionados should not confuse this "Hole in the Rock," still accessible via a rough road from Escalante or by boat from Lake Powell, with another "Hole in the Rock" on Highway 191 south of Moab. The latter is simply a tourist shop carved out of a sandstone bluff and has nothing to do with the San Juan Mission. For that matter either "Hole in the Rock" must not be confused with "Hole in the Wall" of Butch Cassidy fame in Wyoming.

47. Ibid., 109.

48. Ibid., 119.

49. Platte D. Lyman, "Journal of Platte D. Lyman," entry for February 29, 1880, in Miller, *Hole in the Rock*, 167.

50. Albert R. Lyman, "The Land of Pagahrit," *Improvement Era* (October 1909): 934–38. He offers a very embellished, *Book of Mormon*–oriented view of the lake. In the years between the San Juan Mission's layover at the lake and Lyman's article, Lake Pagahrit obviously became a very important watering place for ranchers in this region of the Canyon Country. In the fall of 1915 a huge flash flood, possibly exacerbated by erosion from grazing damage, destroyed the natural dam and drained Lake Pagahrit. Today hikers from nearby Lake Powell can still see the silted remnants of the lake bottom.

51. Miller, *Hole in the Rock*, 138. Another second-generation "Hole-in-the-Rocker," Utah rancher and legislator Charles Redd, recalled years later that "my father was a strong man, and reluctant to display emotion." But when discussion of this final push over Comb Ridge came up in later years "the memory of such bitter struggles was too much for him and he wept": Leonard J. Arrington, *Utah's Audacious Stockman*, 16.

52. On April 4, 1880, Platte Lyman noted in his journal that, counting man-hours, the cost of the expedition had been $4,800. Given how isolated from outside economies southern Utah was at this time, it is difficult to convert this amount to current dollars, but the true cost of the expedition would have been around $100,000 in today's money.

53. *The Autobiography of Samuel Rowley*, quoted in Miller, *Hole in the Rock*, 55.

54. See, for example, Clarence Dutton, "Map of Portions of Utah and Arizona."

55. Miller, *Hole in the Rock*, 28.

56. Lyman, "Journal," April 11 and April 13, 1880, in Miller, *Hole in the Rock*, 170. Although Silas Smith was the official president of the San Juan Mission, he would not arrive for several more weeks. Lyman was the acting leader.

57. Crampton, *Standing Up Country*, 111.

58. Today Hall's Crossing is beneath the waters of Lake Powell, although a modern ferry runs its approximate course between Bullfrog and Hall's Marina. Dandy Crossing, also submerged, lies just below Hite Marina.

59. Robert S. McPherson, *A History of San Juan County*, 103–4.

60. Quoted in McPherson, *The Northern Navajo Frontier*, 56.

61. Peterson, *Look to the Mountains*, 92; and Gary Topping, *Glen Canyon and the San Juan Country*, 153–54.

62. Albert R. Lyman, *The Edge of the Cedars*, 19.

63. Chapter 2, "Space and Time," in Francaviglia, *The Mormon Landscape*. In one specific example Mormon communities often grazed cattle and sheep in common pastures, unlike larger-scale, "range war"–influenced ranches in the rest of the West. In the town of Monticello, which had significant contact with Texan and New Mexican ranchers, most Mormons still keep their cattle and sheep in separate pastures. Although Mormon communalism actually drove out nonlocal ranchers, Mormons nonetheless adopted some of their competitors' practices. In my own personal anecdotal experience, I have noticed elements of "cowboy culture," more specifically drinking alcohol, playing cards, and swearing, among many ranchers in the Canyon Country. All these practices are much more taboo and shunned in regions closer to the church leadership in northern Utah.

64. McPherson, *The Northern Navajo Frontier*, 23.

65. Ibid., 21.

66. In chapter 5 of *All Abraham's Children*, Mauss argues that the continued failure of missionary efforts among the Navajos actually prompted the church to focus more on proselytizing to Central American Indians in the twentieth century. With success among these new groups, the entire mythology of *The Book of Mormon* gradually shifted to emphasize Mesoamerica more in its geography, because its modern inhabitants seemed to be more accurately fulfilling the prophecy of redemption from the Lamanite curse.

67. Peterson, *Look to the Mountains*, 28.

CHAPTER 8. THE RIM OF MORMONDOM II

1. Crampton, "Military Reconnaissance in Southern Utah," 145–46.
2. Ibid., 146. The quotations are taken from official orders given to Andrus by Brig. Gen. Erastus Snow of St. George.
3. Ibid., 152.
4. Ibid., 157.
5. Ibid., 153.
6. Ibid., entry for August 28, 153.
7. Prospectors were squatting in the area of what would become the town of Pahreah as early as the mid-1860s, Mormons first attempted to settle it under occasional Indian attacks in 1868, and it was finally organized as a Mormon ward in 1877. See Thomas W. Smith, "A Brief History of Early Pahreah Settlements."
8. Leland H. Creer, "Mormon Towns in the Region of the Colorado," 11.
9. Bradford J. Frye, *From Barrier to Crossroads*, 1:49.
10. Glynn Bennion, "A Pioneer Cattle Venture of the Bennion Family," 312–23. This Castle Valley on the upper San Rafael should not be confused with the Castle Valley near the Colorado River above Moab, Utah. Technically, the San Rafael formally begins at the junction of Cottonwood, Ferron, and Huntington Creeks, just before its descent into the Canyon Country.
11. In the North Fork of Coal Wash, near a spring, is the inscription "Joseph Swasey Feb The 7 1875."
12. Gilbert, *Report on the Geology of the Henry Mountains*, 151–52.
13. Bennion, "A Pioneer Cattle Venture," 316.
14. Ibid., 323.
15. See Pearl Baker, *Robber's Roost Recollections*; and Richard Negri's oral history compilation *Tales of Canyonlands Cowboys* for more on the development of ranching in the Dirty Devil region around Hanksville.
16. For more on this topic, see Don Walker, "The Carlisles," 268–84; Neil Lambert, "Al Scorup"; chapter 5, "The Livestock Frontier," in Peterson, *Look to the Mountains*; and the chapter "Lake Country Cowboys" in Topping, *Glen Canyon and the San Juan Country*.
17. This idea is best summarized in Flores, "Agriculture, Mountain Ecology, and the Land Ethic."
18. Stegner, *Mormon Country*, 31.
19. Many place-names in the Canyon Country and Great Basin contain the Ute root word "Pah," which denotes the most precious resource in the West: water. I have retained the spelling of the original town "Pahreah" but use the more modern spelling in reference to the Paria River.
20. Smith, "A Brief History of Early Pahreah Settlements," 2–3.
21. Pahreah Ward, Kanab Stake, *Manuscript History and Historical Reports*.
22. A. F. Smithson, untitled letter, *Deseret News*, April 12, 1878.
23. Smith, "A Brief History of Early Pahreah Settlements," 3.

24. Pahreah Ward, Kanab Stake, *Manuscript History*, final entry.

25. Ibid., entry for March 8, 1889.

26. Andrew Jensen, "Compiled Description," in ibid., introduction.

27. George E. Davidson, *Red Rock Eden*, 28–29; and Frye, *From Barrier to Crossroads*, 50. The story of Eph Hanks is told by his sons in Sidney Hanks and Ephraim Hanks Jr., *Scouting for the Mormons on the Great Frontier* (Salt Lake City: Deseret News Press, 1948), although the book is more concerned with promoting faith than with any sort of actual documentation.

28. C. Gregory Crampton actually connects this flood of desperate rather than optimistic settlement to the eventual overtaxing of resources along the Fremont River. See his unpublished manuscript "Mormon Colonization in Southern Utah and Adjacent Parts of Arizona and Nevada," 219–21.

29. Davidson, *Red Rock Eden*, 15.

30. Ibid., 20–23.

31. Powell distinguished between "alcove lands" of harder sandstone, such as the area around Fruita, and "badlands" of shale and clay, such as the area of Caineville and Hanksville: Powell, *Report on the Lands of the Arid Region*, 111–12.

32. Robert J. Meinke, *A Preliminary Ecological and Historical Survey of North and South Caineville Mesas*, 34.

33. Caineville Ward, Wayne Stake, *Manuscript History and Historical Records*, introduction.

34. Miriam B. Murphy, *A History of Wayne County*, 129, 132.

35. *Deseret News*, August 16, 1900.

36. Frederick H. Swanson, *Dave Rust*, 8.

37. Evangeline Godby, "After the Floods, Caineville Would Never Be Quite the Same," *Deseret News* (July 16, 1981), C-1.

38. Ibid.

39. Caineville Ward, Wayne Stake, *General Minutes*, entries for August 16–17, 1909.

40. Ibid., August 20, 1909.

41. Ibid., August 22, 1909.

42. Ibid., September 3, 1909.

43. Godby, "After the Floods."

44. No data for the actual volume of the Fremont River at Caineville for 1909 are available. The biggest flood years in recent history in the Southwest were certainly the El Niño years of 1983 and 1984. In 1984 the Fremont's peak level was 8,800 cubic feet per second (cfs). Even more dramatically, because levels can increase almost exponentially the lower on a river's course the measurement is taken, the highest recorded levels for the Dirty Devil River (into which the Fremont flows) are around 35,000 cfs. In comparison the Colorado River's regular summer flow at Lee's Ferry usually stays at a dam-regulated 10,000 cfs and its highest level in 1983 was 97,000 cfs. By far the highest overall recorded river levels, however, were in 1884, the year that Pahreah was hit. In June of that year the Colorado at Lee's Ferry reached a raging 300,000 cfs as a result of heavy

rains throughout all of its basin, combined with saturated grazing in the mountains. All of these data are available and searchable at the U.S. Geological Service's website: http://nwis.waterdata.usgs.gov/nwis/si. Two books track long-term changes in the Colorado's ecology and flow: Robert H. Webb, *Grand Canyon, a Century of Change*; and Robert H. Webb, Jayne Belnap, and John S. Weisheit, *Cataract Canyon*.

45. George W. Carrol in a special priesthood meeting of all of Caineville's men to "consider the prospect of moving": Caineville Ward, Wayne Stake, *General Minutes*, entry for September 3, 1909.

46. Caineville Ward, Wayne Stake, *General Minutes*, October 31, 1909.

47. David O. McKay, "The Blessing of Work," *Church of Jesus Christ of Latter-Day Saints, 80th Semi-Annual Conference*, October 5, 1909 (http://education.byu.edu/mckay/o9oct5.html).

48. Comments of Elder William Andrews, in Caineville Ward, Wayne Stake, *General Minutes*, September 19, 1909.

49. Ibid., December 14, 1909.

50. Murphy, *A History of Wayne County*, 136–39.

51. Swanson, *Dave Rust*, 15.

52. Quoted in Godby, "After the Floods," C-1.

53. Though the subject is largely beyond the chronological scope of this study, for more information on the ranchers who succeeded the settlements on the Fremont River and grazed the ranges to the east, see Negri, *Tales of Canyonlands Cowboys*.

54. Crampton, "Mormon Colonization in Southern Utah," 221.

55. Lynn Rosenvall, "Defunct Mormon Settlements," 61. All failed settlements in the Canyon Country succumbed to floods except for Elk Mountain Mission, which failed after the Indian attacks, and the Fremont River village of Clifton, which lacked sufficient water.

56. Godby, "After the Floods."

CHAPTER 9. BEYOND AGRICULTURE

1. Roy Webb, "A Foolhardy Undertaking."

2. Although the Denver and Rio Grande Railroad did build a foundational grade for a railroad from Green River to Huntington, Utah, across the canyons of the northern San Rafael Swell, it ultimately decided to take a more northern route to Salt Lake City by way of Price, Utah, further isolating the Mormon towns of the upper San Rafael River.

3. Of course the first Powell expedition of 1869 had launched from Green River, Wyoming, not Green River, Utah.

4. Robert Brewster Stanton and the Denver, Colorado Canyon, and Pacific Railroad, *The Colorado River Survey*, entry from Stanton's diary for May 28, 1889.

5. Stanton, *Colorado River Controversies*, 107.

6. Stanton and the Denver, Colorado Canyon, and Pacific Railroad, *The Colorado River Survey*, entry for May 24, 1889.

7. Robert Brewster Stanton, *Down the Colorado*, 7 (material taken from a previously published serial "Through the Grand Canyon of the Colorado," in *Scribner's Magazine*, 1890, and Stanton's unpublished 1909 manuscript "The Colorado River of the West, and the Exploration, Navigation, and Survey of Its Canyons, from the Standpoint of an Engineer").

8. Ibid., 35–36.

9. Ibid., 64.

10. Ibid., 52–55.

11. Stanton and the Denver, Colorado Canyon, and Pacific Railroad, *The Colorado River Survey*, entries for July 10–15, 1889.

12. Stanton, *Down the Colorado*, 20.

13. Ibid., 106–7.

14. *Deseret News*, February 14, 1872.

15. "Highly Favorable Reports from the Colorado River Placers," *Salt Lake Tribune*, January 4, 1889.

16. Crescent Canyon is today called North Wash.

17. "Green River Gold Fields: Very Favorable Reports Coming from Southeastern Utah about Them," *Salt Lake Tribune*, May 14, 1889. The *Tribune*'s numbers are actually much lower than historian C. Gregory Crampton's figure of "several hundred men," although Crampton's estimates are for the entire rush of the 1890s through all of Glen Canyon: Crampton, *Standing Up Country*, 125. It is unlikely that more than fifty people would have been living at Dandy Crossing at any one time, however.

18. Stanton and the Denver, Colorado Canyon, and Pacific Railroad, *The Colorado River Survey*, entry for June 24, 1889. The estimates of 25 cents per cubic yard that miners gave Stanton were considerably less than the $3 that the *Salt Lake Tribune* was touting at the same time.

19. Ibid., June 24, 1889. See also Brown's separate report on the region's resources on 42.

20. Note in ibid., 42.

21. Stanton, *Down the Colorado*, 19.

22. Ibid. (emphasis in the original). Stanton believed for his entire life that Powell held a sense of proprietorship over the Colorado region. Later, while meeting with Powell in 1892 after the failure of the DCC&P, Stanton wrote that he "seemed to glorify his work and belittle mine." In an 1893 Irrigation Congress meeting in Los Angeles, Powell even made the blatantly untrue statement that no one since his expedition "had passed by boat through the canyons." Stanton, *Colorado River Controversies*, 109–11.

23. Cass Hite, untitled writings in the *Beaver Utonian*, January 13, 1893.

24. Robert Brewster Stanton, "The Hoskaninni Papers," 10–30. See also the Hoskaninni Company's 1899 prospectus on 71.

25. Ibid., 33, 40.
26. Ibid., journal entry for December 9, 1897 (31; emphasis in the original).
27. Ibid., 73.
28. Ibid., 78. Crampton believes that, while Stanton's estimates of gold per square yard were in fact accurate, he grossly overestimated the size of the flakes.
29. Ibid., 140.
30. Ibid., 143.
31. Ibid., 147–49. We do not know how much money Stone personally invested in the Hoskaninni Company, and his personal papers tell nothing about his investment in this venture. By Stanton's account, the initial investments of late 1897 amounted to around $54,000, of which Stone invested $10,342; by 1898 about $200,000 had been spent securing claims along the Colorado River. See Stanton's diary entry for September 18, 1899, in the folder "Hoskaninni Mining Co., Placer Mining on the Colorado River, 1909," Robert Brewster Stanton Papers, Box 1, Folder 13. The total money put into the company by the time it dissolved in 1901 was around $300,000, although we do not know how much of this was Stone's. Adjusted for inflation, total capital invested into the company would have been around $7.4 million. See Stanton, "The Hoskaninni Papers," 147–49.
32. Though it is beyond the chronology of this study, perhaps the best example of the small-scale miner coming out ahead was the case of uranium prospector Vernon Pick, who in 1954 sold his claim to the Delta Mine (also called the "Hidden Splendor") in the San Rafael Swell to the Atlas Mineral Corporation for around $10 million. Atlas never profited from the mine. See Raye C. Ringholz, *Uranium Frenzy*, 133–34.
33. Crampton, *Standing Up Country*, 142; and James M. Aton and Robert S. McPherson, *River Flowing from the Sunrise*, 115–18. For more information on Spencer, see chapter 9 in Reilly, *Lee's Ferry*, 215–48.
34. See the undated letter from summer 1914 from John Hite to Julius Stone in Julius F. Stone, Julius Stone Papers, Box 1, Folder 47. In 1947 Canyon Country guide Harry Aleson wrote to Stone that Hite's Ticaboo gardens were still thriving.
35. Letter from John Hite to Julius Stone, July 2, 1914, Julius Stone Papers, Box 1, Folder 47.
36. Letter from John Hite to Julius Stone, June 39, 1930, Julius Stone Papers, Box 1, Folder 47.
37. "How to Bring Prosperity," *Grand Valley Times*, November 19, 1897 (author uncited).
38. Quoted respectively from two articles in *Emery County Progress*: "Material Resources," September 28, 1901, and "Big Reservoir Scheme," August 24, 1901. The constructed dam and reservoir on Buckhorn Flat, in the northern San Rafael Swell, was apparently not appreciated by all. The *Progress* reported that "some sheep men have taken the liberty on some occasions to turn the water out to

let it run to the San Rafael river besides driving their sheep over the dam and destroying the property...a curse to the country."

39. Outdoor recreation around the turn of the century was largely a product of well-off hobbyists, as is well established in environmental and tourist history. This theme is a major point of both Karl Jacoby's *Crimes against Nature*; and Stephen Fox's *The American Conservation Movement*. See also Robert W. Righter, *The Battle over Hetch Hetchy*, 24–26.

40. Julius Stone's 1932 account of the trip, *Canyon Country: The Romance of a Drop of Water and a Grain of Sand*, ix.

41. Ibid., 70.

42. Julius Stone, "Statement Prepared at the Request of Randolph S. Collins Representing the Solicitor General of the United States," Julius Stone Papers, Box 2, Folder 9.

43. Stone's boats were the most advanced and capable yet to descend the Colorado. Having read the reports of both Powell and Stanton and the description of their awkward and heavy boats, Stone hired Galloway personally to design and supervise the building of four "Cataract Boats" in Ohio. These craft were light and maneuverable, containing fore and aft waterproof compartments to prevent swamping. See David Lavender, *River Runners of the Grand Canyon*, 40–41.

44. Stone, *Canyon Country*, 78.

45. Dave Rust would recall, for example, that his brother Roy, after working through the summer of 1901 for the Hoskaninni Company, "like much of the crew, failed to collect his wages": Swanson, *Dave Rust*, 23.

46. This amusing anecdote is often repeated in river runners' lore and campfire stories, though few published works have mentioned it. The earliest mention I have found of it was in a 1945 letter from river guide Harry Aleson to Stone, in which Aleson sent Stone random bolts and pebbles from the dredge. Aleson also humorously wrote in the letter: "On this decoration day 1945, for sentiment's sake, I removed a heavy pin bolt with plans to mail it to you. The dividend you received from the Stanton Dredge in 1938 is being added to in 1945. Whereas the 7 cups of coffee you cooked in 1938 cost you $714.28 each, you will now require an income tax expert's services from Washington to estimate the value or deduction allowable upon receipt of the pin bolt": Julius Stone Papers, Box 1, Folder 29.

47. By the 1920s a new generation of river runners, armed with the new media of the motion picture, were publicizing the Colorado River in terms familiar to any "extreme sports" enthusiasts today. Most notably the Kolb brothers were holding daily showings of their filmed river expedition at their Grand Canyon studio. See Lavender's *River Runners* for an excellent history of all these river explorers and more. For more detail, Stone himself recommended in his introduction to *Canyon Country* that readers seeking "the thrills of river experiences" read Ellsworth Kolb, *Through the Grand Canyon from Wyoming to Mexico*; and Clyde Eddy, *Down the World's Most Dangerous River*.

48. Letter from Frank Dodge to Julius Stone, dated August 31, 1933, Julius Stone Papers, Box 1, Folder 40.
49. Hank Hassell, *Rainbow Bridge*, 51–53.
50. Byron Cummings, "The Great Natural Bridges of Utah."
51. Hassell, *Rainbow Bridge*, 69.
52. Richard Sellers makes the argument in *Preserving Nature in the National Parks* that the main objective of the National Park Service has always been promoting visitation and not necessarily natural preservation.
53. For example, the only paid employee for decades at Natural Bridges was guide Zeke Johnson, who received a salary of one dollar a month as superintendent of the national monument. For more on the difference between National Parks and Monuments, and the politics behind their designation, see Hal Rothman, *America's National Monuments*, 90–93.
54. Charles L. Bernheimer, *Rainbow Bridge* (1924), 8.
55. Ibid., 4.
56. Ibid., 55.
57. Ibid., 28–29. Later guides and outfitters carried on this illusion of discovery as well. In Glen Canyon veteran Canyon Country river guide Ken Sleight would sometimes lead hikes to Rainbow Bridge without even telling his clients that they were about to see the massive landmark.
58. George C. Fraser, *Journeys in the Canyon Lands of Utah and Arizona*, entry for July 28, 1916 (190).
59. Bernheimer, *Rainbow Bridge*, 31.
60. In July most of the town's men and boys would have been herding in the Abajo Mountains twenty miles to the north.
61. Bernheimer, *Rainbow Bridge*, 32.
62. Stone, *Canyon Country*, 12.
63. Ibid., xiii–xiv (emphasis in the original).
64. J. E. Broaddus, "Doctor Makes Strong Plea in Behalf of Southeastern Utah."
65. Zion was designated a national monument in 1909 and a park in 1919; Bryce a monument in 1924 and a park in 1928. See Wayne Hinton's "Getting Along."
66. Broaddus, "Doctor Makes Strong Plea."

Coda. Modernity Approaches an American Desert

1. The area from Fruita south to Pleasant Creek was designated as Capitol Reef National Monument in 1937. Its boundaries were expanded later, and it was given national park status in 1971.
2. This Grand Gulch of Hall's Creek should not be confused with the better-known canyon of the same name in the San Juan region to the east.
3. "Apostles" are twelve men who sit just below the prophet/president in the Mormon leadership.
4. John A. Widtsoe, *Dry-Farming*, ix.

5. Swanson, *Dave Rust*, 78–79.

6. John A. Widtsoe, "A Journal of John A. Widtsoe, Colorado River Party, September 3–19, 1922," 212.

7. Ibid., 226.

8. Ibid., 203–4.

9. Ibid., 204.

10. Topping, *Glen Canyon and the San Juan Country*, 336. Water development in the Southwest (of the Colorado in particular) is an extensively researched and documented field not discussed here. Two excellent jumping-off points for further examination of attitudes such as LaRue's are Donald Worster's *Rivers of Empire* and Marc Reisner's *Cadillac Desert*.

11. For more on the Progressive impulse to conserve but also develop and streamline natural resources, see Samuel P. Hays, *Conservation and the Gospel of Efficiency*.

12. For more on the Hetch Hetchy Dam controversy, see Righter, *The Battle over Hetch Hetchy*.

13. Specifically, see Abbey's chapter "Polemic: Industrial Tourism in the National Parks," in *Desert Solitaire*, 48–73.

14. Bernard DeVoto, "The West against Itself," *Harper's* 194 (January 1947): 231–56.

15. Jim Stiles, "The Greening of Wilderne$$ in Utah."

16. Elmo R. Richardson, "Federal Park Policy in Utah," 118–19.

17. For more on the interplay between government and ranchers in regard to the Taylor Grazing Act, see Karen R. Merrill, *Public Lands and Political Meaning*.

18. Richardson, "Federal Park Policy in Utah," 117. The Antiquities Act of 1906 allows national monuments with presumed cultural or archaeological resources in need of sometimes immediate protection to be created by the president rather than by the act of Congress that national parks require. See Rothman, *America's National Monuments*, for more information on this problem.

19. Richardson, "Federal Park Policy in Utah," 127. Unlike national parks, which require congressional approval for designation, national monuments are designated by presidential action.

20. Statement of Utah representative James Hansen at U.S. Senate hearings for S. 357: "To Authorize the Bureau of Land Management to Manage the Grand Staircase–Escalante National Monument" (U.S. Senate, 105th Congress, 1st Session, May 1, 1997).

21. Clyde Kluckhohn, *Beyond the Rainbow*, 13. Unlike Kluckhohn's earlier *To the Foot of the Rainbow*, which has had multiple printings, this book is very hard to find. The Utah State Historical Society in Salt Lake City has a photocopied version in its archives.

22. Ibid., 15–17. Jared Farmer has also noted the difference between Kluckhohn's romanticized expectations of a "Wild Horse Mesa" and the more geographically down-to-earth Kaiparowits Plateau: in his *Glen Canyon Dammed*, 89.

23. Kluckhohn, *Beyond the Rainbow*, 194.

24. Ibid., 202.
25. Ibid., 204. Kluckhohn's invocation of the "psychological" value of wilderness—whether genuine or contrived—strongly hints at Pragmatist themes laid out in William James's *The Varieties of Religious Experience: A Study in Human Nature* (1902).
26. Kluckhohn, *Beyond the Rainbow*, 206–7.
27. Ibid., 208.
28. Section 2(c) of the United States Congress's "Wilderness Act: To Establish a National Wilderness Preservation System for the Permanent Good of the Whole People, and for Other Purposes" (Washington, D.C.: 88th Congress, 2nd Session, September 3, 1964).
29. Ruess biographer W. L. Rusho writes that "it has been reported that Wetherill had little respect for Everett, whom he considered a 'pest' who would simply hang around [Wetherill's trading post] for days seeking information and conversation, but who would buy nothing": Rusho, *Everett Ruess*, 151–52.
30. Quoted in Rusho, *Everett Ruess*, 178–79.
31. Ibid., 184.
32. Many Ruess enthusiasts speculate today on the cryptic nature of his self-imposed nickname "Nemo." Ruess had read Jules Verne's 20,000 *Leagues under the Sea* and perhaps may have identified with Captain Nemo's voluntary withdrawal from society. "Nemo" is Latin for "No One," perhaps hinting at some desire on Ruess's part to fade from his old identity.
33. Quoted from a June 29, 1934, letter from Ruess to a friend "Bill," in Rusho, *Everett Ruess*, 160.
34. In 2009 it actually appeared that researchers had finally located the remains of Everett Ruess hidden in rocks near Comb Ridge and even corroborated these remains with an eyewitness account of his being murdered by Navajo thieves. While many parts of this story were intriguing, I personally found it odd that Ruess would have left so many of his essentials in Davis Gulch, crossed the Colorado in winter, and then trudged eighty miles on foot across some of the roughest terrain of the Canyon Country. After significant media attention, detailed DNA analysis of the remains concluded that they were not Ruess's. See David Roberts, "Finding Everett Ruess."
35. Abbey and Hyde's book *Slickrock* included an account of a New Jersey backpacker in the Escalante region whose car was vandalized at a backcountry trailhead simply because she was a backpacker, apparently aligned with conservation efforts, and was assumed not to contribute to the local economy: Abbey and Hyde, *Slickrock*, 57–58. I recall one of the my first forays into the Escalante region with my father in the mid-1990s, when local teenagers at a gas station yelled obscenities at us for our "Utahn for Wilderness" bumper sticker.
36. Since Ruess there have been several other notable cases of overconfident men in their early twenties who assumed that they could survive in harsh wildernesses alone and met with tragic ends, most notably Christopher McCandless,

who starved to death in Alaska's Denali National Park in 1992, and Timothy Treadwell, who lived among Alaskan grizzly bears until being eaten by one in 2003. John Krakauer's book on McCandless, *Into the Wild* (New York: Anchor Books, 1996), specifically mentions Ruess's story. Most recently canyoneer Aaron Ralston very nearly joined the tragic ranks of these young men when he was trapped beneath a boulder in Blue John Canyon in the Canyon Country and only escaped after a self-amputation of his arm.

37. William Cronon, "The Trouble with Wilderness," 89. For more background on the evolution of our cultural definition of "wilderness" see Nash, *Wilderness and the American Mind*.

38. Sarah T. Phillips, *This Land, This Nation*, 19.

39. Introduction to Abbey, *Desert Solitaire*, xii.

40. The essays in Doug Goodman and Daniel McCool (eds.), *Contested Landscape*, give an excellent survey of the wilderness controversy that has so defined the Canyon Country in the last few decades. See also Farmer's *Glen Canyon Dammed* for a very well-rounded view of the many ways in which modern enthusiasts enjoy the Canyon Country.

Bibliography

Books and Articles

Abbey, Edward. *Desert Solitaire: A Season in the Wilderness.* New York: Random House, 1968.

Abbey, Edward, and Philip Hyde. *Slickrock: Endangered Canyons of the Southwest.* New York: Sierra Club/Charles Scribner and Sons, 1971.

Adams, Eilean. *Hell or High Water: James White's Disputed Passage through the Grand Canyon, 1867.* Logan: Utah State University Press, 2001.

Alexander VI. *Papal Bull Inter Cetera II.* Rome, May 4, 1493. In Geoffrey Symcox and Giovanna Rabitti (eds.), Peter D. Diehl (trans.), *Italian Reports on America 1493–1522: Letters, Dispatches, and Papal Bulls. Repertorium Columbianum* 10. Turnhout, Belgium: Brepols, 2001. 34–37

Alexander, Thomas G. "Senator Reed Smoot and Western Land Policy, 1905–1920." *Arizona and the West* 13 (Autumn 1971): 245-64.

———. "Stewardship and Enterprise: The LDS Church and the Wasatch Oasis Environment, 1847–1930." *Western Historical Quarterly* 25, no. 3 (Autumn 1994): 340-64.

Allen, James B. "The Evolution of County Boundaries in Utah." *Utah Historical Quarterly* 23 (July 1955): 261–78.

Allen, John Logan. *Passage through the Garden: Lewis and Clark and the Image of the American Northwest.* Chicago: University of Illinois Press, 1975.

———. "Pyramidal Height-of-Land: A Persistent Myth in the Exploration of Western Anglo-America." *International Geography* 1 (1972): 395–96.

Anderson, Nels. *Desert Saints: The Mormon Frontier in Utah.* Chicago: University of Chicago Press, 1942.

Armijo, Antonio. "Armijo's Journal of 1829–30: The Beginning of Trade between New Mexico and California." Intro. and notes by LeRoy R. Hafen. *Colorado Magazine* 27 (April 1950): 120–31.

Arrington, Leonard J. *Great Basin Kingdom: Economic History of the Latter-Day Saints, 1830–1900.* Lincoln: University of Nebraska Press, 1958.

———. *Utah's Audacious Stockman: Charlie Redd.* Logan: Utah State University Press, 1995.

Aton, James M. *Inventing John Wesley Powell: The Major, His Admirers and Cash-Register Dams in the Colorado River Basin*. Cedar City: Southern Utah State College, 1988.

Aton, James M., and Robert S. McPherson. *River Flowing from the Sunrise: An Environmental History of the Lower San Juan*. Logan: Utah State University Press, 2000.

Bagley, Will. *Blood of the Prophets: Brigham Young and the Massacre at Mountain Meadows*. Norman: University of Oklahoma Press, 2002.

Baker, Pearl. *Robber's Roost Recollections*. Logan: Utah State University Press, 1976.

Barnes, F. A. *Canyonlands National Park: Early History and First Descriptions*. Moab, UT: Canyon Country Publications, 1988.

Barrera-Osario, Antonio. *Experiencing Nature: The Spanish American Empire and the Early Scientific Revolution*. Austin: University of Texas Press, 2006.

Baumgartner, Frederic J. *Longing for the End: A History of Millennialism in Western Civilization*. New York City: St. Martin's Press, 1999.

Beckwith, E. G. *Report of the Exploration of a Route for the Pacific Railroad, Near the 38th and 39th Parallels of Latitude, from the Mouth of the Kansas to the Sevier River, in the Great Basin*. Washington, DC: A. O. P. Nicholson, 1855.

Bellin, Jacques Nicolas. "Carte de L'Amérique Septentrionale." Plate 29 from *L'Hydrographie françoise*. Paris, 1755. DeGolyer Library, Southern Methodist University, Dallas.

Bennion, Glynn. "A Pioneer Cattle Venture of the Bennion Family." *Utah Historical Quarterly* 34 (Fall 1966): 312–25.

Bernheimer, Charles L. *Rainbow Bridge: Circling Navajo Mountain and Explorations in the Badlands of Southern Utah and Northern Arizona* (1924). Ed. Albert E. Ward. Albuquerque: Center for Anthropological Studies, 1999.

Bilinkoff, Jodi. "Francisco Losa and Gregorio López: Spiritual Friendship and Identity Formation on the New Spain Frontier." In *Colonial Saints: Discovering the Holy in the Americas, 1500–1800*, ed. Allan Greer and Jodi Bilinkoff, 115–28. New York: Routledge, 2003.

Billings, Alfred N. "Memorandum, Account Book, and Diary, 1855." Brigham Young University, Harold B. Lee Library Special Collections.

———. "Personal Diary." Utah State Historical Society, Salt Lake City.

Bitton, Davis. "A Re-Evaluation of the 'Turner Thesis' and Mormon Beginnings." *Utah Historical Quarterly* 34 (Fall 1966): 326–33.

Blackhawk, Ned. *Violence over the Land: Indians and Empires in the Early American West*. Cambridge, MA: Harvard University Press, 2006.

Bolton, Herbert E. *Coronado: Knight of Pueblos and Plains*. Albuquerque: University of New Mexico Press, 1949.

——— (ed. and trans.). *Pageant in the Wilderness: The Story of the Escalante Expedition to the Interior Basin, 1776 (Including the Diary and Itinerary of Father Escalante Translated and Annotated)*. Salt Lake City: Utah State Historical Society, 1951.

Broaddus, J. E. "Doctor Makes Strong Plea in Behalf of Southeastern Utah." *Moab Times-Independent*, December 4, 1930.

Brodie, Fawn. *No Man Knows My History: The Life of Joseph Smith, The Mormon Prophet*. New York: Alfred Knopf, 1945.

Brooke, John L. *The Refiner's Fire: The Making of Mormon Cosmology, 1644–1844*. New York: Cambridge University Press, 1994.

Brooks, James F. *Captives and Cousins: Slavery, Kinship, and Community in the Southwest Borderlands*. Chapel Hill: University of North Carolina Press, 2002.

Brooks, Juanita. *Jacob Hamblin, Mormon Apostle to the Indians*. Salt Lake City: Westwater Press, 1980.

———, Juanita. *John Doyle Lee: Zealot, Pioneer-Builder, Scapegoat*. Glendale, CA, A. H. Clark Co., 1962.

Burke, Edmund. *A Philosophical Enquiry into the Origins of Our Ideas of the Sublime and Beautiful* (1757). In *The Works of the Right Honourable Edmund Burke*, section 1, part 2. Cambridge: Oxford University Press, 1906.

Bushman, Richard Lyman. *Joseph Smith: Rough Stone Rolling*. New York: Alfred A. Knopf, 2005.

Caineville Ward, Wayne Stake. *General Minutes*. Vol. 3. Salt Lake City: LDS Church Archives.

———. *Manuscript History and Historical Records*. Vol. 1. Salt Lake City: LDS Church Archives.

Cannon, George Q. "Mission to Arizona, Delivered in the New Tabernacle, Sunday Afternoon, August 10, 1873." *Journal of Discourses* 16 (Liverpool: Joseph F. Smith, 1874): 143.

Carvalho, Solomon Nunes. *Incidents of Travel and Adventure in the Far West with Colonel Frémont's Last Expedition* (1858). Intro. Ava F. Kahn. Lincoln: University of Nebraska Press, 2004.

Cervantes, Fernando. *The Devil in the New World: The Impact of Diabolism in New Spain*. New Haven: Yale University Press, 1994.

Chaffin, Tom. *Pathfinder: John Charles Frémont and the Course of American Empire*. New York: Hill and Wang, 2002.

Chávez, John. *The Lost Land: The Chicano Image of the Southwest*. Albuquerque: University of New Mexico Press, 1984.

Cohen, Bernard. "What Columbus 'Saw' in 1492." *Scientific American* (December 1992): 100–106.

Crampton, C. Gregory. "The Discovery of the Green River." *Utah Historical Quarterly* 20 (October 1952): 299–312.

———. "Military Reconnaissance in Southern Utah, 1866." *Utah Historical Quarterly* 32 (Spring 1964): 145–61.

———. "Mormon Colonization in Southern Utah and Adjacent Parts of Arizona and Nevada." Unpublished manuscript, 1965. Torrey, Utah: Capitol Reef National Park Archives.

———. *Standing Up Country: The Canyon Lands of Utah and Arizona*. New York: Alfred A. Knopf, 1964.

Creer, Leland H. *The Activities of Jacob Hamblin in the Region of the Colorado*. University of Utah Anthropological Papers 33 (1958).

———. *Mormon Towns in the Region of the Colorado*. University of Utah Anthropological Papers 32 (1958).

Cronon, William. "Modes of Prophecy and Production: Placing Nature in History." *Journal of American History* 76 (March 1990): 1122–31.

———. "The Trouble with Wilderness; or, Getting Back to the Wrong Nature." In *Uncommon Ground: Rethinking the Human Place in Nature*, 69–90. New York: W. W. Norton, 1995.

Cummings, Byron. "The Great Natural Bridges of Utah." *National Geographic Magazine* 21 (February 1910): 157–67.

Cutter, Donald C. "Prelude to the Pageant in the Wilderness." *Western Historical Quarterly* 8 (January 1977): 6–14.

Davidson, George E. *Red Rock Eden: The Story of Fruita, One of Mormon Country's Most Isolated Settlements*. Torrey: Capitol Reef Natural History Association, 1986.

Dellenbaugh, Frederick S. *A Canyon Voyage: The Narrative of the Second Powell Expedition Down the Green-Colorado River from Wyoming, and the Explorations on the Land, in the Years 1871 and 1872*. New York: Putnam's Sons, 1908.

———. *Journal, 1871–1873* (microfilm). Utah State University Special Collections, Logan.

Denton, Sally. *American Massacre: The Tragedy at Mountain Meadows, September 1857*. New York: Alfred A. Knopf, 2003.

DeVoto, Bernard. "The West against Itself." Harper's 194 (January 1947): 231–56.

Diamond, Jared. *Collapse: How Societies Choose to Fail or Succeed*. New York: Viking Press, 2005.

Dolnick, Edward. *Down the Great Unknown: John Wesley Powell's 1869 Journey of Discovery and Tragedy through the Grand Canyon*. New York: Harper-Collins, 2001.

Dutton, Clarence E. "Map of Portions of Utah and Arizona Showing Faults and Flexures." Washington, DC: U.S. Geographical and Geological Survey of the Rocky Mountain Region, 1879.

———. *Report on the Geology of the High Plateaus of Utah, with Atlas*. Washington, DC: U.S. Government Printing Office, 1880.

———. "The San Rafael Swell, 1880." Utah State Historical Society, Salt Lake City.

Eddy, Clyde. *Down the World's Most Dangerous River*. New York: Frederick A. Stockes Co., 1929.

Egan, Ferol. *Frémont: Explorer for a Restless Nation*. New York: Doubleday, 1977.

Escobar, Francisco. "Father Escobar's Relación of the Oñate Expedition to California." Ed. Herbert E. Bolton. *Catholic Historical Review* 5 (1919): 19–41.

Fagan, Brian. *The Little Ice Age: How Climate Made History*. New York: Basic Books, 2000.

Farmer, Jared. *Glen Canyon Dammed: Inventing Lake Powell and the Canyon Country*. Tucson: University of Arizona Press, 1999.

———. *On Zion's Mount: Mormons, Indians, and the American Landscape*. Cambridge, MA: Harvard University Press, 2008.

Ferris, Warren A. *Life in the Rocky Mountains: A Diary of Wanderings on the Sources of the Rivers Missouri, Columbia, and Colorado, 1830–1835*. Denver: Old West Publishing Company, 1983.

Firmage, Richard A. *A History of Grand County*. Salt Lake City: Utah Historical Society and Grand County Commission, 1996.

Flint, Richard, and Shirley Cushing Flint (eds.). *The Coronado Expedition from the Distance of 460 Years*. Albuquerque: University of New Mexico Press, 2003.

——— (eds.). *Documents of the Coronado Expedition, 1539–1542*. Dallas: Southern Methodist University Press, 2005.

Flores, Dan. "Agriculture, Mountain Ecology, and the Land Ethic: Phases of Environmental History in Utah." In *Working the Range: Essays on the History of Western Land Management*, ed. John R. Wunder, 157–86. Westport, CT: Greenwood Press, 1985.

Fox, Stephen. *The American Conservation Movement: John Muir and His Legacy*. Madison: University of Wisconsin Press, 1981.

Francaviglia, Richard. *Believing in Place: A Spiritual Geography of the Great Basin*. Las Vegas: University of Nevada Press, 2003.

———. *Mapping and Imagination in the Great Basin: A Cartographic History*. Reno: University of Nevada Press, 2005.

———. *The Mormon Landscape: Existence, Creation, and Perception of a Unique Image in the American West*. New York: AMS Press, 1978.

Fraser, George C. *Journeys in the Canyon Lands of Utah and Arizona, 1914–1916*. Ed. Frederick H. Swanson. Tucson: University of Arizona Press, 2003.

Frye, Bradford J. *From Barrier to Crossroads: An Administrative History of Capitol Reef National Park, Utah*. 2 vols. Denver: Cultural Resources Selections, National Park Service, 1998.

Geary, Edward. *A History of Emery County*. Salt Lake City: Utah State Historical Society and Emery County Commission, 1996.

———. *The Proper Edge of the Sky: The High Plateau Country of Utah*. Salt Lake City: University of Utah Press, 1992.

Gilbert, Grove Karl. *Report on the Geology of the Henry Mountains*. Washington, DC: U.S. Government Printing Office, 1880.

Givens, Terryl L. *By the Hand of Mormon: The American Scripture That Launched a New World Religion*. New York: Oxford University Press, 2002.

Glacken, Clarence. *Traces on the Rhodian Shore: Nature and Culture in Western Thought from Ancient Times to the End of the Eighteenth Century*. Berkeley: University of California Press, 1967.

Godby, Evangeline. "After the Floods, Caineville Would Never Be Quite the Same." *Deseret News* (July 16, 1981), C-1.

Goetzmann, William H. *Exploration and Empire: The Explorer and the Scientist in the Winning of the American West*. New York: Norton, 1966.

————. *New Lands, New Men: America and the Second Great Age of Discovery*. New York: Viking Penguin, 1986.

Goodman, Doug, and Daniel McCool (eds.). *Contested Landscape: The Politics of Wilderness in Utah and the West*. Salt Lake City: University of Utah Press, 1999.

Grattan, Carolyn E. "New St. Joseph, Nevada: A Reexamination of the Mormon Experience on the Muddy River." Master's thesis. University of Nevada, Las Vegas, 1982.

Gregory, Herbert E., William Culp Darrah, and Charles Kelly (eds.). *The Exploration of the Colorado River and the High Plateaus of Utah by the Second Powell Expedition of 1871–1872*. Salt Lake City: Utah State Historical Society, 1949.

Gutiérrez, Ramón. *When Jesus Came, the Corn Mothers Went Away: Marriage, Sexuality, and Power in New Mexico, 1500–1846*. Stanford: Stanford University Press, 1991.

Hafen, Leroy R. (ed.) *Fur Trappers and Traders of the Far Southwest*. Glendale: Arthur H. Clark Company, 1965.

Hafen, Leroy R., and Ann W. Hafen. *The Old Spanish Trail: Santa Fe to Los Angeles*. Glendale: Arthur H. Clark Company, 1954.

Hamblin, Jacob. "Journals and Letters of Jacob Hamblin, 1854–1877" (typescript). Brigham Young University Library, 1969.

Hammond, George P. "The Search for the Fabulous in the Settlement of the Southwest." *Utah Historical Quarterly* 24 (1956): 1–19.

Hanks, Ephraim, Jr. and Sidney Hanks. *Scouting for the Mormons on the Great Frontier*. Salt Lake City: Deseret News Press, 1948.

Hansen, Klaus J. *Mormonism and the American Experience*. Chicago: University of Chicago Press, 1981.

Hassell, Hank. *Rainbow Bridge: An Illustrated History*. Logan: Utah State University Press, 1999.

Hausladen, Gary J. (ed.). *Western Places, American Myths: How We Think about the West*. Reno and Las Vegas: University of Nevada Press, 2003.

Hayden, F. V. "Letter to Secretary of the American Philosophical Society, Oct. 10, 1867," Proceedings of the American Philosophical Society, Vol X (1865–1868): 352–353.

————. *Ninth Annual Report of the United States Geological and Geographical Survey*. Washington, DC: U.S. Government Printing Office, 1876.

————. *United States Geological and Geographical Survey of Territories* 10. Washington, DC: U.S. Government Printing Office, 1878.

Hays, Samuel P. *Conservation and the Gospel of Efficiency: The Progressive Conservation Movement, 1890–1920*. Cambridge, MA: Harvard University Press, 1959.

Hill, Joseph John. "Spanish and Mexican Exploration and Trade Northwest from New Mexico into the Great Basin, 1765–1853." *Utah Historical Quarterly* 7 (January 1930): 3–23.

Hinton, Wayne. "Getting Along: The Significance of Cooperation in the Development of Zion National Park." *Utah Historical Quarterly* 38 (Fall 2000): 313–31.

Humboldt, Alexander von. *Atlas geographique et physique du Royaume de la Nouvelle Espagne* (1811). Stuttgart: Brockhaus, 1969.

Huntington, Oliver B. "History of the Life of Oliver B. Huntington, Written by Himself, 1878–1900." University of Utah, Marriot Library Special Collections, Salt Lake City.

———. *Official Elk Mountain Mission Journal, 1855*. LDS Church Archives, Salt Lake City.

———. "Personal Diary." Utah State Historical Society, Salt Lake City.

Huntington, William. "Interesting Account of a Trip to the Navijos, and of the Ancient Ruins in That Region." *Deseret News* (December 28, 1854), 3.

Jackson, Richard. "Righteousness and Environmental Change: The Mormons and the Environment." In *Charles Redd Monographs in Western History* 5, ed. Thomas G. Alexander, 21–43. Provo: Brigham Young University Press, 1975.

———. "Utah's Harsh Lands: Hearth of Greatness." *Utah Historical Quarterly* 49 (Spring 1981): 5–25.

Jacobs, G. Clell. "The Phantom Pathfinder: Juan María Antonio de Rivera and His Expedition." *Utah Historical Quarterly* 60 (Summer 1992): 200–223.

Jacoby, Karl. *Crimes against Nature: Squatters, Poachers, Thieves, and the Hidden History of American Conservation*. Berkeley: University of California Press, 2001.

James, William. *The Varieties of Religious Experience: A Study in Human Nature*. New York: Penguin, 1982 (originally published 1902).

Keeler, Daniel A. "The Journey of the Billings Party to Elk Mountain in 1855" (unpublished manuscript). Utah State Historical Society, Salt Lake City.

Kelly, Charles. "The Mysterious D. Julien." *Utah Historical Quarterly* 6 (July 1933): 83–88.

———. *Salt Desert Trails: A History of the Hastings Cutoff and Other Early Trails Which Crossed the Great Salt Desert Seeking a Shorter Road to California*. Salt Lake City: Western Printing Company, 1930.

Kennedy, Roger G. *Mr. Jefferson's Lost Cause: Land, Farmers, Slavery, and the Louisiana Purchase*. New York: Oxford University Press, 2003.

Kenton, Edna (trans. and ed.). *The Jesuit Relations and Allied Documents: Travels of the Jesuit Missionaries in North America, 1610–1791*. New York: Albert and Charles Boni, 1925.

Kimball, Spencer W. "The Day of the Lamanite." *Improvement Era* (December 1960): 922–23.

Kluckhohn, Clyde. *Beyond the Rainbow*. Boston: Christopher Publishing House, 1933 (out of print; typescript available at Utah State Historical Society in Salt Lake City).

———. *To the Foot of the Rainbow: A Tale of Twenty-Five Hundred Miles of Wandering on Horseback through the Southwest Enchanted Land* (1927). Albuquerque: University of New Mexico Press, 1992.

Knipmeyer, James H. *Butch Cassidy Was Here: Historic Inscriptions of the Colorado Plateau*. Salt Lake City: University of Utah Press, 2002.

———. "The Denis Julien Inscriptions." *Utah Historical Quarterly* 64 (Winter 1996): 52–69.

———. "Denis Julien: Midwestern Fur Trader." *Missouri Historical Review* 95 (April 2001): 245–63.

Kolb, Ellsworth. *Through the Grand Canyon from Wyoming to Mexico*. New York: Macmillan, 1915.

Krech, Shepard, III. *The Ecological Indian: Myth and History*. New York: W. W. Norton, 1999.

Lambert, Neil. "Al Scorup: Cattleman of the Canyons." *Utah Historical Quarterly* 32 (Summer 1964): 301–20.

Las Casas, Bartolomé de. *Las Casas on Columbus: The Third Voyage*. Ed. Geoffrey Symcox and Jesús Carillo. Trans. Michael Hammer and Blair Sullivan. Repertorium Columbianum 11. Turnhout, Belgium: Brepols, 2001.

Lavender, David. *River Runners of the Grand Canyon*. Grand Canyon Village, AZ: Grand Canyon Natural History Association, 1985.

Lee, Ronald F. *The Antiquities Act of 1906*. Washington, DC: U.S. Government Printing Office, 1970.

Leiby, Austin Nelson. "Borderland Pathfinders: The 1765 Diaries of Juan María Antonio de Rivera." Ph.D. dissertation. Northern Arizona University, 1984.

Leone, Mark P. *Roots of Modern Mormonism*. Cambridge, MA: Harvard University Press, 1979.

Limerick, Patricia Nelson. *Desert Passages: Encounters with the American Deserts*. Albuquerque: University of New Mexico Press, 1985.

Linklater, Andro. *Measuring America: How an Untamed Wilderness Shaped the United States and Fulfilled the Promise of Democracy*. New York: Walker Publishing Company, 2002.

Losa, Francisco de. *The Holy Life of Gregorio López, a Spanish Hermite in the West Indies* (1612). London, 1675.

Lyman, Albert R. *The Edge of the Cedars: The Story of Walter C. Lyman and the San Juan Mission*. New York: Carlton Press, 1966.

———. "Oral History Interview" (Charles Peterson, interviewer, 1970). Utah State Historical Society, Gary Topping Papers, Box 13, Folder 5.

Lyman, Platte D. *The Diary of Platte D. Lyman*. Provo: Brigham Young University, 1946.

MacKinnon, William P. "'Like Splitting a Man Up His Backbone': The Territorial Dismemberment of Utah, 1850–1896." *Utah Historical Quarterly* 71, no. 2 (Spring 2003): 100–24.

Madsen, David. *Exploring the Fremont*. Salt Lake City: Utah Museum of Natural History, 1989.

Madsen, Steven. *Exploring Desert Stone: John N. Macomb's 1859 Expedition to the Canyonlands of the Colorado*. Logan: Utah State University Press, 2010.

Manly, William. *Death Valley in '49: An Important Chapter of California Pioneer History*. New York: Wallace Hebberd, 1929.

Mauss, Armand L. *All Abraham's Children: Changing Mormon Conceptions of Race and Lineage.* Chicago: University of Illinois Press, 2003.

McConkie, Bruce R. *Mormon Doctrine.* 2nd ed. Salt Lake City: Bookcraft, 1966.

McPherson, Robert S. "Canyons, Cows, and Conflict: A Native American History of Montezuma Canyon, 1874–1933." *Utah Historical Quarterly* 60 (Summer 1992): 238–58.

———. *A History of San Juan County: In the Palm of Time.* Salt Lake City: Utah Historical Society, 1995.

———. *The Northern Navajo Frontier: Expansion through Adversity, 1860–1900.* Albuquerque: University of New Mexico Press, 1988.

Meinig, D. W. *The Shaping of America: A Geographical Perspective on 500 Years of History, vol. 3: Transcontinental America, 1850–1915.* New Haven and London: Yale University Press, 1998.

Meinke, Robert J. *A Preliminary Ecological and Historical Survey of North and South Caineville Mesas, Wayne County, Utah.* Boulder: Western Interstate Commission for Higher Education, 1975.

Merchant, Carolyn. *Reinventing Eden: The Fate of Nature in Western Culture.* New York: Routledge, 2003.

Merrill, Karen R. *Public Lands and Political Meaning: Ranchers, the Government, and the Property between Them.* Berkeley: University of California Press, 2002.

Miller, David E. *Hole in the Rock: An Epic in the Colonization of the Great American West.* Salt Lake City: University of Utah Press, 1959.

Morgan, Dale L. *The Humboldt: Highroad of the West.* New York: Farrar and Rinehart, 1943.

Morris, John Miller. *El Llano Estacado: Exploration and Imagination on the High Plains of Texas and New Mexico, 1536–1860.* Austin: Texas State Historical Association, 1997.

Murphy, Miriam B. *A History of Wayne County.* Salt Lake City: Utah State Historical Society and Wayne County Commission, 1999.

Nash, Roderick. *Wilderness and the American Mind.* New Haven: Yale University Press, 1967.

Negri, Richard (ed.). *Tales of Canyonlands Cowboys.* Logan: Utah State University Press, 1997.

Nelson, Lowry. *The Mormon Village: A Pattern and Technique of Land Settlement.* Salt Lake City: University of Utah Press, 1952.

Newberry, John S. *Report of the Exploring Expedition from Santa Fé, New Mexico, to the Junction of the Grand and Green Rivers of the Great Colorado of the West in 1859, under the Command of Capt. J. N. Macomb, Corps of Topographical Engineers, with Geological Report.* Washington, DC: Engineering Dept., U.S. Army, Government Printing Office, 1876.

Nibley, Hugh. "Brigham Young on the Environment." In *To the Glory of God: Mormon Essays on Great Issues—The Environment, Commitment, Love, Peace, Youth, Man,* ed.

Truman Madsen and Charles D. Tate, 3–29. Salt Lake City: Deseret Book Company, 1972.

———. *Nibley on the Timely and the Timeless: Classic Essays on Hugh W. Nibley.* Vol. 1, Religious Studies Monograph Series. Provo: Brigham Young University Religious Studies Center, 1978.

Nuttal, L. John. "Journals: 1857–1904." L. Tom Perry Special Collections, Harold B. Lee Library, Brigham Young University.

Oelshlaeger, Max. *The Idea of Wilderness: From Prehistory to the Age of Ecology.* New Haven: Yale University Press, 1991.

Pace, William B. "Blessing Given by Patriarch Isaac Morely upon the Head of William B. Pace of Payson, March 31, 1854" (typescript, 1941). Utah Historical Society, Salt Lake City.

———. "Diary of the Elk Mountain Mission, 1855–1856" (typescript, 1941). Utah State Historical Society, Salt Lake City.

Pagden, Anthony. *The Fall of Natural Man: The American Indian and the Origins of Comparative Ethnology.* New York: Cambridge University Press, 1982.

Pahreah Branch, Kanab Stake. *Record Book 1878–1898.* Salt Lake City: LDS Church Archives.

Pahreah Ward, Kanab Stake. *Manuscript History and Historical Reports.* Salt Lake City: LDS Church Archives.

Pattie, James O. *The Personal Narrative of James O. Pattie* (1831). Ed. Timothy Flint. New York: Garland Publishers, 1976.

Peterson, Charles S. "Albert F. Potter's Wasatch Survey, 1902: A Beginning for Public Management of Natural Resources in Utah." *Utah Historical Quarterly* 39 (Summer 1971): 238–53.

———. "Grazing in Utah: A Historical Perspective." *Utah Historical Quarterly* 57 (1989): 300–319.

———. *Look to the Mountains: Southeastern Utah and the La Sal National Forest.* Provo: Brigham Young University Press, 1975.

———. *Take Up Your Mission: Mormon Colonizing along the Little Colorado River, 1870–1900.* Provo: Brigham Young University Press, 1973.

———. *Touch of the Mountain Sod: How Land United and Divided Utahns, 1847–1985.* Ogden: Weber State College Press, 1989.

Phelan, John. *The Millennial Kingdom of the Franciscans in the New World.* Berkeley: University of California Press, 1970.

Phillips, Sarah T. *This Land, This Nation: Conservation, Rural America, and the New Deal.* New York: Cambridge University Press, 2007.

Posada, Alonso de. *A Description of the Area of the Present Southern United States in the Seventeenth Century.* Trans. and ed. Alfred B. Thomas. Pensacola: Perdido Bay Press, 1982.

Powell, John Wesley. *The Exploration of the Colorado River and Its Canyons* (1875). New York: Flood and Vincent, 1895. Reprinted: New York: Dover Publications, 1961.

———. "Major Powell's Preliminary Report to Prof. Joseph Henry, Secretary, Smithsonian Institution, Washington, D.C." *Utah Historical Quarterly* 7 (1939): 134–38.

————. *Report on the Lands of the Arid Region of the United States, with a More Detailed Account of the Lands of Utah* (1879). Boston: Harvard Common Press, 1983.

Price, Virginia, and John D. Darby. "Preston Nutter: Utah Cattleman, 1886–1936." *Utah Historical Quarterly* 32 (Summer 1964): 232–51.

Pyne, Stephen J. *How the Canyon Became Grand: A Short History.* New York: Viking, 1998.

Reeve, W. Paul. *Making Space on the Western Frontier: Mormons, Miners, and Southern Paiutes.* Urbana: University of Illinois Press, 2006.

Reid, J. Jefferson, and David E. Doyel (eds.). *Emil W. Haury's Prehistory of the Southwest.* Tucson: University of Arizona Press, 1986.

Reilly, P. T. *Lee's Ferry: From Mormon Crossing to National Park.* Ed. Robert H. Webb. Logan: Utah State University Press, 1999.

Reinhartz, Dennis, and Gerald D. Saxon (eds.). *The Mapping of the Entradas into the Greater Southwest.* Norman: University of Oklahoma Press, 1998.

Reisner, Marc. *Cadillac Desert: The American West and Its Disappearing Water.* New York: Viking, 1986.

Richardson, Elmo R. "Federal Park Policy in Utah: The Escalante National Monument Controversy of 1935–1940." *Utah Historical Quarterly* 33 (Spring 1965): 109–33.

Righter, Robert W. *The Battle over Hetch Hetchy: America's Most Controversial Dam and the Birth of Modern Environmentalism.* New York: Oxford University Press, 2005.

Ringholz, Raye C. *Uranium Frenzy: Boom and Bust on the Colorado Plateau.* Albuquerque: University of New Mexico Press, 1989.

Roberts, B. H. *History of the Church of Jesus Christ of Latter-Day Saints.* Salt Lake City: Church of Jesus Christ of Latter-Day Saints, 1932–53.

Roberts, David. "Finding Everett Ruess." *National Geographic Adventure Magazine* (April–May 2009), accessed online at http://adventure.nationalgeographic. com/2009/04/everett-ruess/david-roberts-text/2.

Ronda, James P. *Finding the West: Explorations with Lewis and Clark.* Albuquerque: University of New Mexico Press, 2001.

Rosenvall, Lynn. "Defunct Mormon Settlements: 1830–1930." In *The Mormon Role in the Settlement of the West*, ed. Richard H. Jackson, 51–74. Provo: Brigham Young University Press, 1976.

Rothman, Hal. *America's National Monuments: The Politics of Preservation.* Lawrence: University of Kansas Press, 1989.

————. *Devil's Bargains: Tourism in the Twentieth-Century West.* Lawrence: University of Kansas Press, 1998.

Ruess, Everett. *The Wilderness Journals of Everett Ruess.* Ed. W. L. Rusho. Salt Lake City: Gibbs Smith, 1998.

Rusho, W. L. *Everett Ruess: A Vagabond for Beauty.* Salt Lake City: Gibbs Smith, 1983.

Sachs, Aaron. *The Humboldt Current: Nineteenth-Century Exploration and the Roots of American Environmentalism.* New York: Viking, 2006.

Sánchez, Joseph P. *Explorers, Traders, and Slavers: Forging the Old Spanish Trail, 1678–1850.* Salt Lake City: University of Utah Press, 1997.

Sandweiss, Martha. *Print the Legend: Photography and the American West.* New Haven: Yale University Press, 2002.

San Juan Stake. "Camp Records, 1879." In *San Juan Stake History.* LDS Church Historian's Office, Salt Lake City.

Schiel, James. *The Land Between: Dr. James Schiel's Account of the Gunnison-Beckwith Expedition into the American West, 1853–1854* (originally published in German, 1859). Trans. Frederick W. Bachmann. Ed. William S. Wallace. Los Angeles: Western Lore Press, 1957.

Schmieding, Samuel. "Visions of a Sculptured Paradise: The Colorado Plateau as American Sacred Space." Ph.D. dissertation. Arizona State University, 2002.

Sellers, Richard West. *Preserving Nature in the National Parks: A History.* New Haven: Yale University Press, 1997.

Shipps, Jan. *Mormonism: The Story of a New Religious Tradition.* Urbana: University of Illinois Press, 1985.

Shlaer, Robert. *Sights Once Seen: Daguerreotyping Frémont's Last Expedition through the Rockies.* Santa Fe: Museum of New Mexico Press, 2000.

Silliman, Bert J. Bert J. Silliman Papers (1951–1957). Utah Historical Society, Salt Lake City, Utah.

Simmons, Marc. *The Last Conquistador: Juan de Oñate and the Settling of the Far Southwest.* Norman: University of Oklahoma Press, 1991.

Simms, Steven R. *Ancient Peoples of the Great Basin and Colorado Plateau.* Walnut Creek, CA: West Coast Press, 2008.

Smart, William B., and Donna T. Smart (eds.). *Over the Rim: The Parley P. Pratt Exploring Expedition to Southern Utah: 1849–50.* Logan: Utah State University Press, 1999.

Smith, Henry Nash. *Virgin Land: The American West as Symbol and Myth.* Cambridge, MA: Harvard University Press, 1950.

Smith, Joseph, Jr. The Book of Mormon: An Account Written by the Hand of Mormon upon Plates Taken from the Plates of Nephi (1830). Salt Lake City: Church of Jesus Christ of Latter-Day Saints, 1985.

———. The Pearl of Great Price: Being a Choice Selection from the Revelations, Translations, and Narrations of Joseph Smith, First Prophet, Seer, and Revelator to the Church of Jesus Christ of Latter-Day Saints. Liverpool: Albert Carrington, 1882.

Smith, Thomas W. "A Brief History of Early Pahreah Settlements and a Pioneer Story of an Encounter with the Indians" (unpublished manuscript, circa 1890). Utah State Historical Society, Salt Lake City.

Smythe, William E. *The Conquest of Arid America.* New York: Macmillan Co., 1905.

Sproul, David Kent. *A Bridge between Cultures: An Administrative History of Rainbow Bridge National Monument.* Denver: U.S. Dept. of the Interior, National Park Service, 2001.

Stanton, Robert Brewster. *Colorado River Controversies.* New York: Dodd, Mead, and Co., 1932; reprint: Westwater Books, 1982.

———. *Down the Colorado*. Ed. Dwight L. Smith. Norman: University of Oklahoma Press, 1965.

———. "The Hoskaninni Papers: Mining in Glen Canyon, 1897–1902." Ed. Dwight L. Smith and C. Gregory Crampton. University of Utah Anthropological Papers 54 (November 1961).

———. Robert Brewster Stanton Papers (1861–1960). Miami University Special Collections, Oxford, OH.

Stanton, Robert Brewster, and the Denver, Colorado Canyon, and Pacific Railroad. *The Colorado River Survey*. Ed. Dwight L. Smith and C. Gregory Crampton. Salt Lake City: Howe Brothers, 1987.

Stegmaier, Mark J., and David J. Miller. *James F. Milligan: His Journal of Frémont's Fifth Expedition, 1853–1854; His Adventurous Life on Land and Sea*. Glendale: Arthur Clark Company, 1988.

Stegner, Wallace. *Beyond the Hundredth Meridian: John Wesley Powell and the Second Opening of the American West*. New York: Houghton Mifflin, 1953.

———. *The Gathering of Zion: The Story of the Mormon Trail*. New York: McGraw-Hill, 1964.

———. *Marking the Sparrow's Fall: Wallace Stegner's American West*. Ed. Page Stegner. New York: Holt and Co., 1998.

———. *Mormon Country*. Lincoln: University of Nebraska Press, 1942.

Stiles, Jim. "The Greening of Wilderne$$ in Utah." Canyon Country Zephyr (June–July 2005). Online at http://www.canyoncountryzephyr.com/oldzephyr/june-july2005/gtw.htm.

Stone, Julius F. *Canyon Country: The Romance of a Drop of Water and a Grain of Sand*. New York: G. P. Putnam's Sons, 1932.

———. Julius Stone Papers (1845–1949). Ohio State University Archives, Columbus.

Swadesh, Frances Leon. *Los Primeros Pobladores: Hispanic Americans of the Ute Frontier*. Notre Dame: University of Notre Dame Press, 1974.

Swanson, Frederick H. *Dave Rust: A Life in the Canyons*. Salt Lake City: University of Utah Press, 2007.

Tanner, Faun McConkie. *The Far Country: A Regional History of Moab and La Sal, Utah*. Salt Lake City: Olympus Publishing Company, 1976.

———. *A History of Moab, Utah*. Moab: Press of the *Moab Times Independent*, 1937.

Thomas, Alfred B. (ed.). *Forgotten Frontiers: A Study of the Spanish Indian Policy of Don Juan Bautista de Anza, Governor of New Mexico, 1777–1787*. Norman: University of Oklahoma Press, 1932.

Thomas, George. *The Development of Institutions under Irrigation, with Special Reference to Early Utah Conditions*. New York: Macmillan Co., 1920.

Thompson, Almon Harris. "Diary of Almon Harris Thompson, Geographer: Explorations of the Colorado River of the West and Its Tributaries, 1871–75." Ed. Herbert E. Gregory. *Utah Historical Quarterly* 7, no. 1 (January 1939).

Topping, Gary. *Glen Canyon and the San Juan Country*. Moscow: University of Idaho Press, 1997.

————. *Utah Historians and the Reconstruction of Western History*. Norman: University of Oklahoma Press, 2003.

Turner, Frederick. *Beyond Geography: The Western Spirit against the Wilderness*. New Brunswick: Rutgers University Press, 1983.

Tyler, Lyman S. "The Myth of the Lake of Copala and the Land of Teguayo." *Utah Historical Quarterly* 20 (1952): 313–29.

Tyler, Lyman S., and H. Daniel Taylor. "The Report of Fray Alonso de Posada in Relation to Quivera and Teguayo." *New Mexico Historical Review* 33 (Oct. 1958): 285–314.

Utley, Robert. *A Life Wild and Perilous: Mountain Men and the Paths to the Pacific*. New York: Holt and Co., 1997.

Van Wagenen, Michael Scott. *The Texas Republic and the Mormon Kingdom of God*. College Station: Texas A&M University Press, 2002.

Van Wagoner, Richard S. *Mormon Polygamy: A History*. Salt Lake City: Signature Books, 1989.

Vélez de Escalante, Silvestre. *The Domínguez-Escalante Journal: Their Expedition through Colorado, Utah, Arizona, and New Mexico in 1776*. Ed. Ted J. Warner. Trans. Fray Angelico Chávez. Salt Lake City: University of Utah Press, 1995.

Walker, Don. "The Carlisles, Cattle Barons of the Upper Basin." *Utah Historical Quarterly* 32 (Summer 1964): 268–84.

Waters, Frank. *The Colorado*. New York: Holt, Rinehart and Wilson, 1946.

Webb, Robert H. *Grand Canyon, a Century of Change: Rephotography of the 1889–1890 Stanton Expedition*. Tucson: University of Arizona Press, 1997.

Webb, Robert H., Jayne Belnap, and John S. Weisheit. *Cataract Canyon: A Human and Environmental History of the Rivers in Canyonlands*. Salt Lake City: University of Utah Press, 2004.

Webb, Roy. "A Foolhardy Undertaking: Utah's Pioneer Steamboaters." *Canyon Legacy: A Journal of the Dan O'Laurie Museum* 5 (1990): 15–16.

————. *If We Had a Boat: Green River Explorers, Adventurers, and Runners*. Salt Lake City: University of Utah Press, 1986.

Weber, David J. *Bárbaros: Spaniards and Their Savages in the Age of Enlightenment*. New Haven: Yale University Press, 2005.

————. *Myth and History of the Hispanic Southwest*. Albuquerque: University of New Mexico Press, 1987.

————. *The Spanish Frontier in North America*. New Haven: Yale University Press, 1992.

West, Elliot. *The Last Indian War: The Nez Perce Story*. New York: Oxford University Press, 2009.

White, Lynn. "The Historical Roots of Our Ecologic Crisis." *Science* 10 (March 1967): 1203–1207.

Widtsoe, John A. *Dry-Farming: A System of Agriculture for Countries under a Low Rainfall*. New York: Macmillan, 1911.

————. "A Journal of John A. Widtsoe, Colorado River Party, September 3–19, 1922." Ed. A. R. Mortensen. *Utah Historical Quarterly* 23 (July 1955): 195–230.

Wiebe, Robert. *The Search for Order: 1877–1920.* New York: Hill and Wang, 1967.

Williams, George H. *Wilderness and Paradise in Christian Thought: The Biblical Experience of the Desert in the History of Christianity and the Paradise Theme in the Theological Idea of the University.* New York: Harper and Brothers, 1962.

Winship, George Parker (ed. and trans.). *The Journey of Coronado, 1540–1542: From the City of Mexico to the Grand Canyon of the Colorado and the Buffalo Plains of Texas, Kansas, and Nebraska, as Told by Himself and His Followers.* New York: A. S. Barnes and Co., 1904.

Winthrop, John. "Reasons to Be Considered for Justifying the Undertakers of the Intended Plantation in New England." *Massachusetts Historical Society Proceedings* 8 (1864–65): 420–25.

Worster, Donald. *Nature's Economy: A History of Ecological Ideas.* New York: Cambridge University Press, 1977.

————. *A River Running West: The Life of John Wesley Powell.* New York: Oxford University Press, 2001.

————. *Rivers of Empire: Water, Aridity, and the Growth of the American West.* New York: Oxford University Press, 1985.

Young, Brigham. "Management of the Kanyons." *Journal of Discourses* 1 (Liverpool: F. D. and S. W. Richards, 1852): 209-20.

Young, Carl. "Wild Cows of the San Juan." *Utah Historical Quarterly* 32 (Summer 1964): 252–67.

Zárate Salmerón, Jerónimo. *Relaciones by Zárate Salmerón.* Ed. and trans. Alicia Ronstadt Milich. Albuquerque: Horn and Wallace Publishers, 1966.

Index